The Skyscraper Curse

The Skyscraper Curse

And How Austrian Economists Predicted Every Major Economic Crisis of the Last Century

M ARK T HORNTON

MISESINSTITUTE

AUBURN, ALABAMA

Mises Institute
518 West Magnolia Ave.
Auburn, Ala. 36832
mises.org

hardback edition: 978-1-61016-683-6
paperback edition: 978-1-61016-684-3
large print edition: 978-1-61016-685-0
epub edition: 978-1-61016-688-1

Contents

Foreword

In the wake of the financial crisis of 2008, the economics profession suffered a blow to what reputation it had. But unlike most of his colleagues, Mark Thornton was vindicated by 2008. Mark has been a voice of sanity at times when the wild interventions of the Federal Reserve have caused otherwise sensible people to lose their minds.

One rule of thumb I've adopted is: whenever the idea that the business cycle may have been tamed forever starts to become mainstream, the bust is around the corner.

After reading this book, you'll see why. Mark discusses the very different records of Irving Fisher and Ludwig von Mises in the 1920s, with the former saying (in late 1929!) that stock prices had reached a "permanently high plateau" and Mises warning that all the artificial credit creation of the world's central banks meant a reckoning was coming.

At the end of the 1960s, presidential economic adviser Arthur Okun announced that wise fiscal and monetary policy was making boom and bust a thing of the past. One month after his book on the subject was released, the United States was officially in recession.

The dot-com bubble of the 1990s continued the pattern. Federal Reserve chairman Alan Greenspan even speculated that we had entered an age in which booms no longer necessarily had to be followed by busts.

I trust you know what happened next.

The most recent financial crisis, which was connected to an especially destructive housing bubble, yielded the same kind of crazy commentary: why, real estate prices *never* fall!

I trust you know what happened next.

In fact, Mark Thornton was one of a handful of economists to warn — as early as 2004 — of a housing bubble and its inevitable consequence. That was a lonely position to adopt in those days. Nobody wanted to hear the words "unsustainable" or "bubble" when buying multiple properties and sitting on them seemed to be a path to certain riches. Of course, Mark was the voice that would have done them the most good had they bothered to listen, because they might thereby have limited their exposure to the bust that was surely coming.

But when all so-called respectable voices are assuring everyone that all is well, it is the wise man who appears to be the crank.

Now had Mark been known for nothing more than being a conscientious historian of these earlier business cycles and an accurate prognosticator of the housing bust and financial crisis, that would be ample reason to respect him as a scholar worthy of our attention and respect.

But of course Mark has done much more than this. In this book, for instance, you will encounter Mark's work on the so-called "skyscraper curse." I shall not here disclose Mark's thesis on the matter; the author of a foreword ought to know his place, and stealing the author's thunder is rather unbecoming.

For now, I can say this: although a correlation between the setting of new skyscraper records on the one hand and plunges into recession on the other had been noted by certain writers, the connection had been generally dismissed as little more than a curious coincidence. Mark, on the other hand, has shown how the two phenomena are connected — not that tall skyscrapers cause the business cycle, of course, but rather that they embody numerous features of the boom period described by Austrian business cycle theory.

Austrian business cycle theory, in turn, is probably the most important piece of economic information and understanding for Americans and indeed the world to understand right now. Again I shall leave the full exposition to Mark. For now, what matters is that according to economists of the Austrian school, the familiar pattern of economic boom and bust is not an inherent feature of the market economy, but instead the product of intervention into the economy by the monetary authority. When the central bank lowers interest rates below what they would have reached on the market, it sets in motion a series of responses by investors and consumers that will prove to be incompatible. The result is the recession, which is the economy's return to health: the economy's unsustainable configuration is unwound, and resources (including labor) are reallocated to lines of production that make sense in terms of resource availability and consumer preferences.

In the pages that follow, Mark explains the theory, applies it to various historical (and present) cases, and rebuts the most common objections.

In short, this collection serves the valuable purpose of defending the market economy against the conventional view that freedom has failed us and we need still more controls. We had plenty of rules and bureaucrats on the eve of the financial crisis. A lot of good that did us. Pretty much none of them saw any problems on the horizon, and the sheafs of rules and regulations were aimed in the wrong direction: while the private sector operated in the equivalent of a Kafka novel, the Federal Reserve was able to carry out its mischief unimpeded.

Here's a crazy thought: maybe this time we might consider a real free market, with sound money and market interest rates, and abolish the giant bubble machine once and for all. Read Mark Thornton and you'll entertain this and other forbidden thoughts.

Thomas E. Woods, Jr.
Harmony, Florida

Introduction

The Skyscraper Index expresses the strange relationship between the building of the world's tallest skyscraper and the onset of a major economic crisis. This relationship only came to light in 1999 when research analyst Andrew Lawrence published a report noting the odd connection between record-height buildings and noteworthy economic crises — that is, the skyscraper curse, a relationship that dated back nearly a century. Without a theory to support it, journalists largely dismissed Lawrence's report as the fun story of the day.

However, from the vantage point of Austrian business cycle theory, or ABCT, Lawrence's report was important for understanding the business cycle: booms and busts. ABCT is the business cycle theory developed by the economists of the Austrian school during the early twentieth century.

In the 1860s, Austrian financial journalist Carl Menger (1840–1921) began to ponder economic activity that he was reporting on in light of the economics of the classical school — that is, Adam Smith (1723–90), David Ricardo (1772–1823), John Stuart Mill (1806–73), and so on. He found huge gaps in the explanation of many basic concepts, such as supply and demand. To close those gaps he developed some fundamental elements of modern economics, such as marginal analysis and the rudiments of opportunity cost, marginal utility, and subjective value.

His students at the University of Vienna learned from him and built on his insights. For example, Eugen von Böhm-Bawerk (1851–1914), who served as finance minister of the Austro-Hungarian Empire, built on Menger's work to show that production can be less or more time consuming, or *roundabout*. From this perspective, we can see that laborers get paid very quickly, while capitalists are paid *interest* for delaying their rewards until the product is actually sold. Böhm-Bawerk showed that interest was based on the *time preferences* of workers and capitalists, savers and borrowers. The interest rate is a critical economic factor because it helps determine the size and complexity of an economy's capital structure. The capital structure is simply the non-natural world around us: all the business assets related to mines, farms, factories, utilities, transportation, warehouses, wholesale and retail businesses, and so on. Austrian economics has been described by Peter Klein as *mundane economics*.[1]

For example, a market economy populated with individuals with low time preferences and interest rates would, over a long period, be characterized by a large accumulation of savings that is turned into large amounts of "brick and mortar" capital and advanced-technology production processes. The division of labor would be highly specialized. People would be wealthy and have a high standard of living.

Ludwig von Mises (1881–1973) was a student of Böhm-Bawerk who extended Austrian analysis into the area of money, solving the classical school's problem of how to connect the workings of the real economy with monetary economics. He accomplished this with his regression theorem, which was based in part on Menger's explanation for the origin of money. Mises also formulated a theory of the business cycle based on the interaction of the interest rate and capital allocation. His approach is based on distortions of the market rate of interest. His student, Friedrich August von Hayek (1899–1992), further elaborated and extended Mises's theory, a contribution for which he was awarded the Nobel Prize for economics in 1974. Their theory is now known as Austrian business cycle theory. (See Roger Garrison for a technical explanation of Austrian macroeconomics.[2])

Inspired by ABCT, my reflections about skyscrapers eventually resulted in an academic working paper, "Skyscrapers and Business Cycles." The manuscript was summarily rejected by several mainstream economic

---

[1] Peter G. Klein, "The Mundane Economics of the Austrian School," *Quarterly Journal of Austrian Economics* 11, nos. 3–4 (2008): 165–87.

[2] Roger W. Garrison, "The Austrian School: Capital-Based Macroeconomics," in *Modern Macroeconomics: Its Origins, Development and Current State*, edited by Brian Snowden and Howard R. Vane (Aldershot: Edward Elgar, 2005).

journals. The replies from the journal editors would often include a short or cryptic explanation such as "This paper does not have a testable hypothesis." The article[3] was eventually published in the *Quarterly Journal of Austrian Economics* in 2005. It uses ABCT to explain how record-breaking skyscrapers are linked to business cycles and economic crises. In particular I drew on the economic theories of Richard Cantillon (1680s–1734?), the first economic theorist and a proto-Austrian economist, in order to establish causal links between skyscrapers and business cycles.

Cantillon showed how the interest rate and the money supply can create changes and distortions in the economy, a phenomenon now referred to as *Cantillon effects*. The paper describes three such effects: (1) the relationship between the interest rate, land prices, and building height; (2) the relationship between the interest rate, the size of firms, and the demand for office space; and (3) the relationship between building height and the enhanced incentive for advanced — or premature — technological innovations in both design and construction.

The time period of my research on skyscrapers and business cycles was crucial for my early identification of the housing bubble. In my February 2004 article " 'Bull' Market?" I used a trend-channel technique to define the initial stage of the bubble. Then in June 2004 I wrote "Housing: Too Good to Be True," a full explanation of how the Federal Reserve's monetary policy had caused a massive housing bubble. I also began giving presentations on this subject to the general public.

As a result of this publicity, I was invited in 2005 to contribute a chapter to a book, *Housing America: Building Out of a Crisis*, edited by Randall G. Holcombe and Benjamin Powell. I submitted the resulting chapter, "The Economics of Housing Bubbles," to the editors the first week of June 2006.

The publisher of the book asked me to remove some text they considered too gloomy and ominous regarding what might happen in the aftermath of the housing bust. I agreed to the changes because the book was to be marketed to people interested in zoning laws, building codes, and urban planning, not economic Armageddon. However, the editors later allowed me to include that removed text, when, after a long publishing delay, the book was finally published in 2009. At that time my gloomy

---

[3]Mark Thornton, "Skyscrapers and Business Cycles," *Quarterly Journal of Austrian Economics* 8, no. 1 (2005): 51–74.

predictions seemed more appropriate. The removed text was placed in a Postscript in the original publication. Indeed the editors were so kind as to mention my chapter prominently at the beginning of their preface:

> The timing is noteworthy because most of the chapters were completed in 2006 when the housing boom across much of the country was reaching its peak. One chapter in particular that deserves mention in this regard is Mark Thornton's, because he was discussing the inevitable collapse of the housing market bubble at a time when many observers were arguing that house prices could continue rising indefinitely. Thornton's chapter does a good job of explaining the collapse of housing prices in hindsight, and it is worth noting that Thornton's hindsight was actually foresight: he was talking about the collapse before it actually occurred.[4]

Between 2004 and 2007 audiences and readers generally scoffed at my analysis. This was a time when the accepted wisdom in mainstream economics and the real estate industry was that "housing prices never go down" and "you can never lose money in real estate." *Mainstream economics* refers to what is widely taught at well-known universities and associated with the neoclassical synthesis, which combines neoclassical microeconomics and Keynesian approaches to macroeconomics.

One of my particularly provocative public lectures, circa 2006, "Luxury Game Day Condominiums," was given to students at Auburn University. As it turned out local building contractors and bankers were also in attendance. The empirical evidence I presented was based on interviews of people who had purchased these game day condos during the housing bubble. The condos had been marketed to football fans of Auburn University who come to Auburn, Alabama, for the six or seven home football games per year. When I did the calculations I discovered that the condo buyers could have stayed at the best hotel in town and eaten all their meals at gourmet restaurants and saved money. I then asked the buyers, "Why buy the condo?" To this the answer would invariably be "I can always sell it for more money later."

---

[4]Randall G. Holcombe, and Benjamin Powell, eds., *Housing America: Building Out of a Crisis* (New Brunswick, N.J.: Transactions Publishers, 2009), p. vii.

The complete bust in housing had not been recognized yet, but everyone in the audience knew that condo prices were falling and that some local projects had been cancelled. The students in the audience roared with laughter at those responses, but the builders and bankers were none too pleased. Of course it was not just local builders and bankers that wanted to keep the bubble going. By now Federal Reserve officials were publically cheerleading for the housing bubble and denying that it existed.[5]

They should have known better, or at least reexamined their models. After all, the housing industry as measured by the Philadelphia Stock Exchange Housing Sector Index peaked on June 30, 2005. On August 8, 2005, my short article "Is the Housing Bubble Popping?" was published.[6] In the article I presented charts that indicated that home-builder stock prices could be headed much lower and that short-term and long-term interest rates could be heading higher. Both trends, which did continue, were harbingers that the housing bubble would eventually pop.

In 2007, the skyscraper curse struck again, the second occurrence since Lawrence's 1999 report. This time it happened in the Middle East in the city-state of Dubai. Located in the United Arab Emirates, between Saudi Arabia and Oman and across the Persian Gulf from Iran, Dubai is a fantasy city. Its ruler has transformed his oil wealth into a highly dynamic city with very tall and ornate buildings, hotels, the world's largest shopping mall, and even man-made islands in the Persian Gulf designed to resemble a map of the world.

It was in Dubai that construction of the Burj Dubai tower began in 2004. It was designed to be a world-record setting skyscraper in terms of all metrics such as height, highest livable floor, the most floors, and so on. The next "skyscraper signal" occurred when construction reached a new record height in late July 2007. In August I reported:

> There is a new record setting skyscraper in the making in the United Arab Emirates. The Skyscraper Index predicts economic depression and/or stock market collapses to occur prior to the completion of the skyscraper.[7]

---

[5]Mark Thornton, "Transparency or Deception: What the Fed Was Saying in 2007," *Quarterly Journal of Austrian Economics* 19, no. 1 (2016): 65–84.

[6]Mark Thornton, "Is the Housing Bubble Popping?" LewRockwell.com, August 8, (2005).

[7]Mark Thornton, "New Record Skyscraper (and Depression?) in the Making," mises.org blog, August 7, 2007.

The tower was renamed the Burj Khalifa and opened in early January 2010. The building was renamed for the ruler of Abu Dhabi who had arranged for billions of dollars in emergency loans to bail out his cousin in Dubai. Clearly the skyscraper curse had hit once again. The media began to take it more seriously. On January 8, 2010, CNN.com's Kevin Voigt reported:

> When the Burj Khalifa officially opened in Dubai on Monday, much of the world press noted the irony of the world's tallest building unveiled just weeks after the emirate's debt crash.
>
> But a look at the history of record-breaking skyscrapers and business cycles suggests otherwise — the opening of every single "world's tallest" building in the past century has coincided with an economic downturn.
>
> One person who wasn't surprised by the economic woes greeting the dedication of the Burj Khalifa (renamed Monday from Burj Dubai in honor of the sheikh of Abu Dhabi, which recently threw Dubai a $10 billion lifeline) was Auburn University economist Mark Thornton.
>
> He predicted tough times for the emirate two years ago in a blog entitled "New Record Skyscraper (and depression?) in the making." He noted that economic depression or stock market collapse usually occurs prior to completion of such skyscrapers.[8]

So the Skyscraper Index's "curse" has correctly forecast all major economic crises for over a century. The skyscraper curse has also experienced a good deal of mainstream media coverage; and so it would seem that the Skyscraper Index theory is accurate and alive and well.

That was until March 28, 2015, when the *Economist* declared the skyscraper curse was dead. In reviewing the current "skyscraper boom" they noted in their unsigned "Towers of Babel" editorial the following:

> Does this frenzy of building augur badly for the world economy? Various academics and pundits, many of them cited by *The Economist*, have long argued as much, but new research casts doubt on it.

---

[8]Kevin Voigt, "As skyscrapers rise, markets fall," CNN.com.

As a side note, the majority of major media who write about my work and this phenomenon fail to cite me as a source, although they have clearly been drawing from my publications. Of the "various academics and pundits" most draw from Andrew Lawrence.[9] *The Economist*'s article did not include me explicitly in the text, but at least they did reference my 2005 journal article at the end as a source.[10] Thank you.

The Economist based its view on a new academic article, "Skyscraper Height and the Business Cycle: Separating Myth from Reality." The article was written by three Rutgers University economists: Jason Barr, Bruce Mizrach, and Kusam Mundra. It was published in the academic journal *Applied Economics* in 2015.

Their article demonstrates that skyscrapers do not *cause* (in a technical economic sense) business cycles as measured by changes in overall economic activity — that is, GDP. Their statistical analysis shows that skyscraper construction and overall economic activity move together, having a common cause or trend. They also found it difficult to find a correlation between the skyscraper announcement and completion dates and changes in GDP.

Let's be perfectly clear here. Skyscraper construction does not *cause* business cycles. The statistical evidence presented in *Applied Economics* actually supports the Skyscraper Index theory.

It should be clear from my "Skyscrapers and Business Cycles" article that there is a third factor at work. Skyscrapers are essentially part of the boom phase of the cycle. The cause of both is artificially very low interest rates and artificially very easy credit conditions. This *cause* results in new record-breaking skyscrapers, a boom in the economy, and eventually a substantial economic crisis — the skyscraper curse.

Immediately, I wrote a letter to the editor of *The Economist* to inform them of the error in the 2015 article and to ask them to change the date they printed for my journal article from 2004 to 2005. The letter was never published and the date of my paper was never corrected. I did receive an email three months later that said the magazine had misplaced my letter. I also submitted a comment (with Lucas Engelhardt) on the article published in *Applied Economics*. Surprisingly, the editors of *Applied Economics*

---

[9]Andrew Lawrence, "The Skyscraper Index: Faulty Towers!" *Property Report*, January 15, 1999 and "The Curse Bites: Skyscraper Index Strikes," *Property Report*, March 3, 1999.

[10]Thornton, "Skyscrapers and Business Cycles."

rejected the comment. Accordingly, this book is dedicated, in part, to the editors of *Applied Economics* and *The Economist*.

The main point of the Skyscraper Index and the resulting curse is to give people a tangible, concrete example of what is happening to the economy during a business cycle. ABCT is necessarily vague on some issues and silent on others. For example, it refers to capital, the structure of production, and goods of higher and lower orders without being specific. The theory presents issues, such as interest rates being artificially low relative to market-determined rates, without providing readers with a mechanism to calculate whether and when they in fact apply.

That does not mean ABCT is unrealistic, hard to understand, or difficult to apply. Austrian economists have always striven to be realistic about the economy and the limits of economic theory, but that necessarily puts limitations on the analysis and forces us to introduce significant caveats to our conclusions. For example, Austrian economists cannot "predict" in the strictest scientific sense. We speculate about the future, given the caveat of *ceteris paribus* — that is, all things being equal — and without illusions that economic theory can help us determine the timing and magnitude of future events. However, we can make "pattern predictions" based on economic theory and an appraisal of the facts.

In contrast, when mainstream economists are faced with the complexities of real economies or with scarcity of data, they resort to unrealistic assumptions, questionable simplifications, and inappropriate data. For most mainstream economists, their *sine qua non* is predicting the future. However, mainstream theories of the business cycle, such as real business cycle theory and various Keynesian theories, cannot predict anything about the future because in their view, the cycle is generated by economic shocks that cannot be anticipated. They can only predict in the sense that they use historical data in their models, like "back testing" stock market strategies. They practice retrodiction, rarely prediction.

The grand benefit of this book then is to show what Austrian economists see with the aid of the business cycle theory. ABCT shows what causes the business cycle, what happens during the business cycle, and that the boom must inevitably end in a bust or economic crisis. The value of resources is squandered in the process and people are harmed. Austrian theory can also show how to best deal with the bust, what to avoid, and how to permanently fix the problem by ending the business cycle, or at least minimizing its impact.

In section 2, I present evidence that demonstrates the real-world usefulness of ABCT by showing that Austrian economists have correctly forecast almost every major economic crisis for over a century. I also present evidence that mainstream economists have a poor record of predicting business cycles and have made some very bad predictions.

To be fair, there have been some mainstream economists who have made correct forecasts of economic crises, but their numbers are few compared to the Austrian economists, especially considering that Vedder and Gallaway[11] have estimated that there are about a hundred mainstream economists for every Austrian-school economist. Obviously, not all predictions by Austrian economists have come true or in a timely manner, including those of this author.

Before leaving section 2, let me be perfectly clear on one key point. Austrian economists have used ABCT to make their predictions about booms and busts since Böhm-Bawerk's time over a century ago. But since the concept of the Skyscraper Index is a relatively new concept, it has not been a part of the Austrian economists' toolkit. The idea of the Skyscraper Index was only discovered in 1999, and the theoretical justification for connecting it to ABCT has only been around since 2005.

Before ending this introduction, a question arises: what are Austrian economists saying about the current economy and government policy? Austrian economists have spoken out against current fiscal and monetary policy, and many have argued that policy has been unconventional, unorthodox, and extreme even by mainstream standards. Austrian economists have recommended drastic changes to current policies, and they have speculated that the economic consequences of the next crisis will be truly horrible. There are obviously differences of opinion, but the Austrian school is united against the current policy regime.

A skyscraper alert has already been issued, in that a groundbreaking ceremony has taken place and construction has begun on the Jeddah Tower in Saudi Arabia, a prospectively record-setting skyscraper. If a skyscraper signal is issued, it will mean that that project's height exceeds the current world record.

In conclusion, the book provides a remedy of how to best deal with the next economic crisis.

---

[11]Richard Vedder, and Lowell Gallaway, "The Austrian Market Share in the Marketplace for Ideas, 1871–2025," *Quarterly Journal of Austrian Economics* 3, no. 1 (Spring 2000): 33–42.

The author would like to acknowledge the assistance and support of many people and to apologize for no doubt forgetting the assistance of many others over the long course of this project.

First and foremost I would like to acknowledge the support of the officers, members, and donors of the Mises Institute who made this book possible. I would also like to thank Paul Cwik, Harry David, David Gordon, Lucas Engelhardt, Jörg Guido Hülsmann, Roger Garrison, Karl-Friedrich Israel, Floy Lilly, Greg Kaza, Jonathan Newman, Patrick Newman, Shawn Ritenour, Louis Rouanet, Joseph Salerno, Susan Schroeder, Judy Thommesen, Paul Wicks, all the economics teachers I've had throughout the years. I would most especially like to thank Robert B. Ekelund, Jr.

Section 1:
The Skyscraper Curse

CHAPTER 1

What Is
the Skyscraper Curse?

The skyscraper, that unique celebration of secular capital-
ism and its values, challenges us on every level. It offers
unique opportunities for insightful analysis in the broadest
terms of twentieth-century art, humanity, and history.

— Ada Louisa Huxtable, *The Tall Building Artistically*
Reconsidered

People have been seeking to discover the cause of the business cycle
since the dawn of capitalism. For an even longer time people have
sought a magic crystal ball that predicts the future. This book provides some insight for both quests.

The skyscraper is the great architectural contribution of modern capitalism, on par with the canals and railroads that transformed the economy of the nineteenth century. However, no one ever thought to connect
it with the quintessential feature of modern capitalism — the business
cycle. James Grant[1] did make a clear connection between real estate and
skyscrapers on the one hand and the business cycle on the other in *The*

---

[1] James Grant, *The Trouble with Prosperity: The Loss of Fear, the Rise of Speculation, and the
Risk to American Savings* (New York: Random House, 1996).

Trouble with Prosperity, and that book could have been an inspiration to Andrew Lawrence.

In 1999, Lawrence published his Skyscraper Index, which purported to show that the building of the tallest skyscrapers coincides with economic booms. Specifically, he showed that the building of the world's tallest skyscraper is a good proxy for dating the onset of a major economic crisis — the skyscraper curse. His index does not apply to the irregular ebbs and flows of the economy, only substantial economic crises.

Lawrence is an investment analyst whose Skyscraper Index records the history of the world's record-breaking skyscrapers and major economic crises. According to his index, when there is a groundbreaking ceremony for a new world-record-height skyscraper the economy is booming, but when the record height is achieved a significant economic crisis soon follows. The "curse" is the economic crisis, which is usually self-evident by the time the opening ceremony occurs. The mystery is, how can record-breaking skyscrapers be connected to economic crises?

Does this represent a cause and effect relationship? Can building a skyscraper cause business cycles? Architectural historian Carol Willis describes a very similar empirical conundrum:

> In the overheated speculation of the 1920s, as land prices rose, towers grew steadily taller. Or should the order be: as skyscrapers grew taller, land prices rose? The variables that contributed to real estate cycles were even more complex than this "chicken and egg" conundrum.[2]

What is the nature of the relationship between skyscraper building and the business cycle? Surely, building the world's tallest building does not *cause* economic collapse. Just as clearly, there are well-known economic linkages between construction booms and financial busts. So what theoretical connections can be made between skyscrapers and business cycles?

Lawrence considered overinvestment, monetary expansion, and speculation as possible explanations for the relationship his index revealed, but he did not explore these issues at length or come to a definitive conclusion. Instead he finished with the notion that his Skyscraper Index was an unhealthy hundred-year correlation. Without an established connection

---

[2]Carol Willis, *Form Follows Finance: Skyscrapers and Skylines in New York and Chicago* (New York: Princeton Architectural Press, 1995), p. 88.

or theory for the Skyscraper Index there are strong reasons to doubt its usefulness.

For example, with the destruction of the World Trade Center and the increased threat of terrorism, the Skyscraper Index may have already lost its usefulness for prediction. However, Edward Glaeser and Jesse Shapiro[3] did not find a statistically significant link between terrorism and the numbers of skyscrapers built. They also note that because of government interventions — for example, building codes — as well as psychological reasons such as a builder's desire for personal fame, the number of skyscrapers may not be market determined.

The business press reported on Lawrence's Skyscraper Index, but without much fanfare. *Investors' Business Daily*[4] seemed somewhat sympathetic to his "impressive" evidence, but asked: "How could something bad come of building the world's biggest skyscraper? After all, bigger is better. Having the biggest building on earth can be a source of national pride."

Also positive was *Barron's*, which seemed to agree that it was an "excellent forecasting tool for economic and financial imbalance."[5] *Business Week* raised the question of how to connect skyscrapers with economic crisis as described by the Skyscraper Index.[6] The first and most concerned report came from the *Far Eastern Economic Review*, which noted that China was planning on breaking the record for the world's tallest building and was constructing three of the ten tallest buildings on the planet to be completed by 2010.[7]

The main reason for the muted response to the Skyscraper Index by the business press is that most economic indicators have eventually failed over time. There have been numerous indicators put forth to help us predict the business cycle and stock markets, but they have not passed the test of time. As Goodhart's law[8] states: "Any observed statistical regularity will

---

[3]Edward L. Glaeser, and Jesse M. Shapiro, "Cities and Welfare: The Impact of Terrorism on Urban Form," NBER Working Paper 8696 (Cambridge, MA: National Bureau of Economic Research, 2001), p. 15.

[4]*Investors' Business Daily*, "Edifice Complex," May 6, 1999.

[5]William Pesek, Jr., "Want to Know Where the Next Disaster Will Hit? Look Where the World's Biggest Skyscraper's Going Up," *Barron's*, May 17, 1999, MW11.

[6]Gene Koretz, 1999. "Do Towers Rise before a Crash?" *Business Week*, May 17, 1999, p. 26.

[7]Alkman Granitsas, "The Height of Hubris: Skyscrapers Mark Economic Bust," *Far Eastern Economic Review* 162, no. 6 (February 11, 1999): 47.

[8]Charles A.E. Goodhart, "Problems of Monetary Management: The U.K. Experience," in

tend to collapse once pressure is placed upon it for control purposes." This is also a likely fate of the Skyscraper Index.

For example, the Super Bowl indicator predicts that if the championship team from the National Football Conference (the old NFL) beats the championship team from the American Football Conference (the old AFL) in the Super Bowl game it should be a good year for the stock market and *ipso facto* a good year for the economy. This is a classic case of a "coincidental indicator." This type of coincidental indicator (with no causal connections) should be differentiated from the traditional type of coincidental economic indicators that track changes in the business cycle. For example, payroll statistics are clearly linked with economic activity over time. If payrolls increase, then there is more economic activity and GDP. There is a real reason why we expect both statistics to change roughly in unison.

When this Super Bowl connection was first noticed in the 1970s by sports writer Leonard Koppett it was nearly perfect.[9] Since then it has lost much of its credibility, with an overall record of about 80 percent but only about 50 percent over the last fifteen years. Therefore, the early success of the Super Bowl indicator manifested just a coincidence and a statistical illusion, as Koppett himself professed.

There are also seasonal indicators like the "January effect," which claims that if stock markets increase in January, then stock markets will increase that year as well. However, this effect has been given multiple justifications, such as year-end bonuses and tax-avoidance strategies. It is also not clear whether the January effect is based on the performance of the stock market during the first week of January or during the entire month. It is also unclear whether it applies only to small-company stocks or the entire stock market. The January effect also suffers from the fact that once everyone is aware of it, it becomes anticipated and therefore no longer offers reliable investment advice or insight into the economy. As a result, such indicators do not have a reliable record for predicting the stock market or business cycles.

Political indicators of the economy are based on the political business cycle theory. This theory maintains that politicians will use monetary

---

Inflation, Depression, and Economic Policy in the West, edited by Anthony S. Courakis (Lanham, MD: Rowman & Littlefield, 1981), p. 116.

[9]Jason Zweig, "Super Bowl Indicator: The Secret History," *Wall Street Journal*, January 28, 2011.

and fiscal policy, along with other policy measures at their disposal, to boost the economy, job growth, and the stock market prior to an election in order to enhance the probability of being reelected. Then after the election they will reverse those policies, creating a recession. Despite its intuitive appeal, the political business cycle theory has found little consistent empirical support. This failure may be the result of the difficulty of knowing what ruling coalition is truly in charge of government or how the different levels of government are interacting over their respective election cycles. These and other problems leave the theory with only a weak link between politics and the economy.

According to Paul Cwik,[10] indicators with good causal-economic links to the economy include the inverted yield curve. When short-term interest rates rise above long-term interest rates, the yield curve becomes *inverted*, and this indicates trouble ahead for the economy. High short-term lending rates may indicate that borrowers are desperate for funds and lenders are reluctant to loan due to the perception of increased risk. The Index of Leading Economic Indicators was once the official crystal ball of the economy. However, in recent years it has had less success predicting changes in the economy. Two other indicators that I use to gauge the global economy are the price of oil and the Baltic Dry Shipping Index, which is a measure of the cost of ocean transportation. When both are high, it is an indication of global economic expansion, a boom, or a bubble. When both are low, it is an indication of economic contraction, a bust, or an economic crisis. However, all of these indicators are error prone and generally only provide a limited advanced notice of cyclical change. Such indicators certainly cannot issue alerts far enough in advance to be helpful for large capital-investment decisions.

Economist Richard Roll explained that economic indicators have only questionable or fleeting value for real-world investing:

> I'm not just an academic but also a businessman. ... [W]e could sure do a heck of a lot better for our clients in the money management business than we've been doing. I have personally tried to invest money, my client's money and my own, in every single anomaly and predictive device that academics have dreamed up. ... I

---

[10]Paul Cwik, "The Inverted Yield Curve and the Economic Downturn," *New Perspectives on Political Economy: A Bilingual Interdisciplinary Journal* 1, no. 1 (2005): 1–35.

have attempted to exploit the so-called year-end anomalies and a whole variety of strategies supposedly docu-
mented by academic research. And I have yet to make
a single nickel on any of these supposed market inefficiencies.[11]

The problems with stock market and economic indicators are many.
Some have a poor track record of predictions, while others have a good
track record but no economic rationale and thus offer little confidence that
they are not just statistical anomalies.

The Skyscraper Index, in contrast, does have a good record in predicting important downturns in the economy. This index is a leading
economic indicator. The announcement of building plans — and in particular, groundbreaking ceremonies — typically occurs during economic
expansions long before the onset of an economic crisis.

The most important question about the Skyscraper Index is why it has
had such a good record of predictive success. Why does it work? What can
it tell us about the structure of the economy over the course of a business
cycle? Before we answer those questions, let us first examine the history of
the index's success in predicting the curse.

---

[11]Richard Roll, "Volatility in U.S. and Japanese Stock Markets: A Symposium," *Journal of
Applied Corporate Finance* 5, no. 1 (Spring 1992): 29–30.

CHAPTER 2

The History of the Skyscraper Curse Reexamined

Y ou could probably go back in history and find examples of the skyscraper curse in structures such as the Egyptian pyramids and medieval cathedrals. Here the review is confined to modern buildings, but we will expand our time horizon to examine records prior to and after the original Skyscraper Index (1907–99). We will also reexamine the one record-setting building, the Woolworth Building, that Andrew Lawrence considered a failure of the index because no curse occurred. As a result of this reexamination, the Skyscraper Index appears more reliable than previously thought.

This reexamination will consider modern buildings with steel-frame construction. The primary criteria for record-breaking projects are the number of floors of livable space and building height, not counting features such as antennas and spires. Those types of adornments are not costly or technologically challenging, compared to difficulties of building taller buildings with more livable space, which have requirements for such things as elevators, plumbing, and temperature control.

The two important inventions that made skyscraper construction feasible were the elevator and the steel-frame construction technique. Prior to the introduction of elevators in the 1850s, construction was typically limited to four-story buildings. Before the introduction of elevators, the lower floors were more highly valued and the higher floors were less highly valued because of the added time and effort of climbing more stairs. This limited the demand to build higher. With elevators, the higher floors became more highly valued, with the exception of first-floor retail space. The introduction of steel-frame construction in the late nineteenth century made it much more cost effective to build taller structures. Steel-beam construction bears the load or weight of taller buildings, and construction can proceed at a faster pace. In contrast, masonry construction requires an ever-larger base to carry the load of taller buildings.

The Equitable Life Assurance Building in New York City is considered by many to be the first skyscraper. Construction was completed in early 1870 and the building opened on May 1. It served as the home of the Equitable Life Assurance Society and was the first office building to feature hydraulic passenger elevators. It had seven floors and set a new record height at 130 feet.

Prior to its opening and approximately when it set the record height, the first Black Friday occurred on September 24, 1869. Jay Gould and James Fisk were attempting to corner the gold market in New York City, but US Treasury officials broke up their plot by selling large amounts of gold. Nevertheless, the economy was adversely affected as the price of gold first skyrocketed and then collapsed. In the aftermath, stocks fell by 20 percent and agricultural exports, the key output of the US economy, declined by 50 percent. According to Robert Kennedy,[1] there were several bankruptcies of brokerage firms "and a severe disruption to the national economy for months." The aftermath has been labeled both a panic and a depression, but not a significant one.

The Home Insurance Building was completed in 1884 in Chicago. It rose to a height of ten floors and 138 feet. Interestingly, two more floors were added in 1890. This building is connected to the panic of 1884 and the depression of 1882–85. While the financial panic was real, the depression that occurred was mostly about deflation and the railroad bubble. According to Victor Zarnowitz,[2] his measure of economic activity indicates that the depression was less severe than the panics of 1873 and 1893 and the depression of 1920–21.

The Auditorium Building in Chicago set a new record of seventeen floors and 222 feet to the top floor in late 1889. Meanwhile the New York

---

[1] Robert C. Kennedy, "Gold at 160, Gold at 130," *Harper's Weekly*, October 16, 1869.

[2] Victor Zarnowitz, *Business Cycles: Theory, History, Indicators, and Forecasting* (Chicago: University of Chicago Press, 1992), pp. 221–16.

Building	Announcement	Record Completion	Opening	Economic Crisis
Auditorium Building- Chicago		1889		Baring Crisis— Panic of 1890
Pulitzer (New York World)	Jun 1889	1890	Dec 1890	Baring Crisis— Panic of 1890
Masonic Temple- Chicago		1892		Panic of 1893
Manhattan Life	Feb 1892	1894	May 1894	Panic of 1893
Park Row	Mar 1896	1899	Apr 1899	No Crisis
Singer Building	Feb 1906	1908	May 1908	Panic of 1907
Metropolitan Life	Jan 1907	1909	Jan 1910	Panic of 1907
Woolworth	Jul 1910	1913	Apr 1913	World War I 1914
40 Wall Street	Mar 1929	1930	May 1930	The Great Depression
Chrysler	Oct 1928	1930	Apr 1930	The Great Depression
Empire State	Aug 1929	1931	Apr 1931	The Great Depression
World Trade Towers	Jan 1964	1970-1971	Dec 1970/ Jan 1972	Bretton Woods- Stagflation, Au standard
Sears Tower	Jul 1970	1973	Sep 1973	Bretton Woods- Stagflation, Au standard
Petronas Towers	Aug 1991	Mar 1996	Sep 1999	Asian Financial Crisis
Taipei 101	Oct1997	2004	Dec 2004	Asian Financial Crisis— Tech Bubble
Burj Khalifa	Feb 2003	Jul 2007	Jan 2010	The Great Recession

World Building, also known as the Pulitzer Building, was completed in 1890 with sixteen to twenty floors (depending on how it is measured) and was 309 feet high, setting a new height record.

This cluster of new-record skyscrapers can be linked to the panic of 1890. Also known as the Baring crisis, it involved the near insolvency of Barings Bank in London. The crisis was international in scope, but the most severe impact did not involve the US economy. It should be kept in mind that the United States was becoming the world economic powerhouse, transforming itself from a largely agricultural economy into a manufacturing and service economy. As farmers went to the cities they often took jobs not only in manufacturing, but also in service sectors, such as insurance and sewing machine salespersons. The service industries were a significant component of the demand for office space and hence skyscrapers.

The Manhattan Life Insurance Building was completed in 1894 with eighteen floors and 348 feet in height, setting a new record. Also completed at this time were the American Surety Building with twenty floors and 303 feet in 1895 and the Masonic Temple with nineteen floors and 302 feet in 1892, but they are not widely considered clear record-breaking skyscrapers. Nevertheless, this cluster of skyscraper construction coincided with the largest contraction in US history, culminating in the largest quarterly decline in real GNP in US history and included the panic of 1893, which is thought to have begun six years of double-digit unemployment, although those statistics are still open to debate among economic historians.

The Park Row Building was completed in 1899. It was twenty-six full floors and is at least 309 feet in height: if the three-story cupolas are included its height is 390 feet, which would make it the world's then-tallest skyscraper. The opening of the building was preceded by the fourth-largest quarterly decline in real GNP over the period of 1875–1918.

The next skyscraper cluster took place between 1904 and 1909. This is the cycle where Lawrence begins his documentation of the Skyscraper Index. It included the Singer Building, which, at forty-seven floors and 612 total feet in height, became the world's tallest skyscraper when completed in 1908. The Metropolitan Life Insurance Company Tower set another new record in 1909 with fifty floors and 700 total feet in height. Both projects were begun prior to the panic of 1907 and were reaching record heights when the panic occurred. The panic occurred at a time when seasonal factors relating to fall harvests coincided with cyclical factors in credit markets. It ignited in October when a bank regulated under the National Banking Act refused to clear funds for the Knickerbocker Trust Company, an unregulated bank. The result was widespread runs on banks and one of the sharpest downturns in US history. This episode is historically important and of continuing relevance because it is widely considered to be the key event that led to the passage of the Federal Reserve Act in 1913.

It is worth noting that the panic of 1907, like many nineteenth-century panics, is now widely considered to have been caused by the regulatory structure imposed by the National Banking Acts (1863 and 1864).

According to Howden,[3] the financial instability during this period was not the result of a lack of regulation or unfettered capitalism. According to Michael Bordo, Peter Rappoport, and Anna J. Schwartz,[4] the National Banking Acts created a system that was "characterized by monetary and cyclical instability, four banking panics, frequent stock market crashes, and other financial disturbances." The poor performance of the subsequently adopted Federal Reserve has led many economists to call into question the suitability of a central bank for solving the problems caused by the National Banking Acts.

The Woolworth Building was the world's next record-breaking skyscraper in 1913. When completed, it stood fifty-seven floors and 792 feet tall. Lawrence saw the Woolworth Building as an exception to, or error in, his Skyscraper Index because there was no curse in the sense that there was no major economic crisis that coincided with the building. There is no famous panic or depression in the history textbooks. Therefore it seems like the Skyscraper Index failed in this case.

However, it would be wrong to consider the Woolworth Building as evidence against the Skyscraper Index. The Woolworth Building project was announced in March of 1910, but at first it was planned to be a modestly tall building. In November 1910 its projected height was increased, but it was still only slated to become the third-tallest building in the world. In January of 1911 the building was re-planned to become one of the tallest buildings in the world at 750 feet, but this figure was later raised still higher to more than 792 feet high.[5] The opening ceremonies for the Woolworth Building were held on April 24, 1913, although it was not fully completed until later.[6]

In fact, the US economy peaked and began to contract in the first quarter of 1913, ahead of opening ceremonies. The economy continued

---

[3]David Howden, "A Pre-History of the Federal Reserve," in *The Fed at One Hundred: A Critical Review on the Federal Reserve System*, edited by David Howden and Joseph T. Salerno (New York: Springer, 2014).

[4]Michael D. Bordo, Peter Rappoport, and Anna J. Schwartz, "Money versus Credit Rationing: Evidence for the National Banking Era, 1880–1914," in *Strategic Factors in Nineteenth-Century American Economic Growth*, edited by Claudia Goldin and Hugh Rockoff (Chicago: University of Chicago Press, 1992), p. 189.

[5]Sara Bradford Landau, and Carl W. Condit, *Rise of the New York Skyscraper: 1865–1913* (New Haven, CT: Yale University Press, 1996), pp. 382–84.

[6]Ibid., p. 390.

to contract until the fourth quarter of 1914. This contraction included the third-worst quarterly decline in real GNP between 1875 and 1918, and was worse than any quarterly performance between 1946 and 1983. Kaza[7] reports that the building's opening ceremony occurred during a twenty-three-month-long contraction between January 1913 and December 1914. This would clearly qualify this period as a severe recession.

The only reason that American history textbooks do not refer to the depression of 1913 or something else was that World War I was already brewing in Europe and hostilities would break out in mid-1914. WWI was the largest conflagration in human history, resulting in over twenty million casualties of all types. However, in the United States the war created a tremendous increase in demand from Europe for US agricultural products, metal production, and armaments, as well as labor. This event singlehandedly provided stabilization for the American economy and pulled it into an expansion, not an ordinary recovery. While economic historians now know that World War II did not get America out of the Great Depression,[8] WWI appears to have prevented the United States from falling into one.

Therefore, it would seem that the Woolworth Building should not be viewed as an exception to or error in the Skyscraper Index. It was simply that World War I in Europe did not provide enough time for the economic slump in the United States to deepen and to justify a historical label such as the depression of 1913.

A reexamination pre-Index of the evidence suggests that the Skyscraper Index is an even better forecasting tool than first presented by Lawrence. First, we have shown that the skyscraper curse occurred several times in the late nineteenth century. Second, the only example of an error of the original Skyscraper Index, when the curse did not happen, has a simple explanation. Our examination of this early period also makes clear that the causes behind both skyscrapers reaching new heights and economic crises emerging are related to government intervention in credit markets.

The next cluster of the world's tallest buildings occurred at the onset of the Great Depression. Three record-breaking skyscrapers were announced during the late 1920s, when the stock market boom was being matched by

---

[7]Greg Kaza, "Note: Wolverines, Razorbacks, and Skyscrapers," *Quarterly Journal of Austrian Economics* 13, no. 4 (Winter 2010): 74–79.

[8]Robert Higgs, "Wartime Prosperity? A Reassessment of the U.S. Economy in the 1940s," *Journal of Economy History* 52, no. 1 (March 1992): 41–60.

booms in residential and commercial construction, as well as in manufacturing. In May 1930, the skyscraper at 40 Wall Street (now the Trump Building) was completed at a height of seventy floors and 927 feet. This was followed by the Chrysler Building in 1930 at seventy-seven floors and a height of 899 feet (925 feet to the roof and 1,046 to the top of the spire). The Empire State Building was completed a year later in May 1931 at 102 floors and 1,224 feet. Clearly, there was a capital-oriented boom in the construction of ever-taller buildings before the Great Depression.

Economists have offered many different explanations for the Great Depression, and Robert Lucas[9] has even claimed that it defies explanation. What is clear is that there was a significant increase in the money stock between the founding of the Federal Reserve and the stock market crash, a significant restructuring in banking and bank regulation, a significant decline in the supply of money after the crash, despite the Fed's best efforts to stop it,[10] a significant number of bank failures, and a variety of other important factors that contributed to the initiation and duration of the depression, including the Smoot-Hawley tariff and President Hoover's and President Roosevelt's New Deal policies.[11]

It is also worth noting that Ben Bernanke,[12] Milton Friedman and Anna Schwartz,[13] and Murray Rothbard[14] all place the blame for the Great Depression on the Federal Reserve, but for different reasons. Bernanke believes the problem was that the Federal Reserve failed to bail out systemically important banks in the 1930s. Friedman and Schwartz believe the problem was that the Fed failed to prevent a drop in the stock of money in the 1930s. Rothbard, using ABCT, found the cause to be the Fed's expansionary monetary policy in the 1920s. These three theories will be reexamined later in the book.

---

[9]Robert E. Lucas, Jr., *Models of Business Cycles* (New York: Basil Blackwell, 1987).

[10]Joseph T. Salerno, "Money and Gold in the 1920s and 1930s: An Austrian View," *Freeman* (October 1999): 31–40. Reprinted in Joseph T. Salerno, *Money Sound and Unsound* (Auburn, AL: Mises Institute, 2010), pp. 431–49.

[11]Murray N. Rothbard, *America's Great Depression*, 5th ed. (1963; Auburn, AL: Mises Institute, 2000).

[12]Ben S. Bernanke, *Essays on the Great Depression* (Princeton, NJ: Princeton University Press, 2004).

[13]Milton Friedman, and Anna J. Schwartz, *The Great Contraction, 1929–1933* (Princeton, NJ: Princeton University Press, 1965).

[14]Rothbard, *America's Great Depression.*

The next major cluster of skyscraper records occurred in the early 1970s. Once again the economy was coming off a strong and sustained boom in economic activity during the 1960s. At the peak of the 1960s boom, construction workers in New York and Chicago were busy building the next group of the world's tallest buildings. They would break records set back in the early days of the Great Depression. The World Trade Center was completed in 1972 and opened in April 1973. Both of the Twin Towers were 110 floors, with 1 World Trade Center at 1,368 feet in height and 2 World Trade Center at 1,362 feet in height. Then in Chicago, the Sears Tower was completed in 1974, which also had 110 floors but reached a height of 1,450 feet.

The economic downturn of early 1970 marked the beginning of a slump more than a decade long with the then-rare confluences of high rates of both inflation and unemployment. The breakdown of the Bretton Woods monetary system, abandoning the last vestiges of the gold standard, wage and price controls, gasoline shortages, and several recessions occurred between 1970 and 1982. There were several straight months in the early 1980s where unemployment was double digits and interest rates exceeded 15 percent. The US stock market declined in value between 1970 and 1982 by an inflation-adjusted 50 percent. The skyscraper curse for this period is known as the stagflation of the 1970s. This indicates that there was a general depression in the US economy between 1970 and 1982. The experience thoroughly discredited the then-dominant Keynesian school of economics, at least temporarily.

The next skyscraper cycle ushered in the 1997 Asian financial crisis and the dot-com bubble. The Pacific Rim countries, such as Hong Kong, Malaysia, Singapore, Vietnam, and South Korea, experienced significant economic growth during the 1980s and 1990s. Japan was the region's leading economy, but it was in recession for much of the 1990s. Observers named the smaller regional economies the Asian Tigers. They were considered miracle economies because they were strong and durable despite being small and volatile. The bubble in East Asia was rooted in technology and export manufacturing, but it was fueled by an expansion of money and credit, much of it foreign money seeking high returns for "investors without borders." This influx of foreign-investment money led to large increases in domestic money supplies and bank lending.

The Petronas Towers were completed in Kuala Lumpur, the capital of Malaysia, setting a new record for the world's tallest building. They are only eighty-eight floors, but 1,483 feet in height, which breaks the old record by 33 feet. The two Petronas Towers were completed just months before the skyscraper curse hit in mid-1997. It marked the beginning of the extreme drop in Malaysia's stock market and those around the region, rapid depreciation of local currencies, and even widespread social unrest. Financial and economic problems spread to economies throughout the region, a phenomenon known as the Asian contagion or, more generally, the Asian financial crisis. The ensuing credit crunch increased bankruptcies and created panic-like conditions.

At the same time, with increased US interest rates and a stronger dollar, the United States became a more attractive investment environment relative to East Asia. Starting in early 1996 this began to hurt Asian exports into the United States. These events essentially transferred the tech bubble from Asia to the United States and to a lesser extent Singapore and Taiwan, which were initially insulated from the crisis.

The next record breaker's planning began in 1997. Construction began in 1999 on Taipei 101 in Taiwan City, the capital of the Republic of China (a.k.a. Taiwan). The 101-floor building set a new world record if you go by the height of livable space of 1,671 feet. This height surpassed the Petronas Towers, and Taipei 101 became the first skyscraper to exceed one-half of a kilometer. The roof was completed in June 2003, but we are not sure when the new record was set. However, its construction closely paralleled the dot-com/tech bubble's bursting. This was the first skyscraper cycle to occur in the developing world and the first in which one record, the Petronas Towers, was broken at the beginning of a crisis and the other, Taipei 101, was completed at the end of the crisis — that is, the dot-com/tech bubble. A wild card here is the tech bubble, which was essentially transferred from the Asian-contagion countries to the United States and non-Asian-contagion countries, such as Taiwan and Korea. Taipei 101 is the first addition to the Skyscraper Index after Lawrence.[15]

The next world-record-breaking skyscraper was the Burj Dubai tower, which began construction in 2004 in Dubai, in the United Arab Emirates. At this time, it was clear to me that in the United States there was what would come to be called the housing bubble. The tower set a new record in the summer of 2007 just as the housing bubble ended and a financial crisis started to become apparent. The building opened to the public in January 2010 in the depths of the financial crisis, with Dubai

---

[15]Andrew Lawrence, "The Skyscraper Index: Faulty Towers!" *Property Report*, January 15, 1999.

bankrupt and needing a multibillion-dollar bailout from a neighboring emirate. The bailout resulted in the name of the building being changed from the Burj Dubai to the Burj Khalifa tower. This is another addition to the Skyscraper Index after Lawrence.[16]

These skyscraper cycles reliably contain common features. A cycle begins with a long period of easy money and credit. This leads to an expansion of the economy and a boom in the stock market. In particular, the relatively easy availability of credit fuels a substantial increase in capital expenditures. Capital expenditures start to flow in the direction of new technologies, which in turn create new industries and transform existing industries. This is when the world's tallest buildings are begun. At some point afterward there is a necessary reversal. Many things could initiate the reversal. The reversal often gives the appearance of panic and mass psychological disorder, but people are being scared by real things such as not meeting profit expectations and projections, increases in interest rates, and problems with meeting sales projections, controlling costs, and retrieving accounts receivable. Finally, unemployment increases, particularly in capital- and technology-intensive industries. While this analysis concentrates on the US economy, the impact of these crises often has international implications.

The skyscraper has many of the characteristic features that play critical roles in various business cycle theories. These features make skyscrapers an important marker of the twentieth century's business cycles, that is, the recurring pattern of entrepreneurial errors in a boom phase that are later revealed during a bust phase to be malinvestments.

It would be very easy to dismiss the Skyscraper Index as a predictor of the business cycle, just as indicators and indexes of other major entrepreneurial advances like canals, railroads, and factories were. The twentieth century skyscraper replaced the factories and railroads, just as the information and service sectors have replaced heavy industry and manufacturing as the prominent sectors of the present US economy.

It should not be surprising that the skyscraper, an important manifestation of the twentieth-century business cycle and indicator of modern global capitalism and commerce, will itself be replaced in the same way by an unknown new capital and technologically intensive investment in the future.

16Ibid.

This chapter has demonstrated that Lawrence's Skyscraper Index can be extended backward and forward in time and that the one instance where the Skyscraper Index was thought to have failed because the skyscraper curse failed to materialize has a perfectly logical explanation. Next we turn our attention to the question of what makes the Skyscraper Index work.

CHAPTER 3

Do You Have a Theory?

We don't really know what starts the speculative bubbles.

— Jesse Abraham and Patric Hendershott, "Bubbles in
Metropolitan Housing Prices"

The Skyscraper Index was based on the most noteworthy business cycles of the twentieth century and can be explained using Austrian business cycle theory (ABCT). In contrast, there is no consensus within mainstream economics about business cycle theory. The Keynesians have several versions, but all are driven by psychology and changes in aggregate demand. This would include behavioral-finance economists such as Robert Shiller who believe that stock markets are irrational. There are also debt-cycle theories put forth by Irving Fisher, Hyman Minsky, and Joseph Schumpeter. There is the real business cycle theory (RBCT), which is associated with the Chicago school and embraces the role of external shocks, such as technological change. There is a political business cycle theory based on the election cycle, and there are even Marxist theories.

The problem with most business cycle theories is that they are really just descriptions of business cycles rather than economic theories of business cycles. Each description emphasizes particular features that are then elevated to the status of causal forces. Each stage of the business cycle is characterized by several features — for example, speculation, unstable supply of money, changes in aggregate demand, changes in social mood, and external real factors, or shocks. As a result, business cycle theories could be characterized as perspectives in which the economist has identified particular features of the economy to blame, along with their preferred remedies.

As such, business cycles are reoccurring sequences of varying length of expansions, downturns, contractions, and upturns in many types of economic activities such as production, employment, income, sales, housing starts, money, credit, and prices. Interest rates, inventories, fixed capital, and loans outstanding tend to be procyclical. Keynesian theories emphasize that business cycles must be fought with aggressive government policies, such as deficit spending, bailouts, public works projects, and monetary stimulus. Real business cycle theorists take the opposite approach and recommend a passive policy of letting the government and economy absorb the impact of external shocks.

Austrian business cycle theory has significant advantages over mainstream theories:

First, whereas mainstream theories find the cause of business cycles to be either psychological or technological, ABCT identifies a cause of the business cycle that is economic in nature — namely, artificially low interest rates, which start a chain of events that can be understood using simple economic tools, such as supply and demand.

Second, mainstream theories assume away the complexities of the real-world economy, while ABCT incorporates complexity in its analysis.

Third, ABCT incorporates the psychological and technological features of mainstream theories and shows them to be predictable rather than random and unexpected shocks.

Fourth, by identifying an economic cause of the business cycle, ABCT reveals a solution for ending the business cycle and the endless cycle of psychological and technological shocks and wasted resources.

For ABCT, the cause of the boom and subsequent bust is when the central bank reduces the market rate of interest below the natural rate of interest by increasing the supply of money and credit. The natural rate of interest is the market rate of interest set by savers and borrowers in the absence of intervention by the central bank and is adjusted for both risk and price inflation. This rate, therefore, signals the general time preference of society. Artificially low interest rates are not calculable because we cannot know what the natural market rate would be except by indirect measures such as the amount of open-market operations conducted by the Fed — that is, its net government-bond purchases. However, we can understand the impact of artificially low interest rates by looking at another, more straightforward, example of a government price control — in this case, a price ceiling set by rent-control laws. Such laws keep the rental rates on apartments artificially low. These laws lead to shortages of apartments, physical depreciation of apartment buildings, and misallocation of apartments. For example, with rent-control laws, you might find a large family occupying a one-bedroom apartment and a single individual living in a three-bedroom apartment due to the shortage of apartments. The key difference with artificially low interest rates in the loanable-funds market is that the Fed can make up for any deficiencies and prevents a shortage by printing money out of thin air.

Market for Loanable Funds

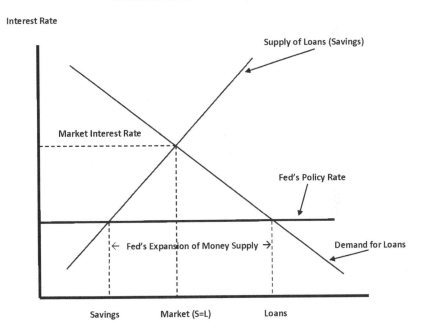

Prior to Fed involvement, the amount of savings and borrowing are equal at the market-determined interest rate. Actual loan rates of interest vary from loan to loan based on the combination of the base rate, risk premium, inflation premium, and processing costs. After the Fed has reduced this rate to artificially low levels it creates a shortage of loanable funds, which it then corrects by buying government bonds from banks for cash.

Banks now have more cash, which they can use to make loans. The direct consequences of this policy are to reduce savings, increase lending and debt, and lower lending standards so that individuals with lower credit ratings obtain loans and individuals with higher scores can obtain a larger amount of loans.

For consumers this means a greater debt burden and a reduction of future income because of less saving and interest income. For entrepreneurs this means a larger amount of borrowing. The lower interest rates also make longer-term investments appear more profitable relative to shorter-term investments. For example, low rates might induce a farmer to switch from growing corn, an annual crop, to growing apples, a multi-decade-length project. Lower interest rates induce foresters to let their trees grow longer, winemakers to let their wine age longer, and publishers to have larger print runs of their books. It also induces entrepreneurs to make production structures more roundabout.

The simplest example concerning roundabout production is of an isolated person who catches fish by hand and obtains one fish per day. If that person spends one day not fishing, but instead makes a net, that person could obtain three or four fish per day. Fishing by hand is direct production, while making the net and then fishing is more roundabout.

For a more modern example, let us examine the alternative ways we can communicate with each other. The most direct way of communicating with someone is to walk over to them and begin talking. A more roundabout method would be to first run a telephone line between your location and their location and use telephones to communicate. Using phones to communicate implies the prior existence of a vast variety of capital goods for the production of wires, phones, telephone poles, and so on. The amount and complexity of capital goods for cellular phone service is even more astounding. Phones are therefore more roundabout than the "walk and talk" method, but are much more productive. Austrian economists focus on this process of technological change. Investment in more roundabout production processes means that investors are investing in new ways of doing things that were previously on the shelf but were not feasible or in general use. Spending money on research and development is investment in new technologies to be available in the future. These technologies generally involve even more-roundabout production processes. In this manner, ABCT shows how the interest rate plays a direct role in the so-called technological shocks of the RBCT.

ABCT also tries to deal with the complexity of the economy rather than assuming it away. Mainstream theories generally have a mathematical model manipulating aggregate statistics such as consumption, investment, and government spending. The mainstream approach treats capital as a homogeneous factor of production that can be retooled and relocated with a wave of a magic wand.

In contrast, ABCT examines structures of production that span from the discovery of raw materials to the final product available for sale in retail stores. There are many stages of production in every structure of production, and each stage employs specific and nonspecific labor and specific and nonspecific capital goods. For example, an oil refinery contains a multitude of capital goods that are very specific to refining oil, but also capital goods such as pipelines and tanker trucks that are nonspecific capital goods because they can be used to transport many different things. To these, the entrepreneur adds very specific labor (e.g., petroleum engineers), nonspecific labor (e.g., truck drivers), and other inputs from previous stages of production (e.g., crude oil) in order to produce gasoline, a consumer good. Therefore, ABCT can show that nonspecific capital and labor can more easily be reallocated if conditions in the gasoline market deteriorate, but highly specific capital and labor are much more difficult to reallocate. Either the market value of oil refineries and the salaries of petroleum engineers must fall dramatically or they must remain unemployed.

The structure of production of all goods and services is highly complex. It is so complex that mainstream economics assumes it away. Even being complex, we can know some things about it and some things that affect it. The structure of production of a new product begins with a very short and direct structure. For example, with the invention of the automobile hundreds of small companies started making their own hand-fitted parts and assembling cars one at a time.

My first "portable" computer was built just for me by a computer technician using purchased parts, and it was the first one in town. This "portable" was the size of a suitcase that would barely fit in the overhead compartment of an airplane and weighed almost twice as much as a fully packed suitcase. Over time structures of production tend to get longer and the number of companies that sell the final consumer product often decreases.

For example, mass-produced interchangeable parts and the assembly line production technique for automobiles were introduced and quickly adopted. These technologies made production more efficient and increased the specialization of labor. They also made the structure of production more roundabout: machines had to be created to make interchangeable parts and assembly lines, technologies had to be created to replicate those machines, and so on. Today we find the structure of the automobile industry incredibly complex, with thousands of firms spanning the globe. These firms provide everything from computer graphics software to design new automobiles to the caps for the air valves on tires. Parts are transported to assembly factories, and then automobiles are shipped to auto dealerships. For mainstream economists the idea of perfect competition is the initial chaos of thousands of individual automobile companies, while for Austrians the whole process of the initial chaos evolving over time into a small number of mega-sized automobile manufacturers is competition. Mainstream economics' ideal market form requires a large number of buyers and sellers, perfect information, a homogenous product, and several other conditions. For Austrian economists the only requirement for competition is no government barriers for entrepreneurs entering or exiting an industry.

Another difference between Austrians and mainstream economists concerns the role of money. For the mainstream economists money is neutral and is similar to their view of capital. Money can be injected into any point in the economy and it will not cause disruptions, distortions, or redistributions of wealth. In other words, new money does not affect the real economy or relative prices. For them it only raises the so-called price level and reduces the purchasing power of money. In the mainstream view, new money seamlessly seeps throughout the economy without resulting in any relevant changes in demands, relative prices, or production.

In contrast, Austrians base their analysis on the real impacts money can have on the economy. Let us contemplate a doubling of the money supply in the economy, as Richard Cantillon did in 1730. He concluded that new money could not possibly be neutral and then gave several examples of new money and how it would disturb an economy and cause redistributions. His examples included the discovery of silver mines and a large number of wealthy immigrants moving into a nation with their money. He showed that new money changes prices and production to meet the new demands of wealthy mine owners, miners, and new immigrants.

Our example is a central bank that wishes to try an experiment with newly printed money. After carefully acquiring the names of all pickup truck and NASCAR enthusiasts in the economy, it credits each of their bank accounts with $10 million. Austrian economists would expect to see ticket prices for the Daytona 500 increase dramatically, and they might speculate about the introduction of a Daytona 1000, but mainstream economists would expect no change. Austrian economists would expect that the price of the Ford F-450, the most expensive pickup truck in the market today, would increase and that Ford would produce a larger quantity of such trucks and might even build a new assembly plant or even design more expensive versions of its line of pickup trucks.

The pickup truck and NASCAR enthusiasts, the Daytona 500, and the pickup truck producers would all gain relative to everyone else. However, when all the money was spent, what would happen to the new capital that the Daytona 500 and Ford have invested? Mainstream economists tell us that there would be no effect on incomes, wealth, production, and new products or that any such disturbance would only be short lived and unimportant.

In recent years, the Fed's use of zero–interest rate policy (ZIRP) and quantitative easing (QE) has made it possible for hedge fund managers, Wall Street bankers, and bond dealers to become extraordinarily wealthy. As a result of this immense wealth, real estate prices in Manhattan have increased dramatically and many new luxury-condo skyscrapers have been constructed. The experience at art auctions also tells a similar story. The price of artwork of artists of the currently fashionable contemporary-art genre, such as Jean-Michel Basquiat, Christopher Wool, and Jeff Koons, has skyrocketed to millions of dollars, while the minor works of such famed artists as the impressionist Pierre-Auguste Renoir can be purchased for perhaps less than $100,000.

In reality, with conventional monetary policy there are some straightforward ways in which the economy is distorted by artificially low interest rates. There is more lending and investment and entrepreneurs tend to favor longer-term, more roundabout means of production. For example, in the current environment of extremely low interest rates, especially for large corporations, Amazon has found it profitable to use robots rather than employees to fulfill orders from customers, despite the low-wage environment. The most direct way to fulfill orders is to have employees read orders, retrieve products, and package the products for delivery. A more roundabout method would be to design and build robots to replace the employees; create software for the robots to fulfill orders; reorganize warehouses and order-fulfillment centers to operate with robots; and train some employees to maintain and interact with the robots.

To watch the robots move around Amazon facilities, one might get the feeling that the company is somehow cheating on its various competitors. Additionally, when one looks at the price of Amazon stock one might guess that the company is earning huge profits, akin to a worldwide monopoly. Sales in 2015 were an enormous $35.7 billion, up 22 percent over 2014. Profits were also up a staggering 125 percent at $482 million in 2015. However, that means they are only making about 1 percent profit on sales. Amazon has a market capitalization of $300 billion and a price-to-earnings ratio of over 500.[1] In other words, investors cannot imagine anything going wrong for the company. Wilson[2] reports that one analyst predicts the company will be worth $3 trillion in less than ten years.

Some of the conventional disturbances caused by an increased money supply include a redistribution of wealth from savers to borrowers because borrowers obtain loans at lower rates, savers get a lower return on their savings, and the value of savings and debt is diminished by price inflation. The biggest beneficiary of this redistribution is the federal government, which has trillions of dollars of debt. The other primary redistribution from an increased money supply is the redistribution from people working for wages or living on fixed incomes to people with variable incomes, primarily but not exclusively in the financial sector.

Keynesian business cycle theories are based on psychological factors while real business cycle theory rests on external shocks such as technological change. ABCT incorporates both psychology and technology. With artificially low interest rates the economy will experience more investment and consumption. The price of assets will increase and unemployment will fall, even below the so-called natural rate of unemployment. Wages, incomes, and profits will all increase. During this boom Austrians expect the psychology of investors and entrepreneurs to be highly positive. Retirement stock accounts will increase substantially, variable-income workers in the service economy, such as waiters and massage therapists, will earn higher incomes, and novices will earn windfall incomes by endeavors such as flipping houses and day trading stocks. Given the above story about Amazon, it would also not surprise Austrians that a great deal of new technology would come about; in fact with ABCT it would be expected. The very nature of

---

[1]David Goldman, "Amazon Shares Plummet as Profit Disappoints," CNN.com, January 28, 2016.

[2]David Wilson, "Cisco, Apple Fail to Reach $1 Trillion. Is Amazon Next?" Bloomberg.com, May 9, 2016.

making an economy more roundabout implies new recipes for production and the introduction of new technologies. So there is a built-in rationale for a technology shock during a boom.

Every boom eventually peaks, and then the economy enters into a corrective phase, or bust. The reasons for transition are important and will be discussed, but for now let's stick to our example of the bust phase; in light of the mainstream business cycle theories, this is largely just reversing aspects of the boom phase. The price of assets will fall, and the unemployment rate will increase above the natural rate. Wages, incomes, and profits will fall, and the incomes of service workers will decline. House flippers will flop. Naturally the positive psychology of the boom will disappear and the social mood will turn gloomy. Austrians expect this to happen. We would be very surprised if it did not happen.

In terms of technological change, it is hard to undo technology once it is introduced, so Austrians generally expect large losses where there had been the largest investments in new technology, the real estate related to that new technology, and the people who financed that new technology. Some RBC theorists argued that the financial technology used in the housing bubble was responsible for both the bubble and the bust. They blamed the new financial instruments, such as collateralized debt obligations, mortgage-backed securities, and asset-backed securities. For RBCT this financial technology was both a positive shock up to 2007 and then a negative shock. Indeed, the financial technology is the primary, but not only, reason why it was, after all, a *housing* bubble. Without these new financial products, Fannie Mae, Freddie Mac, the Community Reinvestment Act, and the tax advantages of homeownership, it would have been simply a generalized bubble throughout the economy, rather than specifically a housing bubble.

For now let us look first at the process of economic growth and contrast it with the business cycle in light of ABCT. It is important to know that true economic growth is dependent on the existence of increased savings. When people spend less of their income on consumption goods and save their money, they leave more resources in the economy to be used by others. As compensation, they will have more savings and interest income so that in the future they can increase their consumption beyond their income, or even forgo working altogether.

Entrepreneurs need savings, whether it is acquired through bank loans, the sale of stocks and bonds, or retained earnings from their companies. They need money to acquire capital goods, to hire labor, and to pay other expenses. Companies will use savings to maintain their capital from physical depreciation and they will invest in new capital goods that present better profit opportunities because of technological advantages. This will make the production structures more roundabout, efficient, and productive. More savings makes it possible to pay for things such as more employee payroll and inventories prior to the consumer ultimately paying for the final product. In other words, all the resources hired and used from the acquisition of raw materials to the final assembly and sale of consumption goods have to be financed in some way. More savings results in greater productivity and production.

Now let us contrast economic growth with the business cycle. Instead of an increased preference for saving and future income, now the lower interest rate and source of new loanable funds comes as a result of the monetary policy of the central bank. At the lower interest rate people will save less, not more. They will consume more. Investment will increase, particularly in longer-run, more-roundabout production technologies, but also for consumption purposes.

Reducing saving and increasing consumption and debt makes consumers less wealthy and puts them in a more precarious economic position. Investing in more-roundabout production processes also puts entrepreneurs in jeopardy. For example, instead of two entrepreneurs developing two new factories for the production of new advanced computer chips, four such projects are proposed and financed at the artificially low rates. The entrepreneurs study their projects, which are not identical but are very similar, in order to determine where to construct such factories and what are the best places to find construction workers, engineers, scientists, and factory workers. Also, what are the best sources of the very-specific capital goods, such as chip-making machines and cleanroom technology? With existing chips selling better than expected due to increased consumption in the economy and promises of a new advanced chip on the way and financed at low interest rates, the stock price of these companies goes much higher. With such activities happening in many industries, the economy is booming.

Now we turn our attention to supply and demand issues as the entrepreneurs start running into some unforeseen circumstances. With twice the normal number of factories under construction, the price of land best suited for the factories is higher than expected. The availability of labor — first construction workers, but eventually the engineers, scientists, and factory workers — is less than anticipated and therefore wages and benefits are higher than were projected. The demand for the advanced chip-making machines and clean-room technology is also much higher than anticipated, so their prices are also higher than expected. Because there are four factories instead of two, the cost of all four projects will be higher than anticipated. Some components of the projects could be ordered in advance to avoid such cost increases, but not all them.

As the factories come online and start producing, other problems arise. The industry-wide supply of advanced computer chips is much greater than the entrepreneurs originally anticipated. As a result, the price of such chips falls and is lower than anticipated when the projects were initiated. The result of having undertaken four projects instead of two is that prices and revenues are lower than anticipated. Computer chips can be sold in advance too, but such hedging provides only short-term protection.

The overall demand for such an advanced computer chip is also likely to be adversely affected by the artificial interest rates. Recall that artificial rates increased consumption and reduced saving. This means that consumers were busy buying things such as the previous generation of smart phones and other chip-containing products, but now they have less savings and more debt. If half of your intended consumer base now has $10,000 in credit card debt and only $100 in their checking accounts, there is going to be a reduced demand for new chip-containing gadgets. This means fewer chips sold and even lower prices. The central bank can try additional doses of artificial credit, but it cannot print resources. It can only create more malinvestments and greater consumer debt. Notice that if there is a general glut of production capacity in an economy the result could be price deflation, the bogie man for mainstream economists.

With market-determined interest rates, an increase in the demand for loans by chip-making companies and entrepreneurs more generally would result in higher interest rates. When the interest rate is determined by the central bank, there is nearly a perfectly elastic supply of loans at the policy interest rate.

You can see the impact of artificially low interest rates today in the boom in higher orders of capital goods: the record-setting stock markets and general weakness in goods of the lowest order, consumption goods. Central bankers have feverishly used their one tool of money printing, but that has only created asset bubbles, malinvestments, and relative weakness in the Consumer Price Index, which is what ABCT expects. Once central bankers give up and put away their tool, asset prices will crash, malinvestments will be revealed, and consumer prices will be *relatively* strong.

Some might wonder here about the Austrian view of entrepreneurs. How can the same people who can figure out such amazing ways of improving the economy and its structures of production be fooled, repeatedly, by the Fed? Yes, Austrian economists do view the entrepreneur as a critical player in the economy, but entrepreneurs are not omniscient and we expect them to fail on a regular basis, constrained and controlled by competition, the system of profit and loss, and their capitalist backers. Engelhardt[3] shows how easy credit conditions provide low-quality entrepreneurs access to credit that they would not have access to under tighter credit conditions.

In a nutshell, ABCT warns that artificially low interest rates create malinvestments and a boom or bubble in the economy. This necessarily sets the stage for a recession, bust, or economic crisis when the cluster of entrepreneurial errors is revealed. This is an economic business cycle theory, although it anticipates and incorporates the technological shocks and psychological instability of the competing mainstream theories. ABCT shows us how the biggest policy errors by the central bank result in economic crises and skyscraper curses and more entries in the Skyscraper Index.

---

[3]Lucas Engelhardt, "Expansionary Monetary Policy and Decreasing Entrepreneurial Quality," *Quarterly Journal of Austrian Economics* 15 no. 2 (Summer 2012): 172–94.

CHAPTER 4

How To Get Milk

Economists understand very little about how technological progress occurs.

> — Alan Greenspan, "Testimony of Chairman
> Alan Greenspan"

Before we leave the topic of the problems and blessings of round-aboutness of production and the structure of production, it will be very useful to see a natural, concrete example of it in action. It then will become easier to understand the unnatural cases involving malinvestments and the skyscraper curse.

Making production processes more roundabout results in greater production in terms of the quantity produced and a lower cost on a per-unit basis. Entrepreneurs would not want to make production processes more roundabout unless they thought they would create more profits as a result. More roundabout production takes more time, more steps, and a more extensive division of labor. It also uses new technology.

Entrepreneurs do make mistakes, of course, but the only systematic errors they make are when they are fooled into rearranging production because of artificially low interest rates and easy credit conditions. When the central bank lowers its target interest rates it also makes credit conditions easier in that banks will make a larger volume of loans, which means they weaken their lending standards in order to facilitate the larger volume of loans.

A good example of a very direct production process, in contrast to a more roundabout one, is a farmer who goes to the barn, milks a cow, and then returns to the house and feeds the milk to his family.

An example of a more roundabout, although still very direct, production process comes from my childhood. We lived on the edge of a small town. Just beyond our house were fields and barns. Dairy cattle would feed on the grass in the fields. Later they would return to the barns to be milked. The milk would then be transported a short distance — a couple miles — in a small tanker truck to one of three small dairies in my hometown. There the milk would be processed and packaged. Early the next morning a dairy man in a white suit would arrive at our house and place several quart-size glass bottles of milk in an insulated dairy box outside of our back door and pick up any empty bottles we had placed there. If we wanted an ice cream sundae, we had to go to the dairy during retail hours.

By the time I graduated from high school the entire system had changed. The small dairy farms had been largely replaced with larger farms. The small four-wheel tanker trucks had been replaced by large eighteen-wheel tankers. An eighteen-wheel tanker truck brought the raw milk from the farms to the dairy factory about thirty miles from our house, and a different eighteen-wheel refrigerated truck brought cartons of milk and ice cream as well as boxes of butter to the supermarket. All three of the small hometown dairies eventually went out of business. They were replaced by much larger, factory-size dairies many miles from our home. Instead of having the milk bottles delivered directly to our house, we now purchased dairy products at the local supermarket, an institution that was also a relatively new phenomenon.

The dairy factory system is a much more roundabout production process. It takes more time. The milk travels a round-trip journey of more than sixty miles instead of the less-than-four-mile journey in the old days. There is a greater amount of capital as well as advanced technology involved and there is also far less labor per unit of milk. The overall cost of milk is lower, and with competition between large dairy wholesalers and supermarkets, so is the price.

In order to attain a more roundabout production process there are several requirements. It requires entrepreneurs with a vision of the most profitable action among all possible actions. It requires investment in more capital goods and new technology. Of course, all of this rearranging of production is going to take a great deal of time and even more time for it to be profitable.

Therefore, the entrepreneurs need to have access to savings. They need to have either their own savings or someone else's savings on a long-term basis in order to proceed. Hence there must be more overall savings in an economy in order to achieve more roundabout production and all the benefits it entails. Savers must have lower time preferences and be willing to delay some consumption in the present. Savers will be rewarded with interest income, with which they will be able to make a greater number of purchases in the future and at lower prices because of the increase in production of goods. The whole process is regulated by the rate of interest, the price system, and the system of profit and loss.

This process is sometimes referred to as creating economies of scale. But notice that while there are economies of scale in this example, *everything* about the production process changed. The most successful approach was not preordained or known in times past. The entire recipe or technology of production has changed. All the capital goods — including the milking machines, the trucks, and the machinery inside the dairies — are different. Notice further that the change in the dairy industry is going to induce changes in other industries, including technology and investment in the mechanical milking machines industry. All of this requires a careful synchronization process, which is obviously beyond the scope of central planning. The process is driven by the rate of interest. So we will now see what happens when the interest rate is misleading and results in an economic bust and, in severe cases, the skyscraper curse.

CHAPTER 5

Cantillon Effects

It makes very little difference how new money is injected.

— Scott Sumner, *TheMoneyIllusion*

In previous chapters, I described economic growth and development as a process whereby lowering time preferences leads to an accumulation of savings that are invested in more-roundabout production processes, which in turn increase future consumption possibilities, labor productivity, and wages and incomes.

We now turn our attention to what happens with an increase in the money supply, rather than an increase in savings. This is critically important. The mercantilist idea that increasing the money supply increases prosperity was exposed as an error centuries ago by Richard Cantillon.[1] However, modern mainstream economists, including the monetarists, Keynesians of various sorts, and the now-fashionable market monetarists, fully embrace the idea that printing money is necessary for prosperity.

In fact, the major central banks of the world have embarked on an unprecedented policy of monetary expansion both before and after the financial crisis of 2008. These central banks are led by people with advanced degrees in "economics," and they have large research staffs of people with

---

[1]Richard Cantillon, *Essai sur la Nature du Commerce en Général*, translated and edited by Henry Higgs (1755; London: Cass, 1931), chap. 1.

PhDs in mainstream economics. The result is a world currency war whereby each currency is printed in an effort to implement an economic expansion by a beggar-thy-neighbor policy, another widely discredited idea.

The beggar-thy-neighbor policy involves printing money to reduce the value of your domestic currency vs. foreign currencies. Reducing the value of your currency reduces the relative price of your exports and makes foreign products relatively more expensive so that you increase exports and domestically produced goods and reduce imports. The problem is that you also increase the price of imports and decrease efficiency. Ultimately this policy does not work: in the end you are worse off.

What happens when the supply of money increases? One of the first to examine this question was Richard Cantillon, writing in the 1730s in the wake of the Mississippi and South Sea Bubbles. Murray Rothbard wrote that Cantillon should have the premier honor among economists:

> The honor of being called the "father of modern economics" belongs, then, not to its usual recipient, Adam Smith, but to a gallicized Irish merchant, banker, and adventurer who wrote the first treatise on economics more than four decades before the publication of the *Wealth of Nations*. Richard Cantillon (c. early 1680s–1734) is one of the most fascinating characters in the history of social or economic thought.[2]

I have written elsewhere about looking at Cantillon's contributions through a modern and contemporary lens.[3]

The *Essai sur la Nature du Commerce en Général* was completed shortly before Cantillon was murdered in 1734. Due to French censorship laws it was not published until 1755, and under mysterious circumstances. The book was initially very influential. It is believed he wrote *Essai* to explain the Mississippi and South Sea Bubbles, but he ended up creating an entire theoretical apparatus and what we now call Cantillon effects.

Cantillon investigated several possible causes of an increase in the domestic money supply including money's importation from foreign countries and the discovery of new gold and silver mines. His important insight

---

[2]Murray N. Rothbard, *Economic Thought before Adam Smith: An Austrian Perspective on the History of Economic Thought* (Brookfield, VT: Edward Elgar, 1995), vol. 1, p. 345.

[3]Mark Thornton, "Richard Cantillon and the Origins of Economic Theory," *Journal of Economics and Humane Studies* 8, no. 1 (March 1998): 61–74.

was that the effect of this new money depended on who had control of this new money and where it was injected into the economy. New money has a disruptive impact on an economy and can cause what we now call the business cycle.

Mainstream economists typically limit the discussion of Cantillon effects to the redistribution of wealth that accompanies an increase in the money supply.[4] The first recipients of the money experience an increase in wealth, while those who do not receive it experience a decrease in wealth.[5] Rouanet provides extensive empirical evidence of the Cantillon effect in terms of changing the distribution of income.[6] However, this redistribution of wealth is only the first step in Cantillon's much deeper analysis of the effects of an increase in money.

For example, if the increased money came from new silver mines, then the money would be in the hands of the owners of the mines and the miners themselves. Cantillon speculated that these now-rich people would consume more meat and wine, instead of bread and beer. This would in turn increase the price of meat and wine and decrease the price of grain. As a result, these price changes would lead farmers to increase the land devoted to raising cattle and vineyards, rather than grain. These are structural changes to the economy, and obviously the mine owners and miners are better off. The peasants who lived on bread and beer would be worse off because the decreased production of grain would mean higher bread and beer prices. Cantillon further theorized that money flows, prices, and the structural changes that were built on them could be reversed and that various businesses would be ruined as a result.

Mainstream economists dismiss all of these real changes in an economy as first-round effects. They do not believe there are any important real-economy impacts from an increase in the money supply, and if minor alterations did occur, it would only lead to temporary, inconsequential changes in the structure of production and income distribution.

To emphasize the importance of where the new money is injected into an economy, Cantillon noted that if the new money came into the hands

---

[4]Andreas Marquart, and Philipp Bagus, *Blind Robbery! How the Fed, Banks, and Government Steal Our Money* (Munich: FinanzBuch Verlag, 2016).

[5]Mark Thornton, "Cantillon on the Cause of the Business Cycle," *Quarterly Journal of Austrian Economics* 9, no. 3 (Fall 2006): 45–60.

[6]Louis Rouanet, "Monetary Policy, Asset Price Inflation and Inequality." Master's Thesis, School of Public Affairs, Institut d'Etudes Politiques de Paris, 2017.

of entrepreneurs, the rate of interest would fall, but if the new money came into the hands of consumers, the rate of interest would rise. If entrepreneurs found themselves with twice the amount of money they previously had, then they would have less demand for loans to finance their purchases of raw materials and to pay their labor. Therefore the rate of interest would be lower. If instead the new money were to double the amount of money that consumers possessed, then they would increase their purchases of goods. This would cause entrepreneurs to borrow more in order to supply the increased demand for goods, which would result in a higher interest rate. Either channel of increased money would put upward pressures on prices. In both cases, the group that receives the money first benefits, while those who receive it later, or not at all, are harmed by the higher prices.

Furthermore, Cantillon was the first to develop the theory of the price-specie-flow mechanism. This theory shows that a country that receives a bounty of new money will eventually experience higher prices. Some types of goods can be produced either domestically or imported from other countries. As the new money causes domestic prices to rise, there is an increased tendency for people to buy imported goods, and therefore money is sent to other countries. In this way, Cantillon showed that domestic industries that benefit and expand because of the increased supply of money will eventually be ruined because their expanded capacity will no longer be profitable in the face of low-priced foreign competition.

The general form of a Cantillon effect is that there is increased money coming into an economy from somewhere. The first recipients benefit. They spend it according to their preferences, and this causes certain prices to go up. The sellers of those goods benefit from the new money, while others who only face higher prices are hurt. Entrepreneurs respond to the higher prices by increasing their capacity to produce those goods by acquiring specific capital goods, raw materials, and labor. As the economy moves toward monetary equilibrium, the industry-specific capital goods are exposed as unprofitable, and if it is difficult to repurpose them for alternative uses, the adjustment process threatens those entrepreneurs with bankruptcy. The main point of Cantillon's broader analysis is that changes in money result in changes in relative prices, which will change production plans and result in a different pattern of fixed investment such that new money changes the real economy and results in winners and losers.

Cantillon's analysis regarding injection of new money has been adopted and extended by Ludwig von Mises and F. A. Hayek as a foundation of Austrian business cycle theory (ABCT). In the modern theory the increase in the money supply is usually restricted to an expansion of bank reserves by the central bank and an expansion of bank loans. In ABCT, this reduces the interest rate below the natural rate and initiates a boom in the prices of capital goods as well as company stocks and real estate. This, in turn, leads to the production of fixed capital goods that will later be revealed as malinvestments, in turn leading to bankruptcies, if not a skyscraper curse.

Chapter 6

Cantillon Effects in Skyscrapers

M oney makes possible the good things in life: our ability to trade with one another and the ability to form groups to work for beneficial purposes, as well as saving, investing, economic growth, and development. Without some form of money, advanced society would not be possible. However, as we saw in the previous chapters, increases in the supply of money, which mainstream economists now view as indispensable, are really the source of many evils of economic life.

Increases in the supply of money result in higher consumer prices, a process now known as *inflation*. This means that many people with jobs suffer diminishing purchasing power of their wages over time. Economic historians have long agreed that such inflation is the enemy of labor. Free market monies, such as gold and silver, typically increase in value over time, which is beneficial for wage labor and encourages work and saving, as the purchasing power of wages and savings tends to increase over time.

Increasing the money supply causes an unnatural redistribution of wealth. People who receive the money first become wealthier because they spend the money before prices have risen. People who receive the money later or not at all become poorer because they pay the higher prices. In the case of money coming from the Federal Reserve, the biggest winners are the US government; its large contractors, such as weapons manufacturers, big banks, and Wall Street. As a result, the financial sector of the US economy has grown enormously and economic inequality, measured in terms of income and wealth, has increased dramatically since the United States went completely off the gold standard in 1971. The financial-services sector has grown from about 4 percent of the US economy then to over 8 percent now. Thomas Piketty[1] has famously shown that inequality of income and wealth has increased greatly in the United States and elsewhere. However, the entire increase in inequality has come after 1970 and the abolition of the Bretton Woods gold standard. The period beforehand, when we were on the gold standard, is one of increasing equality.

The big losers receive the money after prices have already risen. The losers would include private-sector workers and people on pensions or fixed income — in other words, the labor class. Inflation also harms savers and bond investors, as well as taxpayers who find themselves in higher tax brackets when wages catch up with price inflation. Simply put, paraphrasing Senator Phil Gramm of Texas, the people pulling the wagon are harmed and reduced in number, while the people sitting in the wagon benefit and increase in number.

Finally, inflating the money supply causes the business cycle, and this is the least well-understood aspect of the Fed's increasing of the money supply. It is not just natural swings in the economy; it is artificial, squanders resources, and ruins lives. This will be illustrated with the case of skyscraper construction.

Inflating the money supply is directly connected to interest rate manipulation. When the Fed buys government bonds from banks, it gives them dollars, which they can reinvest in more government bonds, mortgages, commercial loans, and consumer loans. This process artificially reduces interest rates. It also completes the movement of government bonds from the US Treasury, to the big banks, to the balance sheet of the Fed. It can sit there until it comes due, at which time the Fed can purchase more government bonds. The Fed is required to return any leftover interest income from these bonds to the US Treasury, so this process is the equivalent of an interest-free loan. Also, as monetary expansion turns into price inflation and lowers the value of the dollar, it effectively reduces the value of the national debt, a process referred to as *monetizing the national debt*. It is a convoluted process, but you can see why those who benefit do not want to reform it. It is quite a racket for the politicians, the big banks, and their highly paid facilitators at the Fed. This is the process that brings about

---

[1]Thomas Piketty, *Capital in the Twenty-First Century* (Cambridge, MA: Harvard University Press, 2014).

artificial gyrations in interest rates and creates Cantillon effects and business cycles.

The Cantillon effects that we can see in record-breaking skyscrapers are symptomatic of what is going on in the economy; it is just more difficult to point to some particular project or new technology and claim that it is a malinvestment caused by the Federal Reserve and artificially low interest rates. So remember, skyscrapers themselves do not cause business cycles, the Fed does.

Many people consider the skyscraper a form of art, but their construction is essentially a business that must respond to incentives and constraints. Therefore skyscraper construction can be expected to follow closely even small changes in relative prices. In reevaluating the early skyscraper artistically, Ada Louise Huxtable[2] noted:

> Essentially, the early skyscraper was an economic phenomenon in which business was the engine that drove innovation. The patron was the investment banker and the muse was cost-efficiency. Design was tied to the business equation, and style was secondary to the primary factors of investment and use. ... The priorities of the men who put up these buildings were economy, efficiency, size, and speed.

That is not to say that the early skyscrapers were without artistic merit, or that later structures failed to improve artistically; quite the contrary. Nevertheless, post-WWI skyscrapers continued to emphasize profits and technology. The early skyscraper drew from existing technology and was considered an engine of innovation. Even in modern times, design continues to grow and evolve, but for Helmut Jahn,[3] the "structural rationale for such a tall structure is technically and economically inescapable." For Huxtable,[4] "Architecture simply doesn't count. ... With pitifully few exceptions in the past, New York's skyscrapers have never reached for anything but money." Art, technology, government regulations, and even ego must be considered factors, but the skyscraper is essentially captive to economic forces and motives. Therefore when architects are asked what makes for

---

[2]Ada Louise Huxtable, *The Tall Building Artistically Reconsidered: The Search for a Skyscraper Style* (Berkeley: University of California Press, 1992).

[3]Quoted in ibid., p. 117.

[4]Ibid., p. 105.

the super skyscraper, economic forces are considered preeminent. Psychological factors related to ego are created in the credit driven boom.

In this context it is important to remember that changes in the price of land, building materials, and the interest rate will have important implications for skyscraper construction. Changes in the rate of interest have three separate Cantillon effects on skyscrapers. All three effects are reinforcing, and all three effects are interconnected to the transformation of the economy toward more roundabout production processes. When the rate of interest is artificially reduced, all three effects contribute to the desire to build taller structures. The world's tallest buildings are generally built when the interest rate is reduced substantially below the natural rate for a sustained period of time. In contrast, when the interest rate is forced above the natural rate the economic effects reduce the value of existing structures and the demand for tall buildings. Construction can come to a complete standstill.

The first Cantillon effect is the impact of the rate of interest on the price of land. The most obvious cause of this result is that lower interest rates reduce the opportunity cost of borrowing to buy the land and to build structures. As a result, owners of land and real estate experience an increase in their wealth. This relationship is confirmed by Jeremy Atack and Robert Margo,[5] who examined the market for land in New York City during the nineteenth century. Their evidence suggests that land values tended to increase during deflationary periods, when interest rates tend to be low, but less so during inflationary periods, when interest rates tend to be higher because of the inflation premium in interest rates. Paul Cwik[6] demonstrates that the interest rate has an impact on the net present value of working capital and longer-lived fixed capital. As a casual observation, when interest rates are artificially low, you tend to see more "land for sale" signs along roads and interstate highways because land prices are higher in general.

A lower rate of interest also tends to increase the value of land, because the interest rate is used by entrepreneurs as a proxy for the discount rate. In evaluating any investment project, entrepreneurs estimate the net pres-

---

[5]Jeremy Atack, and Robert A. Margo, "'Location, Location, Location!' The Market for Vacant Urban Land: New York 1835–1900." NBER Historical Paper 91, National Bureau of Economic Research (Cambridge, MA, August, 1996).

[6]Paul Cwik, "Austrian Business Cycle Theory: Corporate Finance Point of View," *Quarterly Journal of Austrian Economics* 11, no. 1 (2008): 60–68.

ent value of a project by looking at the projected income stream from the investment over a long period of time and adjusting it for interest payments over time. The income in the first year does not have to be discounted much at all, that is, just one year's interest expense, but that same income in year twenty-five has to be discounted by twenty-five years of interest expenses and may be worth nothing in terms of net present value. Net present value of an income stream has to exceed risk-adjusted cost of an investment for the project to be undertaken. High interest rates lead to heavy discounting of income streams, whereas low interest rates lead to less significant discounting, which makes long-term projects seem relatively more profitable.

For example, consider an investment project that is expected to produce $1 million in income above operating costs per year for ten years. In the tenth year of operation, if the discount rate is 4 percent, the calculated net present value of that year's $1 million net income is $675,000. However if the discount rate is 8 percent then the calculated net present value of that year's income is only $463,000.

From this we can see that land values rise because lower rates of interest reduce the opportunity cost, or full price, of owning land and drive up the net present value of income streams from using land. Treating the rate of interest as the cause, a reduction in the interest rate will increase the demand for land and result in an increase in land prices. The impact of lower discount rates will tend to favor longer-term investment projects using land, such as skyscrapers.

It has been often said that the three most important things about real estate are location, location, and location. When the rate of interest is falling, the land best suited for the production of the longer-term, more capital-intensive, and more roundabout methods of production will increase in price relative to land better suited for shorter-term, more direct methods of production. As land prices rise, the yield required from any piece of land to make ownership of it profitable must also rise. Combined with a lower cost of capital brought about by a lower rate of interest, land owners will seek to build more-capital-intensive structures, and at the margin, this will cause land to be put to alternative uses.

In the central business district this means more-intensive use of land and thus taller buildings. Higher prices for land reduce the ratio of the per-floor cost of tall vs. short buildings and thus create the incentive to build taller buildings to spread the land cost over a larger number of floors and more leasable space. Thus, higher land prices lead to taller buildings.

In my hometown there are a variety of one- and two-story structures currently being demolished to make way for the construction of multifloor structures. These projects are stimulated by artificially low interest rates and the search for yield on investment funds. In this manner, the height aspect of the projects is driven by land prices.

The second Cantillon effect from lower rates of interest is the impact on the size of firms. A lower cost of capital encourages firms to grow in size and to take advantage of economies of scale, such as the example of the dairy industry in transition. Here, companies that expand based on artificially low interest rates benefit, at least temporarily, at the expense of companies that do not and exit the industry. As part of this larger-scale, more roundabout production process, firms develop central offices or headquarters for their accounting, management, marketing, human resources, and product-development departments. This increases the demand for office space in central business districts. This demand in turn raises rents and encourages the construction of taller office buildings within the central business district.

The phenomenon of firms growing in size and scope in response to artificially low interest rates can be seen in the history of merger-and-acquisition waves. Mergers between two firms occur when both firms believe they can profit from combining their operations. Acquisitions and takeovers occur when one firm believes it can manage the combined assets of the firms in a more profitable manner. Lower interest rates reduce the cost of the capital to buy out investors of the other firm. Mergers and acquisitions have occurred in clusters or waves during periods of low interest rates and easy credit conditions (the boom), and because they often start operating as a united company during the bust, their record of success has not been great.

Saravia[7] shows that waves of mergers and acquisitions that have been experienced in the past are consistent with Austrian business cycle theory (ABCT). Not only do low interest rates help finance mergers and especially acquisitions, but the demand for such business deals is a reflection of the "resource crunch" of ABCT as shown in the previous example of the expansion of the advanced computer-chip industry. Ekelund, Ford, and Thornton[8] show that when mergers are delayed by government "red tape," the

---

[7]Jimmy A. Saravia, "Merger Waves and the Austrian Business Cycle Theory," *Quarterly Journal of Austrian Economics* 17, no. 2 (Summer 2014): 179–96.

[8]Robert B. Ekelund, George Ford, and Mark Thornton, "The Measurement of Merger Delay in Regulated and Restructuring Industries," *Applied Economics Letters* 8, no. 8 (2001): 535–37.

resulting acquisitions and mergers tend to be unprofitable because they are often completed during an economic downturn. Thornton[9] has furthered the discussion of why so many mergers and acquisitions turn out to be miscalculations.

The third Cantillon effect is the impact of interest rates on the technology of constructing record-tall buildings. Record-breaking skyscrapers require innovation and new technology in order to be profitable. Buildings that reach new heights pose numerous engineering and economic problems relating to such issues as building a sufficiently strong foundation, ventilation, heating, cooling, lighting, transportation (e.g., elevators, stairs, and parking), communication, electrical power, plumbing, fire protection, and security systems, as well as wind resistance, structural integrity, and even window cleaning. There are also a host of public issues connected with increases in employment density brought about by tall structures, such as transportation congestion and environmental concerns. For example, Sukkoo Kim[10] showed how increases in skyscraper-building and, in particular, improvements in skyscraper technology lead to increases in employment density. Here, advanced technology businesses benefit at the expense of incumbent technology businesses.

Beyond the mere technology it takes to build the world's tallest building, every vertical beam, tube, cable, pipe, or shaft in a building takes away from leasable space on each floor built, and the more floors in the structure, the greater the required capacity of each system in the building, whether it is plumbing, ventilation, or elevators. So designers, architects, and building contractors cannot simply increase the size of each system to increase capacity. They must come up with new, more efficient systems to reach record heights. Consequently, there is a tremendous desire to innovate with technology in order to conserve on the size of these building systems or to increase the capacity of those systems. Therefore, as the height of construction rises, input suppliers must go back to the drawing board and reinvent themselves, their products, and their production processes.

---

[9]Mark Thornton, "Review of The Synergy Trap: How Companies Lose the Acquisition Game, by Mark L. Sirower," Quarterly Journal of Austrian Economics 2, no. 1 (Spring 1999): 85–86.

[10]Sukkoo Kim, "The Reconstruction of the American Urban Landscape in the Twentieth Century," NBER Working Paper 8857, National Bureau of Economic Research (Cambridge, MA, April 2002).

M. Ali and Kyoung Sun Moon[11] describe how designers and engineers have a tremendous need to innovate to conserve on the requirements of building systems. For example, one elevator shaft with a floor size of 2×2 meters would take up the space equivalent of ten efficiency-sized apartments in a hundred-floor building. At standard speeds it would take about ten minutes to get to the top floor of the Burj Khalifa tower, plus the time it took for the elevator to arrive on your floor and any additional stops on the way to your destination. Ames[12] reports that KONE Corporation engineers have created a new elevator cable that weighs less than 7 percent of the weight of traditional steel cables, which each weigh over twenty tons for a 400-meter-high building. Obviously, a twenty-ton cable would require an enormous amount of power to operate. Therefore, as building heights rise, technology must be advanced to conserve on the building systems' footprint.

Another example of this type of technological effect is in heating and cooling systems for especially tall skyscrapers. Record-breaking skyscrapers require a tremendous capacity for heating and cooling; and traditionally, hot and cool air or water would have to be pumped long distances, which is both inefficient and requires a great deal of space for all the ductwork and plumbing. A recent solution to this problem is a system called variable-refrigerant-flow zoning and split-ductless systems. Instead of massive amounts of air or water transported throughout a building, only the refrigerant — for example, Freon — is moved to each zone. It is transported in small copper tubing rather than bulky ductwork or water pipes, which take up horizontal space between each floor as well as vertical space. Each zone can have its own temperature, and the flow of refrigerant is variable according to the needs, rather than just on and off. The total amount of equipment is less, it is easier to maintain, and it is said to be 25 percent more energy efficient. Surely this is a great invention, but one that would not have come along as early as it did in the age of the mega-skyscraper. In other words, enormous amounts of resources were expended to obtain small gains in efficiency due to the artificially high demand to build very tall skyscrapers. When the next economic crisis comes, the demand for

---

[11]M. Ali, and Kyoung Sun Moon, "Structural Developments in Tall Building: Current Trends and Future Prospects," *Architectural Science Review* 50, no. 3 (September 2007): 205–23.

[12]Nick Ames, "Elevator Installation Prep Begins at Kingdom Tower," ConstructionWeek-Online.com, May 10, 2015.

these advanced technologies could collapse because either no one is building such skyscrapers or they are only building much smaller buildings.

Construction systems must also be reinvented to tackle new record-breaking construction projects. For example, pumping concrete higher to build taller structures requires innovation in concrete-pumping technology; the same can be said for cranes and moving laborers to and from their worksite on the building. Again, in the economic crisis that follows, these systems and all the capital combinations that support them could either go unused or used at greatly diminished levels.

All three Cantillon effects resulting from lower rates of interest are interrelated and reinforcing. All three are generally recognized by people involved in the construction of large office buildings including architects, bankers, contractors, design specialists, engineers, entrepreneurs, government regulators, often the tenants themselves, and finance specialists such as bond dealers.

Higher interest rates discourage the construction of taller buildings and of construction in general because capital is scarcer and land is less in demand and available at lower prices. Higher interest rates also create financial difficulties for the owners of existing structures because of the decreased demand for office space and condos. Companies engaged in construction and their suppliers face a decrease in the demand for their services, the impact of which falls hardest on those firms that specialize in the production of the tallest buildings and the suppliers of the specialized construction systems and building systems for ultrahigh construction.

In other words, the technologies and industrial capacities that were induced by the artificially low interest rates are now greatly incapacitated and mostly idle. The buildings themselves are likely to have excess capacity, with too few tenants and lower-than-expected leasing rates.

The interest rate is what makes the construction business, in part, such a speculative business. Homebuilders build spec houses and face the risk of finding a buyer at a profitable price. Developers build speculative office buildings, which in contrast to many corporate headquarters are investments that rely on an uncertain flow of rental income. Separating the winners from the losers is not so much a matter of greed as it is a matter of time and calculation. Skyscraper expert Carol Willis explained the difference between normal times and boom times:

> In normal times, when costs of land, materials, and construction are predictable, developers use well-tested

formulas to estimate the economics of a project. These calculations are based on the concept of the capitalization of net income. This value takes into account the net income for thirty or forty years. ... [T]he conventional market formulas and the concept of economic height were widely known and followed in the industry. Most speculative building was not risky, but reserved in its calculations and highly responsive to market desires.[13]

All of these normal calculations that help ensure profit and avoid loss are not, however, reliable during the boom phase of the business cycle.

In booms, the so-called rational basis of land values is disregarded, and the answer to the question "What is the value of land?" becomes "Whatever someone is willing to pay." Some speculators estimate value on new assumptions of higher rents; others simply plan to turn a property for a quick profit. ... But due to the cyclical character of the real estate industry, the timing of a project is crucial to its success, and the amount a property reaps in rents or sale depends on when in a cycle it is completed or comes onto the market.[14]

Building the world's tallest building has been a matter of particularly bad timing by entrepreneurs, and even if they were able to successfully steal away enough tenants from the remaining pool of renters, the economic problem for society is that valuable resources are lost in the process of constructing buildings that are bad investments and underutilized. See, Patric Hendershott and Edward Kane,[15] who estimated that there was more than $130 billion wasted in the commercial construction boom of the 1980s. The Empire State Building was nicknamed the Empty State Building because of its high vacancy rates until after World War II.

However, it is not the entrepreneur's formula that is at fault, but a system-wide failure that has occurred periodically throughout the twentieth

---

[13]Carol Willis, *Form Follows Finance: Skyscrapers and Skylines in New York and Chicago* (New York: Princeton Architectural Press, 1995), p. 157.

[14]Ibid., pp. 157–58.

[15]Patric H. Hendershott, and Edward J. Kane, "Causes and Consequences of the 1980s Commercial Construction Boom," *Journal of Applied Corporate Finance* 5, no. 1 (Spring 1992): 68.

century and before, and is known as the business cycle. Hoyt[16] found the building cycle was a "motion of a definite order" lasting eighteen years, on average, from peak to peak. Willis raised the key issue as it relates to skyscrapers:

> Indeed, a key question about cycles is, if their pattern is so predictable, why don't people foresee the inevitable bust? This conundrum can perhaps be answered by looking more closely at the dynamics of speculation and at a typical skyscraper development.[17]

Hoyt suggested that the cycle is long enough for people to forget the lessons of the previous cycle and thus not be able to apply it to the next cycle. However, the building cycle is much more volatile and unpredictable than this eighteen-year average would suggest. Together with the impact of local economic conditions and government intervention, the combination of factors blurs any usefulness of the simple knowledge that business cycles exist and have an average duration. Indeed, the people who experience one business cycle are often not even the same as the people who experience the next cycle. As Willis noted:

> After the collapse of an inflated market, it is easy to look back on the grave errors of judgment that preceded a crash; yet the basic indicators of the twenties economy seemed to promise unimpeded growth. Pent-up demand for office space after World War I, the expanding numbers of the white-collar workforce, and the increasing per-person average for office space all fueled the building industry. Each year, the summaries of annual construction figures reported record numbers.[18]

Willis did correctly identify that "easy financing underlie[s] all booms," but this does not answer her conundrum, because easy financing and low interest rates are also at the heart of genuine economic growth. The entrepreneur's problem is that profit calculations cannot show for sure whether interest rates will remain low and projects will succeed (i.e., economic

---

[16]Homer Hoyt, *One Hundred Years of Land Values in Chicago: The Relationship of the Growth of Chicago to the Rise in Its Land Values, 1830–1933* (Chicago: University of Chicago Press, 1933).

[17]Willis, *Form Follows Finance*, p. 159.

[18]Ibid., p. 164.

growth), or rates will rise and projects will fail (i.e., the business cycle). Furthermore, it should be made clear that in ABCT, low interest rates and "easy financing" are terms defined not on the basis of their magnitudes, but in relation to their natural rates, which of course are not calculable outside of a free market.

CHAPTER 7

The Curse Misses New York. Is Auburn, Alabama, Next?

A s of November 2013, it was official. New York City had won the title of having the nation's tallest structure. The heated controversy between New York and Chicago was settled when the Council of Tall Buildings and Urban Habitat, based in Chicago, decided that the 408-foot spire sitting atop One World Trade Center could be included in the total height of the building.

The revised height of 1,776 feet made One World Trade Center the tallest structure in the United States. We are told that One WTC is more than a building. It both serves as a monument to those murdered on 9/11 and honors our Declaration of Independence. Not to disrespect those who died, but this "record" is a sham because the useable, productive height of the building is only 1,368 feet. The remaining 400-odd foot difference is just uninhabitable window dressing.

This dubious record should nonetheless be a kind of warning to us that the skyscraper curse, the forerunner of economic crisis, is lurking near.

The Shard Building, in London, broke ground in 2009 and was completed in 2012, becoming the tallest building in Europe. This was a clear signal of the European economic crisis, the PIIIGS fiscal disaster — in Portugal, Italy, Ireland, Iceland, Greece, and Spain — and the grave and ongoing concerns over the long run viability of the euro. Japan joined the fraternity with the Tokyo Skytree broadcasting tower, which was completed in 2012 and is now the tallest structure in Japan. Not to be outdone,

China set a new national skyscraper record with the Shanghai Tower, which opened in 2014. China also broke ground but suspended construction on Sky City tower in part because of fear of the skyscraper curse. It too would have set a new world record.

World-record-breaking skyscrapers are a signal of economic crisis. Like world-record-breaking art prices, such as the $142 million selling price of a painting by Francis Bacon of his friend Lucian Freud at Christie's in New York in 2013, such records are signs of economic excess. Just remember that such excess usually occurs in markets manipulated by central banks.

These are the spectacular results associated with the skyscraper curse, but you also might be able to see signs of it at work in small-town America. For example, there are no true skyscrapers being built in Auburn, Alabama, home of Auburn University and the Mises Institute. But there has been a great deal of building big and tall for this small city in eastern Alabama.

Luxury student-apartment building leads the way, followed by high-end restaurants and retail space. Recently two student-apartment buildings were torn down to make room for yet bigger buildings. The city government is also spending truckloads of money on street improvements and a state-of-the-art high school. More recently, old single-floor buildings have been demolished downtown to make room for multistory high density apartments.

What are people thinking? Don't they realize we are in one of the weakest recoveries on record and headed for another recession? Has no one in Auburn realized there is an enormous amount of student debt and that the job market for holders of college degrees is weak? Is it greedy bankers and construction companies run amuck? Is it out-of-control architects and chefs that are to blame? Or is it the spoiled rich college kids who demand luxury apartments and locally grown veggies at the high-end restaurants they frequent?

The rush to build bigger, taller, and more luxurious buildings actually has little to do with any of these groups, but it has divided us as a city. On the one hand, there are many people upset because all this construction is changing "the loveliest village on the plains." Local residents are seeing "Keep Auburn Lovely: Save Our Village" signs popping up all over town. They oppose the building spree.

On the other hand, construction workers, cement dealers, building-supply companies, and heavy-equipment operators must love the fast-paced business and full-time jobs with overtime. They love it while heavy dump trucks and cement trucks rush their loads through town.

The problem actually starts in Washington, DC, in an unremarkable building at Twentieth Street and Constitution Avenue NW that houses the Board of Governors of the Federal Reserve. The board, along with the president of the New York Fed, and a rotating selection of regional Federal Reserve Bank presidents, forms the Fed's Open Market Committee (FOMC), which sets the policy targeting the interest rate that banks charge other banks for very short-term loans — the federal funds rate.

When the Federal Reserve's Open Market Committee sets the target lower, it sets off a tendency for interest rates to fall across the economy. When it raises the target for the federal funds rate, interest rates tend to rise across the economy. For the last seven and a half plus years they have kept the target under a quarter of 1 percent. This type of policy has never been pursued before. This explains the ultralow rates on your savings account and home mortgage over the last several years.

It also explains the luxury-building mania. When the Federal Reserve first lowered rates, bankers who were burned by bad mortgages after the collapse of the housing bubble, along with luxury game-day condo builders, would not take the bait. Once bitten, twice shy. However, eventually low interest rates become too tempting to resist, especially as new bankers and construction companies come onto the scene.

Lower rates have several effects, including less saving and more spending. Low rates also increase stock market prices because lower rates increase the value of corporations, reduce the cost of borrowing, and induce individuals to move money from bank accounts to stock market accounts and to be more fully invested in stocks. When the policy is successful at increasing stock prices, people reduce savings further and spend more on luxury goods. Lower rates also boost borrowing and investment.

If you think that the combination of reduced savings and increased luxury spending sounds contradictory and dangerous, you are correct.

In any case, lower interest rates also tend to increase the price of land, particularly in the central business district. In contrast, higher interest rates encourage land and real estate owners to part with their properties at lower prices. Higher land prices make development deals harder to generate profits. The solution is to build more intensively and to make buildings taller. A $1 million piece of land could be made profitable by building just one story, but if that same lot is $2 million then you might have to build three stories to make it profitable. A one-story building is relatively inexpensive to build compared to a three-story building, which requires stairways, elevators, and sturdier construction techniques. However, the three-story building also produces two and a half times more rentable space.

Is it better to just build something, even if it is the wrong something? Well, even if interest rates could stay near zero forever, it would still mean we are deploying our resources incorrectly. The things we are building will not be as profitable as originally projected, and the excess capacity means that long-existing projects will also become less profitable. In other words, eventually, their economic values will be less than the amount invested in them. It will also make it more difficult to pay back the loans, especially if you reduce savings and increase your borrowing and luxury spending.

These circumstances are in no one's long-term best interest. But apparently, eliminating the cause in Washington is currently beyond our collective ability.

CHAPTER 8

When Will the Next
Skyscraper Curse Come?

In 2014, there should have been a skyscraper alert issued for China. Groundbreaking ceremonies took place on what was expected to be the world's tallest skyscraper, called Sky City tower. This project was noteworthy not just as an attempt to build a record-breaking skyscraper of 2,749 feet in height, but also because of the remarkably short construction schedule due to the construction company's prefabricated construction process. Initially, on-site construction was delayed until April 2014. Later, the government cancelled the project due to environmental concerns over nearby wetlands. That reversed the need to broadcast a skyscraper alert.

The confluence of regional skyscraper signals in Europe, North America, and China, along with a skyscraper alert clearly suggested the possibility of a burgeoning world-wide economic crisis. This pattern would be very much like previous episodes of skyscraper records including the panic of 1907, the Great Depression, the stagflation of the 1970s, the Asian contagion / dot-com bubble, and the housing bubble. In line with these skyscraper-based predictions, a fundamental case can be built around the notion of a looming world economic crisis. Most of the world's major economies are facing pressing economic difficulties, including the United States, Europe, Russia, Brazil, Japan, and China. Additionally, central banks have been engaged in a worldwide currency war since the housing bubble, on a scale that has never been experienced in human history. It should not be surprising that super tall buildings are being built at an astonishing rate.

Not only is the world teeming with real estate speculation and sky-scraper-building from China, to New York, to London and the Middle East, *there is a new world-record-setting skyscraper being constructed in Jeddah, Saudi Arabia.* The Kingdom Tower is designed to be over one kilometer in height, or more than eleven football fields. It is scheduled to be completed in 2020. As designed, the Kingdom Tower will exceed the height of the Burj Khalifa by more than 500 feet, although only a few floors of inhabitable space. If events proceed as the skyscraper curse predicts, the beginning of construction of the Kingdom Tower signaled a crisis alert, as a new record-breaking skyscraper has had its groundbreaking ceremony. This will change to a skyscraper signal when a new record height has been achieved between now and 2020.

The skyscrapers can sometimes tell us about the geography of world economic bubbles. The last bubble occurred in the oil-rich Middle East, and the next one would also be in the Middle East. Both bubble projects were begun when oil prices exceeded $100 a barrel.

It is interesting to note that according to *Television Post,*[1] Prince Alwaleed, the owner of the Kingdom Tower project, recently and unexpectedly sold most of his large stake of stock in News Corp., Rupert Murdoch's media conglomerate, to raise nearly $200 million. The move was said to have been part of an overall review and rebalancing of the prince's $20 billion portfolio. This is probably a smart move given the collapse of oil prices and the hefty price tag of $1.2 billion for the prince's Kingdom Tower.

With more financing in place, the next world's tallest skyscraper project is moving forward. The final piece of financing that is necessary to bring the $1.2 billion Kingdom Tower project in Saudi Arabia to record heights has been obtained. Media reports also show that the structure has risen to more than seventy-five meters (246 feet), and construction is proceeding at an uninterrupted pace, although there remain many concerns about the project's viability. (Subsequently, the project experienced more delays.)

For example, above-ground construction on the long-delayed Kingdom Tower, now called the Jeddah Tower, started in September 2014, but there was considerable doubt that the financing for the one-kilometer

---

[1] *Television Post,* "Prince Alwaleed Sells 5.6% Stake in News Corp for $188 Million," March 2, 2015.

(3,280.84 feet) tower could be obtained, given the shaky financial conditions in Saudi Arabia.

But the Jeddah Tower is only the latest phase in an enormous boom that began setting new records in 2014. As I reported in February 2015:

> Super tall buildings, or skyscrapers, are being built at an astonishing rate. Ninety-seven buildings that exceed 200 meters (656 feet) high were constructed in 2014, setting a new record. The previous record was eighty-one buildings completed in 2011. The total number of skyscrapers in existence now is 935, a whopping 350 percent increase since the year 2000.[2]

If completed as planned, Jeddah Tower will be the tallest building in the world. Jackie Salo, in the *International Business Times,* reports:

> Saudi Arabia's Kingdom Tower in Jeddah is slated to become the world's highest skyscraper when it is erected in 2020, knocking Dubai's Burj Khalifa tower from its perch as tallest building at 2,716 feet. The new tower will claim the title if it reaches its planned height of 3,280 feet. ...The 200-floor Kingdom Tower will be part of a reported $8.4 billion project to construct Jeddah City. Construction of the skyscraper will entail 5.7 million square feet of concrete and 80,000 tons of steel.[3]

In other words, the Tower could be the next record-breaking skyscraper, which is just part of an even more massive project. That means it's time for a new skyscraper alert (as of January 1, 2016).

Remember, a skyscraper alert is an indicator that suggests a significant economic crisis will occur in the near future, even though economic conditions currently appear good. This alert could have been issued earlier, because an alert is defined based on the groundbreaking ceremonies of a world-record-breaking skyscraper, not the initial announcement of the project, which in this case occurred in August 2011. At that time there was still considerable doubt the project would be completed as planned.

---

[2]Mark Thornton, "Where Is the Skyscraper Curse Today," *Mises Daily*, February 24, 2015.

[3]Jackie Salo, "World's Tallest Skyscraper Is Saudi Arabia's Kingdom Tower? Jeddah Building Projected to Break Height Records," *International Business Times*, December 1, 2015.

Skyscraper alerts indicate significant looming danger in the economy, but the danger is not necessarily imminent. The next pivotal date for the Jeddah Tower project is when it reaches the height to break the old record and a skyscraper signal is given. That date is difficult to estimate given the uncertainty of construction. Media reports indicate that the project will be completed in 2020 without indicating whether that date is the completion date or the opening ceremonies.

So, will this latest frenzy of new construction tip us off to the next bust? The Skyscraper Index is silent on the issue of timing, so the dating of when the skyscraper curse becomes apparent is just guesswork. It seems that the boom reaches its peak around the time the new record height is set, and this is when a skyscraper signal should be issued. The skyscraper signal means that economic danger is looming. In most episodes, record-breaking skyscrapers generally have their completion dates and opening ceremonies when the economic crisis is readily apparent.

The important thing to remember is that skyscrapers do not cause economic crises. Rather they are just very noticeable examples of the distortions taking place throughout the economy when interest rates are kept artificially low by the central bank. This point will be thoroughly reinforced in the next chapter.

CHAPTER 9

It Is Not
the Skyscraper's Fault

The notion that a record-breaking skyscraper can *cause* economic crises sounds ridiculous, and it is very much absurd. There is no causal relations between skyscraper construction and the skyscraper curse.

The causality that does exist is between artificially low interest rates causing *both* record-breaking skyscrapers and economic crises. Artificially low rates also cause distortions throughout the economy. Very low rates over extended periods of time are what bring about the record skyscrapers and the economic crises. The skyscraper itself is merely an identifiable manifestation of what is happening throughout the economy.

There are distortions, also known as Cantillon effects, directly tied to the skyscraper, such as what happened with the new lightweight elevator cable. Resources had to be diverted to research and development of the new elevator cable from other investment possibilities. A new production facility and production process had to be designed to produce the cable in a profitable fashion. Distribution could probably take place with existing company facilities, but certainly the marketing aspect of the product would have to be built from scratch. When the economic crisis comes, all these resources could have very low value. What happened to the elevator cable company is taking place in all areas of the economy, although it is not universal.

This type of distortion is occurring throughout the economy as entrepreneurs succumb to the lure of artificially low interest rates and embark on investments in more roundabout and advanced production techniques. These investments will later be discovered to be malinvestments in what has been described as a cluster of entrepreneurial errors, a phrase first used by British economist Lionel Robbins[1] in his description of the Great Depression of the 1930s.

Much of the interest in the Skyscraper Index can be linked to its ability to forecast the business cycle and to predict the business cycle. In my view, its primary and best use is not to be able to predict the future, but to be able to describe the types of real changes that occur in an economy exposed to artificially low interest rates. Those changes can then be linked to the troubles we experience in the economic crises that follow. Thus, it *helps* us to understand the business cycle. Unfortunately, many economists ignore the business cycle or do not believe in economic causes of the business cycle. I am afraid that if this situation is not rectified soon, Karl Marx might turn out to be right about business cycles. He argued that business cycles will intensify over time and bring about the demise of capitalism.

In what follows I review an editorial from *The Economist*[2] that was published March 28, 2015, under the title "Towers of Babel." The editorial was based on an academic article published by three Rutgers University economists. Unfortunately, the editorial staff of *The Economist* accepted the wrong, naïve understanding of cause and effect when it comes to skyscrapers. They did not refer to me by name in the editorial, but they did reference my 2005 article as a reference for what, in their minds, is the wrong point of view.

The editorial begins by noting that the world is in a major skyscraper boom and that such booms have often been an ominous signal of tough economic times ahead — the skyscraper curse. *The Economist* had long reported on and agreed with the Skyscraper Index, but they were no longer sure:

> Does this frenzy of building augur badly for the world economy? Various academics and pundits, many of them cited by *The Economist*, have long argued as much, but new research casts doubt on it.[3]

---

[1]Lionel Robbins, *The Great Depression* (London: Macmillan, 1934).

[2]"Towers of Babel: Is There Such a Thing as the Skyscraper Curse?" March 28, 2015.

[3]Ibid.

They then explain the economics of skyscrapers, noting that taller buildings mean more potential revenues. However, they correctly note that the marginal costs of construction also increase with taller buildings. This part of the editorial is a great capsule summary of my 2005 paper, although the role of the interest rate is not introduced. They then mention Jason Barr's 2010 article,[4] which seems to provide some support for the Skyscraper Index.

Then they turn to the paper, "The Skyscraper Curse: Separating Myth from Reality."[5] Two sets of evidence from that paper are presented. The first set examined the question of why the biggest towers are built near the peak of the business cycle and whether that relationship could help you predict changes in Gross Domestic Product (GDP). They found that the time between announcement date of record setters and business cycle peaks is very long and that only half of the skyscraper opening dates occurred during a downward phase of the business cycle: "In other words, you cannot accurately forecast a recession or financial panic by looking at either the announcement date or the completion date of the world's tallest building."

The problem with this is that no one familiar with the Skyscraper Index would use the announcement dates and completion dates as a consistent forecasting tool. The World Trade Center towers were announced in the early 1960s, nearly a decade before the first tower opened. Also, many announced record-breaking buildings never get off the drawing board or off the ground, or are not built as planned. The better dating method for identifying the existence of a bubble and future trouble would be to look at groundbreaking ceremonies. Such ceremonies are an indication that plans have been approved, financing and permits have been obtained, land has been purchased, and any necessary testing has been started or completed.

When looking for signs of trouble — that is, the skyscraper curse — a better date would be when the project has actually beaten the old record, or is approaching that point. The Burj Khalifa tower broke the old record in the summer of 2007, when economic conditions seemed good, but it was two and half years before it was completed and opened to the public. As a word of caution, none of these dating processes are some kind of

---

4Jason Barr, "Skyscrapers and the Skyline: Manhattan, 1865–2004," *Real Estate Economics* 38, no. 3 (2010): 567–97.

5Jason Barr, Bruce Mizrach, and Kusam Mundra, "Skyscraper Height and the Business Cycle: Separating Myth from Reality," *Applied Economics* 47, no. 2 (January 2015): 148–60.

exact, precise, or magical process; they are just rules of thumb based on experience. However, by using announcement and completion dates, the Barr, Mizrach, and Mundra study exaggerated the amount of error that actually exists. Plus, as *The Economist* notes, it is based on a very small sample size of fourteen. The role of clusters or cycles of record-breaking skyscrapers should also not be ignored.

To rectify the small sample size, the study's authors turned to a second set of data that includes the tallest building completed each year in four countries, which expanded the number of data points to 311. They compared data on tall but not necessarily record-breaking buildings to changes in local per capita GDP, not severe economic crises. As a result, they found that skyscraper construction and per capita GDP were *cointegrated*. When two time-series data sets are cointegrated it means that they move, in general, in the same direction and are thought to be the result of the same causal forces. For example, national income and national consumption will tend to move in the same direction, with small variations. You can think of a dog owner walking the dog on a leash as being cointegrated. The dog might be out front and then move behind the owner, but they are both following the same basic path. The fact that Barr, Mizrach, and Mundra found that skyscrapers and GDP are cointegrated means the two data sets move in the same general direction and implies, in other words, that skyscraper construction does not cause the business cycle, and that both statistics are caused by some other factor or factors.

One major problem with this data is that the Skyscraper Index is not based on general skyscraper construction, but instead on record-breaking skyscrapers. As we have seen before, because of the technology requirements and economic constraints, building two, hundred-story buildings is not the same thing as building one 200-story building. Another problem is that the skyscraper curse involves an economic crisis, not the ordinary ebbs and flows of the typical business cycle.

But let us ignore these fundamental problems with their evidence. The evidence that skyscraper construction and per capita GDP are cointegrated and move together with a common cause *is exactly what is predicted by the Skyscraper Index!* Both statistics move together and have the common cause of artificially low interest rates. The Skyscraper Index tells us that artificially low interest rates cause record-breaking skyscrapers, usually in clusters, as well as a bubble in the economy and eventually an economic crisis — the skyscraper curse. In other words, none of their evidence undermines the Skyscraper Index; it supports it.

Stunned by the editorial, I wrote *The Economist* a letter to the editor to try to clarify the meaning and status of the Skyscraper Index. That letter of March 30, 2015, is reprinted here verbatim:

Dear Editor of *The Economist*:

Thank you for discussing my research and referencing my journal article from the *Quarterly Journal of Austrian Economics*. ("Is there such a thing as a skyscraper curse?" March 28th) I would note that Mr. Barr, Bruce Mizrach and Kusum Mundra's research actually supports my thesis that misaligned interest rates cause both record setting skyscrapers and economic crisis. The fact that skyscraper height and GDP are cointegrated is no surprise and actually supports the case for a skyscraper curse. Also, I claim no precision with respect to the exact timing of events, especially with respect to "announcements" and "completions." Groundbreaking and record achieving dates are actually more relevant, yet are still imprecise. They say a picture is worth a 1000 words and I think you're graphic of the timing of record setting skyscrapers and economic crisis says it all.

Mark Thornton, PhD.
Senior Fellow (economist)
Ludwig von Mises Institute
Auburn, AL 36830 (USA)

Unfortunately, they did not print my letter. I was contacted more than three months later and they explained that my letter had been misplaced.

Based on discussions with Lucas Engelhardt, we decided to go back to the original academic journal article and reexamine their findings. Based on that examination, we determined that a comment should be written on the article. Once a common practice, the comment is not nearly as common today, but it still exists at many academic economic journals, including *Applied Economics*, where the original Barr, Mizrach, and Mundra article was published. Originally, we thought the title of the comment should be "Skyscraper Height and the Business Cycle: Separating Data from Reality," but we chose instead to go for the conventional approach. The comment is reproduced below.

SKYSCRAPER HEIGHT AND THE BUSINESS CYCLE:
SEPARATING MYTH FROM REALITY, A COMMENT

In a recent paper in this journal (*Applied Economics*), Jason Barr, Bruce Mizrach and Kusum Mundra[6] test for the existence of a Skyscraper Curse, which Lawrence (1999) states is the "eerie correlation" between the building of record-breaking skyscrapers and economic crisis. Thornton (2005) shows the theoretical connections between record-breaking skyscrapers and economic crisis. However, the evidence that Barr et al. (2015) presents brings into doubt the existence of the Skyscraper Curse. Based on their evidence the *Economist* declared: "you cannot accurately forecast a recession or financial panic by looking at either the announcement or the completion dates of the world's tallest building."

Here we reexamine Barr et al. (2015) and come to a completely different conclusion. Their evidence does not refute the Skyscraper Curse and most of the more rigorous evidence actually supports it. With the Skyscraper Curse, output and height should be cointegrated and output should Granger cause height. Their evidence here is not only strong, but is more broadly applicable beyond the more narrow issue of record-breaking skyscrapers and once-in-a-lifetime economic crises.

Barr et al. (2015) use Granger causality and cointegration tests to analyze the relationship between skyscraper height and output. They use annual time series data for the tallest building completed each year and real per capita GDP for the United States, Canada, China, and Hong Kong as their measure for output. Their evidence shows that both height and output have a common trend indicating a cointegrated relationship. Granger causality tests show that output causes height, but height does not cause output.

---

[6]Barr, Mizrach, and Mundra, "Skyscraper Height and the Business Cycle."

The evidence from Granger causality and cointegration tests actually supports the theory of the Skyscraper Curse. No one believes that simply building a record-breaking skyscraper actually causes an economic crisis. The record-breaking skyscraper is more of an illustration of the types of microeconomic and technical changes to the overall structures of production that take place throughout the economy in response to artificially low interest rates.

Thornton (2005) clearly describes the Skyscraper Curse theory in terms of a third causal factor, artificially low interest rates, that cause both record-setting skyscrapers and unsustainable economic booms and, eventually, economic crisis. There have been several studies such as Barr (2012) that have suggested that such a third factor is responsible for the building of record-setting skyscrapers, such as builder competition, social status, and ego. However, in contrast to these psychological factors, artificially low interest rates provide an economic explanation for 1. Record-breaking skyscrapers, 2. The boom-bust cycle, and 3. Changes in social psychology. Therefore the results of the Granger causality and cointegration tests are completely in line with the expectations of Thornton's (2005) model.

In contrast to their Granger causality and cointegration test results, the evidence in Table 1 of Barr et al. (2015) does strongly bring into question the existence of the Skyscraper Curse. They use the dates that record-setting skyscrapers were publically announced and the dates that those buildings were opened to the public and find little correlation with either of these dates and the business cycle.

However, there are multiple problems with their evidence. First, neither of these dates would be expected to be well correlated with the business cycle and especially with major economic crises, except in one sense. Announcement dates should generally occur during the boom phase of the cycle. They did find that 10 of 14 announcements did occur correctly in an expansion and

1 occurred at the very peak of the cycle. The 3 remainders occur because the "nearest US peak" is arbitrarily used, placing the 3 announcement dates after a previous peak. Additionally, using NBER peak and trough dates is not a true test of the Skyscraper Curse which is restricted to major economic crises.

Thornton (2014) suggests that announcement dates should be ignored and that instead, ground-breaking dates should be considered "skyscraper alerts" indicating that bubble-related investment opportunities exist, but danger is ahead. Furthermore, the date of record-completion, in the sense that the record-breaking height has been achieved, is a "skyscraper signal" suggesting that economic danger is imminent. Opening dates may be many months or even years in the future from record-completion dates and record-breakers often open in the midst of an economic crisis.

Barr et al. (2015) also downplay the Skyscraper Curse by noting that "the range of months between the announcement and peak is tremendous, varying from 0 to 45 months." However, this variation is the result of using the announcement date so that, for example, the World Trade Towers was announced in January 1964, but the ground-breaking date for construction began in August 1968. They also use US cycle dating for two foreign records, Petronas Towers and Taipei 101. These record-breakers are normally connected to the Asian Financial Crisis of 1997–98 and also to the Tech Bubble-Bust (1997–2001), but these events bear little relationship with either the announcement or opening dates.

There remain several anomalies in Table 1. The Woolworth Building was announced in July of 1910 and opened in April 1913, but there is no economic crisis of note connected to it. However, the economy did peak and began contracting in the first quarter of 1913 and continued to contract until the fourth quarter of 1914. This contraction included the third worst quarterly decline in real GNP between 1875 and 1918, and was worse than any quarterly performance between 1946 and 1983. The founding of the Federal Reserve System in 1913 and the coming of World War I in Europe in 1914 provided stabilization for the American economy as exports to Europe soared. These 2 exogenous factors prevented the Woolworth Building from being associated with the Skyscraper Curse because the intervention of World War I reversed the deepening economic slump and prevented a historical label (e.g., "Depression of 1913–15") from being created.

Table 1 also lists the Pulitzer (1890) and Manhattan Life (1894) buildings, which along with the Masonic Temple in Chicago (1892) and Auditorium Building (1889) represent a wave of record-breaking skyscrapers that preceded the beginning of the largest contraction in US history, culminating in the largest quarterly decline in real GNP in US history, which was then followed by the Panic of 1893 and 6 years of double-digit unemployment.

With these clarifications, 13 of the 14 buildings listed by Barr et al. (2015) come into agreement with the Skyscraper Curse model. The Park Row Building, which was announced in 1896 and opened in 1899 does not seem to fit the model, but is in synch with the emergence of the then new steel frame construction technology. If you take skyscraper waves and historical context into account, record-breaking skyscrapers are indeed associated with major economic crises and the Skyscraper Curse does add to our ability to foresee macroeconomic risks, even if the complexities of history prevent predictions of timing from being precise. We agree with Barr et al. (2015) and the *Economist* that the Skyscraper Index and its Curse is of little value in forecasting the normal ebb and flow of the macroeconomy.

We were quite surprised to learn many weeks later that our comment had been rejected by *Applied Economics*. The editor sent us two referee reports. Neither of the reports dealt directly with our primary comment, and both were defensive of the Barr, Mizrach, and Mundra paper.[7] We noticed that in one of the reports, the referee identifies himself as one of the authors of the Barr, Mizrach, and Mundra paper, writing, "It is hard to reject a comment that agrees with your paper." However, he managed to fight that urge and did reject our comment. It is not unheard of to send an author of an article a comment on their paper to referee, but it does seem odd to give them veto rights without the editor having read the paper and comment, which seems obvious in this case.

It is no embarrassment for a journal to publish a flawed paper. It happens on a regular basis. It is part of the academic process. For example, new econometric techniques have brought into question many early empirical papers. Hundreds of papers have been written on the Phillips Curve, and no doubt many are mistaken and now irrelevant. In the case of Barr, Mizrach, and Mundra, their paper is actually not wrong per se; they just came to the wrong conclusions based on their evidence. Even their secondary evidence could be salvageable. This experience provides a clear window into the messy world of academic publishing.

We expanded the comment into a paper with additional empirical evidence, and this paper was accepted for publication at the *Quarterly Journal of Austrian Economics*.[8] There are other important developing lines of research on the Skyscraper Index, two of which I will report on next. One study looks at the Skyscraper Curse at the state level, the other examines the microeconomics of the Curse at the city level and helps explain the old real estate adage that what matters is "location, location, location."

---

[7]Barr, Mizrach, and Mundra, "Skyscraper Height and the Business Cycle."

[8]Elizabeth Boyle, Lucas Engelhardt, and Mark Thornton, "Is There Such a Thing As a Skyscraper Curse?" *Quarterly Journal of Austrian Economics* 19, no. 2 (Summer 2016): 149–168.

CHAPTER 10

Should I Stay, or Should I Go?

If I go there will be trouble
And if I stay there will be double.
So you gotta let me know
Should I stay or should I go?

— The Clash, *Should I Stay or Should I Go*

The decision of where to locate your residence is difficult to make. Most of the factors that play a role in your decision-making are basically economic factors. So might this kind of decision-making process be somehow involved in the skyscraper curse? Economist Lucas Engelhardt thought so and wrote an insightful paper about it.

I have reiterated throughout this book that record-breaking skyscrapers and the skyscraper curse are merely symptomatic of what is going on throughout the economy when it is influenced by artificially low interest rates for a long period of time. We have already seen that it causes such things as local-record-breaking building heights in places such as Auburn, Alabama, advanced construction technologies, and advanced architectural innovations.

Many factors come into play with respect to the choice of the location of your residence. A big factor is that the cost of your house or apartment is one of your biggest expenses. Rent or mortgage payments are typically the largest single payments in your monthly budget. Once you have paid off your mortgage your standard of living can increase significantly.

Another big factor is that the decision is a long-term choice. If you plan to buy a house or condominium, then there are transaction costs such as moving expenses, realtor commissions, and attorney fees. You can reduce some of these expenses by placing a greater work burden and risk burden on yourself, but you cannot make them go away. Such costs occur every time you move.

These cost considerations also impact decision-making on the choice of apartments. If you sign a lease, then you are obligated to pay rent over the length of the lease. You also have moving costs, whether you pay a moving company or do the moving yourself. The upshot is that people typically spend time and effort acquiring information to make such decisions and typically do not make thoughtless and abrupt choices. So when you ask yourself, "Should I stay or should I go?" remember that there is a significant cost of moving.

Some of the factors that people consider when contemplating moving are housing prices and the amount of the monthly payment; the amount of property, income, and sales taxes; local amenities; the quality of local schools and shopping opportunities; crime rates; and commute time. The location of churches will also affect some people's choices. There are trade-offs among all these factors. For example, people with young children will tend to put up with higher taxes if the local schools are good and crime rates are low. Another example is that some people would be willing to put up with long commute times if housing prices and taxes are low, local amenities and schools are good, and crime is low.

Lucas Engelhardt[1] made a contribution to our understanding of the Skyscraper Index by providing a fuller theoretical explanation of why we should expect an uneven increase in land prices, rather than a general, even increase in land prices. By using location theory, Engelhardt shows theoretically why we should focus on very high skyscrapers rather than just tall buildings in general. In other words, he does not reject the notion that lower interest rates increase land prices and the height of buildings, but he provides theoretical support for the idea that land prices will increase relatively more in central business districts.

---

[1]Lucas Engelhardt, "Why Skyscrapers? A Spatial Economic Approach." Unpublished manuscript, 2015.

Of the three Cantillon effects, his focus is on the first effect, where artificially low interest rates change land prices, which leads to taller buildings. In my 2005 paper[2] the justification for taller buildings in this first effect was not really based on economic theory, but on real estate economics. However, I did provide some theoretical support for the uneven increase in land prices in the second Cantillon effect, where low interest rates caused an increase in company size, which in turn caused an increased demand for office space in central business districts.

Engelhardt uses William Alonso's[3] *bid-rent* model with a purely residential city where all employment opportunities are in the central business district. While not realistic, these assumptions are reasonable. In the model, each household budgets part of its income to pay rent and commuting expenses, and part of its time to cover the commute. The further you get from the central business district, the higher the commuting costs, which diminishes the amount you are willing to pay for rent. As you get closer to the central business district, your commuting time and expense decreases and your willingness to pay higher rent increases.

This trade-off is pretty familiar to many people: do you live near your job and pay higher rent, or do you live in the suburbs and endure substantial commuting cost and time? It is a trade-off between housing costs and commuting costs.

If commuting costs are very high, rents will be very high near the central business district (i.e., a steep trade-off), but if transportation costs are very low (e.g., free, ubiquitous high-speed trains), then rents will be similar near the center to what they are on the periphery (i.e., a shallow trade-off). But what determines the steepness of the trade-off? The quality of transportation services is obviously important, but also very costly to manipulate. For example, Dana Rubinstein[4] reports that government transportation projects are notorious for being long delayed and over budget, with some projects exceeding $2 billion per mile. Engelhardt chose to focus on wage rates and interest rates, which pertain more generally across cities.

---

[2]Mark Thornton, "Skyscrapers and Business Cycles," *Quarterly Journal of Austrian Economics* 8, no. 1 (2005): 51–74.

[3]William Alonzo, *Location and Land Use: Toward a General Theory of Land Rent* (Cambridge, MA: Harvard University Press, 1964).

[4]Dana Rubinstein, "Where the Transit-Build Costs Are Unbelievable," *Politico*, March 31, 2015.

Here he employs Murray Rothbard's[5] concept of the *discounted marginal revenue product* of labor. Normally the difference between this and the mainstream concept of *marginal revenue product* is negligible, but Rothbard's concept does introduce the interest rate and time preference into our theorizing about decision-making by adding time discounting to the mainstream concept.

When interest rates are very low you are less concerned with when you are paid because you lose very little interest. If interest rates are very high, then you want to receive your wages very quickly. Likewise, people who are paid daily are unconcerned about the interest rate, but people who are paid monthly or annually could be very concerned about changes in interest rates.

With respect to the skyscraper curse, when interest rates become artificially low, the discount rate on future sales of products decreases and thereby creates an increased demand for products; and this creates an increased demand for labor and higher wages rates. For example, if the interest rate on inventory paid by an automobile dealership falls from 10 percent to 1 percent, the dealer will want to carry a much larger inventory to better approach maximal profits. This increased inventory, reflected across the economy, will cause higher levels of production, employment, and wages.

What impact will these higher wages have on choice of location? Higher wages will have two distinct effects. First, higher wage rates will result in larger household budgets and a larger budget to pay for rent and commuting costs. Second, the higher wage rate makes a person's commute time more expensive in terms of opportunity costs. For example, a lawyer who makes $500 per hour serving clients would have to consider a move from a 60-minute commute per day to a 120-minute commute per day as increasing their opportunity cost by $125,000 per year! Likewise, a lawyer who moved and reduced commute time from 60 minutes per day to living in his office and having no commute time would potentially increase their revenue by $125,000 per year.

Engelhardt finds that falling interest rates have an unambiguous impact on higher-wage individuals and the land closest to the central business district, although with lower-wage individuals and land near the periphery the effect is ambiguous. This means that artificially low interest

---

[5]Murray N. Rothbard, *Man, Economy, and State* (Auburn, AL: Mises Institute, 1962).

rates induce people to want to move closer to the central business district. This in turn tends to increase land prices and causes taller buildings to be built. So during an artificial boom we would expect things like very tall condominium buildings to be built in central business districts.

If you relax the model and allow for office buildings the results are even stronger because businesses want to minimize travel costs for their employees, customers, and input suppliers. Therefore, they want to locate in the central business district, thereby driving land prices even higher. Engelhardt's findings provide additional evidence for the Skyscraper Index and the skyscraper curse and his research highlights how artificial interest rates can influence our lives on a very personal level.

CHAPTER 11

Razorbacks and Wolverines

Razorbacks are wild pigs that are bulky, strong, fast, and ferocious. They inhabit a very large range in large numbers and are omnivorous and highly adaptable. Wolverines are the largest species of weasel, about the size of a small bear. This fast, muscular carnivore has a well-deserved reputation for strength and ferocity. Do these creatures have anything to do with the skyscraper curse?

No, they don't, but they did inspire an important article by Greg Kaza.

When I give public lectures on the skyscraper curse, I am inevitably asked whether it can be applied on continental, national, and state levels, rather than just a global scale. For example, would a national-record-breaking skyscraper result in a national curse? My answer to those questions is yes, but that is only based on anecdotal evidence.

Greg Kaza[1] examined the Skyscraper Index evidence at the state level in the United States. He chose the states of Arkansas and Michigan. Greg is from Michigan and earned his master's degree in international finance from Walsh College, in Michigan. He has served as executive director of the Arkansas Policy Foundation since 2001. The team names for the University of Arkansas and the University of Michigan are respectively the Razorbacks and Wolverines.

---

[1]Greg Kaza, "Note: Wolverines, Razorbacks, and Skyscrapers," *Quarterly Journal of Austrian Economics* 13, no. 4 (Winter 2010): 74–79.

He used the National Bureau of Economic Research's (NBER) estimates of economic expansions and contractions in the US economy. He compared that data with data on the tallest buildings in both states. What he found was confirmation of the Skyscraper Index at the state level. According to Kaza:

> Michigan's tallest skyscrapers in the early 20th century, Detroit's Dime Building and Penobscot Annex, were completed in 1913, a recession year. Detroit's Guardian and Penobscot buildings were finished in 1928–29 on the Great Depression's eve. Today, Michigan's tallest building is the Detroit Marriott at the Renaissance Center, completed in an expansion (1977). Its final tower, however, was finished in the July 1981–November 1982 contraction.[2]

So the experience in Michigan would seem to confirm the Skyscraper Index. It should also be pointed out that with regard to the Detroit Marriott, the American automobile industry, centered in Detroit, Michigan, was still a vital force relative to the rest of the economy in the 1970s, although that would soon change.

The results were similar in the state of Arkansas. The state is largely an agricultural economy, although that has changed some with the rise of Wal-Mart, which has its headquarters in Bentonville, Arkansas. According to Kaza the state followed the familiar pattern:

> A similar effect can be observed in Arkansas. Little Rock's Pyramid Life Building (1907), Union Life Building (1913), Donaghey Building 2 (1926), Tower Building (1960), Bank of America Building (1970) and Region's Bank Building (1975) were all completed around NBER contractions. The lone exception, Metropolitan Tower (formerly the TCBY Building) was completed in 1986, a year of expansion.[3]

The Metropolitan Tower might have been completed during a national expansion of the economy, but such was not the case in Arkansas. As the

---

[2]Ibid., p. 76.
[3]Ibid., pp. 76–77.

building was being built, the state of Arkansas was entering a very strong economic contraction. According to Henderson, Gloy, and Boehlje:

> U.S. agriculture could not sustain the 1970s prosperity and, similar to the 1920s, U.S. export activity collapsed during the 1980s. After peaking at $96 billion in 1980, real U.S. agricultural exports fell sharply. A weak global economy, world debt problems, a strong exchange value of the dollar and trade barriers — including a Russian grain embargo — cut U.S. agricultural exports (Draben-stott 1983). In 1986, agricultural exports bottomed at $47 billion, half the levels posted five years earlier.[4]

So the lone failures of the Skyscraper Index in Arkansas and Michigan are really about the difficulties that can arise using national statistics on state-level phenomena.

Kaza raises two other important points. The first point is that the tallest buildings in twenty states were completed in years of NBER contractions. It might be interesting to examine the other thirty buildings to see whether their record-breaking dates, in contrast to completion dates, might have occurred during an economic expansion. The second point is that he found, using NBER dating, that the Woolworth Building, which opened in April 1913, did so in a twenty-three-month-long contraction in the US economy between January 1913 and December 1914. This was a long and severe contraction. However, it was not long enough or deep enough to gain a moniker achieved by other skyscraper-cursed buildings.

While Lucas Engelhardt[5] shows that the skyscraper-curse analysis can be integrated into the microeconomic analysis of labor markets and location theory, Kaza[6] has shown that it can also be situated into lower levels of geographic analysis.

---

[4]Jason Henderson, Brent Gloy, and Michael Boehlje, "Agriculture's Boom-Bust Cycles: Is This Time Different?" *Economic Review* (4th quart. 2001): 88.

[5]Lucas Engelhardt, "Why Skyscrapers? A Spatial Economic Approach." Unpublished manuscript, 2015.

[6]Kaza, "Note: Wolverines, Razorbacks, and Skyscrapers."

CHAPTER 12

The Curse of the Federal Reserve

Section 1 of this book has been about the Skyscraper Index, which was created by Andrew Lawrence in 1999. The index chronicles the puzzling connection between the building of record-breaking skyscrapers and the onset of severe economic crises. The resulting crises are dubbed skyscraper curses.

The skyscraper curse refers to the major economic crises that follow in the wake of record-breaking skyscrapers. In retrospect, *curse* is a poor choice of words. One use of *curse* indicates an irritation or annoyance, like psoriasis or a trouble-making daughter, distinct to the individual. A second use refers to being afflicted, at a much higher level of negativity, by a mystical being or worldly but religious person, such as a voodoo doctor. The third use refers to the use of swear words by one individual who is complaining about someone or something. The central contribution of section 1 has been to explain that the skyscraper curse is neither self-inflicted nor related to the use of curse words. It is also not about mystical beings or religious figures. The modern curse is about the imposition of severe economic harm imposed by the worldly beings at the Federal Reserve.

The Skyscraper Index has a remarkable record of showing a very close correlation between world-record-breaking skyscrapers and the onset of major economic crises. This section has extended that history back into the nineteenth century and forward in time since the index's creation in

1999. It has also shown that the original exception to this historical record, the Woolworth Building, was not an exception at all, but simply an accident of history. We also can see that the index can be used to analyze this phenomenon at lower levels of aggregation, such as the state level and the urban level (the problem of urban sprawl).

Of course, if you had not read this section, you might have doubted the reliability of the index. As I have reiterated several times, the use of the Skyscraper Index as a forecasting tool is not highly recommended. Just as canals are no longer a central component of the economy's transportation network, skyscrapers could easily lose their key position in the economy in the future. Another reason for caution is that major economic crises can be initiated by other causes than central banks, such as wars and pandemics. Plus, there is no precise mechanism to employ for forecasting, so there remain good reasons to be doubtful or at least skeptical in this regard.

Most promising indicators eventually fail, especially those that seem whimsical and have no fundamental basis, while others are of little use to guide long-term capital-investment expenditures. This section has provided the grounding or fundamental basis for the Skyscraper Index in economic theory and Austrian business cycle theory (ABCT). An artificially low-interest rate monetary policy pursued by central banks distorts capital-investment plans of entrepreneurs. This monetary policy follows the path from the interest rate setting policies of the central bank to open-market operations between the New York Fed and big banks. This eventually hits Main Street and results in more debt and misguided investments. We compared the natural process of economic growth and development driven by real savings with the disastrous results when apparent growth and development is driven artificially by central banks.

Most mainstream economists do not have an economic theory of business cycles. They see the economy as a simple machine that works just fine at the macro level as long as there are no technological or psychological shocks. These shocks are random and cannot be known in advance. Therefore they cannot be predicted or prevented. ABCT incorporates both technical and psychological change. Plus, ABCT theorists expect those changes to happen and can form expectations about when and where those changes will take place in the presence of artificially low-interest rate monetary policy.

By embracing the complexity of the economy with the aid of concepts such as the structure of production and the roundabout production process, ABCT can even provide insight into where the crisis will most likely be the most severe. The analysis of Cantillon effects is also helpful here because this is where the distortion causes malinvestment in product-specific capital goods. Austrian economists have disdain for magic wands in their economic analysis, whereas such wands play a crucial role in mainstream economic analysis.

We now turn our attention to the forecasting ability of Austrian economists regarding economic crises and compare that with the forecasting ability of mainstream economists. Hint: it has nothing to do with skyscrapers.

Section 2:
And How Austrian Economists Predicted Every Major Economic Crisis of the Last 100 Years

CHAPTER 13

Who Predicted the Great Depression?

It has often been claimed that Austrian economist Ludwig von Mises predicted the Great Depression, but that is not quite true. He did predict in 1924 that a large Austrian bank would eventually fail, and he turned down a prestigious job at another large Austrian bank in 1929 because he did not want his name associated with its failure. Mises was clearly expecting a severe economic crisis, but as Murray Rothbard[1] has shown, what made the Great Depression "great," in that it was both severe and long lasting, were the policies implemented in response to the original crisis. Austrian business cycle theory (ABCT) is generally silent with respect to the timing and magnitude of the economic crisis.

The most important consideration here is that Mises published a thorough theoretical critique of existing monetary policy in the United States and elsewhere in 1928. That book is *Monetary Stabilization and Cyclical Policy*. Now we will look at opposing views regarding the business cycle of the late 1920s, most notably contrasting the views of Ludwig von Mises and his American counterpart, Irving Fisher.

The first "new era" of the twentieth century took place during the 1920s. People started to believe that this period of extended economic growth was actually one of self-sustaining growth and perpetually increas-

---

[1]Murray N. Rothbard, *America's Great Depression*, 5th ed. (1963; Auburn, AL: Mises Institute, 2000).

ing prosperity. World War I had ravaged the developed world, central banks had been established across the globe, and the United States had become a leading economic and military power. The Progressive Era had reinvented America largely through constitutional change. Women now had the right to vote, there was a new federal income tax, and alcohol was prohibited across the nation. America also had joined the rest of the developed world by establishing a central bank with the passage of the Federal Reserve Act in 1913. The world was at peace and with a series of federal tax cuts in place, the United States had a very prosperous, although unstable, economy during the 1920s.[2]

There was also a technological revolution as important as the world has ever experienced. This was the decade when the airplane and automobile went into mass production. In communication, it was the onset of mass availability of the telephone and radio. Motion pictures were invented, along with household appliances such as the dishwasher, electric toaster, and refrigerator. The use of petroleum products and electricity increased dramatically while the use of manual power decreased significantly. Assembly line production became ubiquitous and was seen as the key to industrial progress.

The period of economic boom and stock market bubble during the 1920s is often referred to as the "Roaring Twenties." Few people seemed to think it was unusual that the world's three tallest buildings were being built either on or close to Wall Street, in New York City. However, it was far from a utopian time given all the crime, corruption, and violence created by alcohol prohibition, and there were clearly imbalances and instability in the economy. None of this, however, could discourage or dissuade the optimists that this was indeed a "new era."

Edward Angly[3] compiled quotations from newspapers and public records to chronicle the "new era" thinking during the bubble and its aftermath. A prime example of this thinking came from Herbert Hoover in his speech accepting the Republican Party nomination for president, where he proclaimed on August 11, 1928:

---

[2]Robert B. Ekelund, Jr., and Mark Thornton, "Schumpeterian Analysis, Supply-Side Economics, and Macroeconomic Policy in the 1920s," *Review of Social Economy* 44, no. 3 (December 1986): 221–37.

[3]Edward Angly, *Oh Yeah?* (New York: Viking Press, 1931).

> Unemployment in the sense of distress is widely disappearing. … We in America today are nearer to the final triumph over poverty than ever before in the history of any land. The poor-house is vanishing from among us. We have not reached the goal, but given a chance to go forward with the policies of the last eight years, and we shall soon with the help of God be in sight of the day when poverty will be banished from this nation. There is no guarantee against poverty equal to a job for every man. That is the primary purpose of the economic policies we advocate.[4]

Not surprisingly Hoover believed the prosperity of the 1920s owed itself to the economic policies of his Republican Party, but his future policies to save jobs would be responsible for turning the economic crisis into the Great Depression.

Industrialists also saw a new era. Magnus Alexander, the president of the National Industrial Conference Board, said in 1927: "There is no reason why there should be any more panics." The president of the Pierce-Arrow Motor Car Company, Myron Forbes, claimed on New Year's Day, 1928, that there "will be no interruption of our present prosperity," while Irving Bush, the president of the Bush Terminal Company proclaimed in November that "we are at the beginning of a period that will go down in history as the golden age."

Charles Schwab, the chairman of Bethlehem Steel, noted in March 1929 that "I do not feel there is any danger to the public in the present situation" and in an October speech to the American Iron and Steel Institute reassured members that "in my long association with the steel industry I have never known it to enjoy a greater stability or more promising outlook than it does today." As is typical of new-era philosophy, in October 1931, he blamed the depression on psychological factors: "The overliquidated prices of many securities are a sign of too short perspective and too excitable temperament."

The financial press was similarly intoxicated with the economic bubble, with the *Wall Street Journal* reporting on October 26, 1929, "Conditions do not seem to foreshadow anything more formidable than an arrest of stock activity and business prosperity like that in 1923. Suggestions that

---

[4]Ibid., p. 9.

the wiping out of paper profits will reduce the country's real purchasing power seem far-fetched." Syndicated columnist Arthur Brisbane reported four days later that "those that foolishly talk about a national panic, will please remember that the income of this nation is one hundred billion dollars per year." In November he reported that "business is good, money is cheap" and that "it ought to be a good year."

Shortly thereafter he encouraged his readers by reporting that "all the really important millionaires are planning to continue prosperity" and that "if every man would learn to talk about the country's progress and future as a young mother talks about her new baby, there would be no danger of hard times." On New Year's Day, 1930, he declared the economic crisis was over, noting: "Now that the 'big wind' that swept through Wall Street, blowing away paper profits, has died down, there are sad hearts, but no real losses." And one week later he wrote, "It is safe to say that the peak of idleness has about been reached, with better conditions coming." As the economy worsened and unemployment continued to mount, Brisbane's assurances became increasingly bizarre and macabre. On January 2, 1931, he wrote: "Sometimes when things go wrong, it is a comfort to be reminded that nothing matters very much. If the earth fell toward the sun, it would melt like a flake of snow falling on a red-hot stove."

Politicians were big promoters and defenders of new-era thinking. Secretary of the Treasury Andrew Mellon told the American people near the peak of the boom that there "is no cause for worry. The high tide of prosperity will continue." After the stock market crashed and unemployment began to rise, he reassured Americans on New Year's Day of 1930:

> I see nothing, however, in the present situation that is either menacing or warrants pessimism. During the winter months there may be some slackness or unemployment, but hardly more than at this season each year. I have every confidence that there will be a revival of activity in the spring and that during the coming year the country will make steady progress.[5]

Republican officials continued to report throughout 1930 that the economy was fine, that conditions were satisfactory, that the worst was already over, that things would improve in a couple of weeks, and that signs of recovery were everywhere. However, by the end of 1930 some panic and confusion

---

[5]Ibid., p. 23.

had entered into Republican ranks. On October 15, 1930, Simeon Fess, the chairman of the Republican National Committee, complained:

> Persons high in Republican circles are beginning to believe that there is some concerted effort on foot to utilize the stock market as a method of discrediting the administration. Every time an Administration official gives out an optimistic statement about business conditions, the market immediately drops.[6]

This statement is a sign of both alarm and paranoia and, if true, indicates that the "market" had finally entered a phase of disbelief in the pronouncements from the White House because of a large number of past inaccuracies.

Irving Fisher was the most prominent American economist of the period and is still considered by mainstream economists to be one of the greatest economists of all time. He was an enthusiastic supporter of Herbert Hoover and believed that the great economic prosperity of the 1920s was attributable in part to alcohol prohibition, which he championed, but more importantly he felt the prosperity was based on his theory concerning the "scientific" stabilization of the dollar that had been undertaken by the Federal Reserve. Naturally, with both alcohol prohibition and dollar stabilization firmly in place, Fisher was completely blindsided by the Great Depression. On the eve of the great stock market crash of September 5, 1929, Fisher reassured investors that he foresaw no problem in the stock market:

> There may be a recession in stock prices, but not anything in the nature of a crash. Dividend returns on stocks are moving higher. This is not due to receding prices for stocks, and will not be hastened by any anticipated crash, the possibility of which I fail to see. A few years ago people were as much afraid of common stocks as they were of a red-hot poker. In the popular mind there was a tremendous risk in common stocks. Why? Mainly because the average investor could afford to invest in only one common stock. Today he obtains wide and well managed diversification of stock holdings by purchasing shares in good investment trusts.[7]

---

[6]Ibid., p. 27.

[7]Ibid., 37.

Unfortunately, while Fisher continued to preach that stocks had reached a "permanent high plateau" throughout October 1929, stocks lost one-third of their value. Diversification via investment trusts, which were like the mutual funds of today, might have encouraged people to invest in stocks, but it did little to protect their wealth. The market value of investment trusts fell 95 percent over the two years following his prediction, and the Dow Jones stock index lost nearly 90 percent of its peak value.

Well after the fact, Irving Fisher identified in his 1932 book *Booms and Depressions: Some First Principles* most precisely and perceptively what he meant by a new era. In trying to identify the cause of the stock market crash and depression he found most explanations lacking. What he did find was that new eras occurred when technology allowed for higher productivity, lower costs, more profits, and higher stock prices:

> In such a period, the commodity market and the stock market are apt to diverge; commodity prices falling by reason of the lowered cost, and stock prices rising by reason of the increased profits. In a word, this was an exceptional period — really a "New Era."[8]

The key development of the 1920s that clouded Fisher's perception was that monetary inflation did not show up in price inflation as measured by price indexes. As Fisher[9] noted: "One warning, however, failed to put in an appearance — the *commodity price level did not rise.*" He suggested that price inflation would have normally kept economic excesses in check, but that price indexes have "theoretical imperfections":

> During and after the World War, it (wholesale commodity price level) responded very exactly to both inflation and deflation. If it did not do so during the inflationary period from 1923–29, this was partly because trade had grown with the inflation, and partly because technological improvements had reduced the cost, so that many producers were able to get higher profits without charging higher prices.[10]

---

[8]Irving Fisher, *Booms and Depressions: Some First Principles* (New York: Adelphi Company, 1932), p. 75.

[9]Ibid., p. 74.

[10]Ibid., p. 75.

Fisher had stumbled to a near-correct understanding of the problem of new-era thinking. Technology can drive down costs and increase profits, creating periods of economic euphoria, where economic signals would otherwise inject greater caution and clearer thinking. In other words, the Fed had kept interest rates artificially low, stimulating investments in technology beyond normal levels and thereby creating deflationary pressures in commodity prices.

However, he never lost his faith in scientific management of the economy or his devotion to the idea of a stable dollar, despite the implication that his stable-dollar policy had caused the Great Depression. Fisher's detailed analysis and painstaking investigations of the crash also did little to improve his economic forecasting:

> As this book goes to press (September 1932) recovery seems to be in sight. In the course of about two months, stocks have nearly doubled in price and commodities have risen 5½. European stock prices were the first to rise, and European buyers were among the first to make themselves felt in the American market.[11]

He attributed this "success" to reflationary measures by the Fed that were of deliberate "human effort more than a mere pendulum reaction."[12] Unfortunately, not only was his prediction wrong, the world was only at the end of the beginning of the Great Depression and the "human effort" that he thought was the tonic of recovery was actually the toxin of lingering depression. He scoffed at the "mere pendulum reaction" of the market economy that can correct for the excesses in the economy by liquidating capital and credit, a concept that he clearly opposed. However, James Grant[13] and Tom Woods[14] have shown that this type of "pendulum reaction" worked extremely well during the short depression of 1920–21.

Was the Great Depression predictable? Was it preventable? The failure of the market economy to "right itself" in the wake of the Great Crash is the most pivotal development in modern economic history, and its impact

---

[11]Ibid., p. 157.

[12]Ibid., p. 158.

[13]Grant, James. 1996. *The Trouble with Prosperity: The Loss of Fear, the Rise of Speculation, and the Risk to American Savings* (New York: Random House).

[14]Thomas E. Woods, "Warren Harding and the Forgotten Depression of 1920," *Intercollegiate Review* (Fall 2009): 22–29.

has continued to shape mass ideology and to determine public institutions and policy. Unfortunately, few saw the development of the stock market bubble, understood its cause, or predicted the bust and the resulting depression.

In Austria, economist Ludwig von Mises apparently saw the problem developing in its early stages because of his theoretical insight concerning institutional and ideological changes. The world economy was controlled by central banks instead of the classical gold standard, and artificially reduced interest rates were widely considered to be a good thing. Mises forecast to colleagues the crash of the large Austrian bank Credit Anstalt as early as 1924. In a eulogy for his teacher Eugen von Böhm-Bawerk, Mises wrote in August 1924:

> And no citizen of this country [i.e., Austria] shall forget the minister of finance, the last Austrian minister of finance [i.e., Böhm-Bawerk], who, in spite of all obstacles, earnestly aimed at balancing the public budget and *preventing the upcoming financial catastrophe*. (emphasis added)[15]

As mentioned at the beginning of this chapter, Mises published a book-length critique of Irving Fisher's ideas on monetary policy in 1928, titled *Monetary Stabilization and Cyclical Policy*. There he targeted Fisher's "stable dollar" policy and its reliance on the price index as a key vulnerability that would bring about the economic crisis, concluding: "Because of the imperfection of the index number, these calculations would necessarily lead in time to errors of very considerable proportions."[16]

Mises found that Fisher's attempt to stabilize purchasing power was riddled with inherent technical difficulties and was incapable of achieving its goals: "In regard to the role of money as a standard of deferred payments, the verdict must be that, for long-term contracts, Fisher's scheme is inadequate. For short-term commitments, it is both inadequate

---

[15]Ludwig von Mises, "The Economist Eugen v. Böhm-Bawerk, on the Occasion of the Tenth Anniversary of His Death," translated Karl Friedrich Israel, *Quarterly Journal of Austrian Economics* 19, no. 2 (Summer 2016): 170. Originally published in *Neue Freie Presse*, Vienna, August 27, 1924.

[16]Ludwig von Mises, "Monetary Stabilization and Cyclical Policy [Geldwertstabilisierung und Konjunkturpolitik]," in *The Causes of the Economic Crisis: And Other Essays before and after the Great Depression*, edited by Percy L. Greaves (1928; Auburn, AL: Mises Institute, 2006), p. 82.

and superfluous."[17] He then demonstrated how Fisher's type of monetary reforms cause booms and that these booms inevitably result in crisis and stagnation. He attributes the popularity of Fisher's scheme to political influence and bad ideology:

> The fact that each crisis, with its unpleasant conse-
> quences, is followed once more by a new "boom," which
> must eventually expend itself as another crisis, is due only
> to the circumstances that the ideology which dominates
> all influential groups — political economists, politicians,
> statesmen, the press and the business world — not only
> sanctions, but also demands, the expansion of circulation
> credit.[18]

Mises had addressed the same problems in a 1923 work, but named Fisher and his scheme in 1928. In addition to demonstrating the inevitability of the crisis, he clearly identified its cause, where most others could not:

> It is clear that the crisis must come sooner or later. It is
> also clear that the crisis must always be caused, primarily
> and directly, by the change in the conduct of the banks.
> If we speak of error on the part of the banks, however,
> we must point to the wrong they do in encouraging the
> upswing. The fault lies, not with the policy of raising the
> interest rate, but only with the fact that it was raised too
> late.[19]

He showed that the central bank's attempt to keep interest rates low and to maintain the boom only makes the crisis worse. Despite the tremendous odds against the adoption of Mises's own solution — that is, the traditional gold standard — he ended his analysis with a prescription for preventing future cycles:

> The only way to do away with, or even to alleviate, the
> periodic return of the trade cycle — with its denouement,
> the crisis — is to reject the fallacy that prosperity can be

---

[17]Ibid., p. 84.

[18]Ibid., p. 128.

[19]Ibid., p. 131.

produced by using banking procedures to make credit cheap.[20]

Mark Skousen[21] notes that in addition to Ludwig von Mises, Mises's student F. A. Hayek is said to have predicted the collapse of the American boom in early 1929 (but probably not in written form). Felix Somary, who like Mises was a student at the University of Vienna, issued several dire warnings in the late 1920s; and in America economist Benjamin Anderson also warned that the Federal Reserve's policies would cause a crisis, but like Somary, they were largely ignored. Mises and followers of his business cycle theory clearly had the upper hand over Fisher and the proponents of his stable-dollar policy.

Members of the Austrian school of economics were uprooted by WWII, with Mises in New York and Hayek in London and others scattered in academic posts at other prestigious universities. Despite the Austrians winning the prediction game against Fisher, Keynesian economics would soon rise to control economic thought as the Austrian school went into a general decline. Politically this was tied to the rise of fascism, Nazism, and FDR's New Deal.

Fortunately, in the wake of WWII, the world returned to a Bretton Woods–style gold standard, and free market economies were established in Germany and Japan. The world quickly recovered from the war and the fascist-style economics that dominated prior to WWII. It would be a quarter century before the next economic depression hit the United States.

---

[20]Ibid., p. 153.

[21]Mark Skousen, *Economics on Trial: Lies, Myths, and Realities* (Homewood, IL: Business One Irvin, 1991).

CHAPTER 14

The "New Economists" and the Depression of the 1970s

During the 1960s, when Keynesian economics came to completely dominate the economics profession, there was a large influx of the so-called new economists into government service. The disastrous results included the "Keynesianization" of the economy and what is best described as an economic depression that lasted throughout the 1970s and into the early 1980s. The long economic expansion of the 1960s came to a screeching halt just as 1 and 2 World Trade Center started to impact the Manhattan skyline.

Like the 1920s and 1990s, the decade of the 1960s was a period of remarkable prosperity in the United States as measured by statistics such as GNP and the unemployment rate. In contrast, the 1950s included several periods of stagnation and mild recessions. During the 1960s the economy grew at a brisk pace, and employment and wages grew as well. America was able to fight the Cold War, the Vietnam War, the War on Poverty, and win the space race, simultaneously. The only noticeable negative effect was a mild uptick in price inflation toward the end of the decade.

According to academic economist Arthur Okun[1] the economic expansion was the result of two primary factors. The first was scientific management of the economy by the "new economists" who were brought to

---

[1]Arthur Okun, *The Political Economy of Prosperity* (Washington, DC: Brookings Institution, 1970), p. 57.

Washington to help fine-tune the economy with fiscal and monetary policy — that is, Keynesian economics. The second was the new technology that was introduced in the economy — particularly computer technology, consumer electronics, and technological advances related to space exploration.

Okun was the chairman of President Nixon's Council of Economic Advisors from 1968 to 1969. Right before the crash he described the economic expansion as "unparalleled, unprecedented, and uninterrupted." Okun believed that the economy was on a new "dramatic departure" from the past. According to Okun:

> The persistence of prosperity has been the outstanding fact of American economic history of the 1960s. The absence of recession for nearly nine years marks a discrete and dramatic departure from the traditional performance of the American economy.[2]

After declaring the business cycle dead, he went on to demonstrate that research on the business cycle was now a thing of the past and that a "new" approach to the economy had replaced it. In fact, he even took the precarious step of ridiculing those who stubbornly stuck to the old economics, where business cycles were viewed as an inevitable feature of the market economy. In fact, he charged this old school with viewing recessions in a positive light for correcting past excesses, just as Dr. Pangloss, a character in Voltaire's play *Candide*, preaches optimism: everything, including negative things, is for the best, and we have the best of all possible worlds. Here I believe he is referring to Austrian economists, such as Ludwig von Mises and F. A. Hayek. Okun's "latter-day Machiavellis" probably refers to political-business-cycle theorists who at this time were political scientists:

> When recessions were a regular feature of the economic environment, they were often viewed as inevitable. Indeed, the Doctor Panglosses saw them as contributors to the health of our best of all possible economies, correcting for the excesses of the boom, purging the poisons out of our productive and financial systems, and restoring vigor for new advances. And the latter-day Machiavellis saw potentially great political significance in the timing of turning points. They spun out fantasies, suggesting or suspecting — depending upon whether their party was

---

[2]Ibid., p. 31.

in or out of office — that the business cycle would be controlled so that the inevitable recession would come between elections and would be replaced by a vigorous economic recovery during the campaign period.[3]

Okun confidently declared that the death of the business cycle was "proof par excellence" that economic controversies can be solved. How was the business cycle killed? Okun found that the slayer was not new theories or policy tools, but simply a more confident and scientifically rigorous implementation of existing tools, which resulted in efficient scientific management of the economy — that is, Keynesian economics:

> More vigorous and more consistent application of the tools of economic policy contributed to the obsolescence of the business cycle pattern and the refutation of the stagnation myths. The reformed strategy of economic policy did not rest on any new theory.[4]

For Okun, the New Deal had employed fiscal stimulus, which would later be espoused by Keynesian theory.[5] He believed the old canard that WWII got us out of the Great Depression. As far as he was concerned those two episodes provided evidence of the success of countercyclical fiscal policy. He also viewed the old "fiscal religion" of limiting the size of government and keeping its budget in balance as nothing more than myth and superstition. Overthrowing those fallacies of the past and embracing scientific management of the economy had allowed economists to fully apprehend and subdue the business cycle: "The activist strategy was the key that unlocked the door to sustained expansion in the 1960s."[6] All remaining errors could be dealt with by fine-tuning of the activist strategy.

It was unfortunate for Okun that the publication of his book, *The Political Economy of Prosperity*, occurred just one month before the next economic recession began. Civilian unemployment increased from well below 4 percent to just over 6 percent by the end of 1970. The rate then retreated to 5 percent in 1973 only to skyrocket to 9 percent in mid-1975 — the highest rate since the Great Depression. The unemployment rate

---

[3]Ibid., p. 32.

[4]Ibid., p. 37.

[5]Ibid., p. 43.

[6]Ibid.

remained above the "natural rate" of 5 percent for the next two decades, including ten months of double-digit unemployment during 1982–83.

The experiment of the new economists also resulted in higher price inflation, as would be expected from the "stimulating" fiscal and monetary policy of the 1960s. From the beginning of 1946 to the beginning of 1965 — twenty years — the Consumer Price Index increased by 71.4 percent, but it then increased another 20 percent by the end of the 1960s. From 1965 — when the experiment began in earnest — to the end of 1980 the CPI increased by 176.6 percent. The grand experiment greatly increased the price inflation experienced by consumers.

More importantly, revolutionary changes occurred in money and banking. The US Treasury stopped issuing silver coins in 1964, and Gresham's law ensured that Americans were soon using nothing but "clad" coins that only looked like the old silver coins. Silver-certificate notes were recalled in 1968 in exchange for Federal Reserve Notes. Then, in August 1971, Nixon initiated a "new economic policy" that closed the international gold window (where foreign central banks could still redeem dollars for gold), the last vestige of the pre-1913 classical gold standard.

The United States had printed too much money during the 1960s and had caused a "run" on the dollar by foreign central banks, which sought to cash in their dollar holdings for gold. Despite US promises to the contrary, Nixon also instituted comprehensive wage and price controls in an attempt to block the rising price inflation before his reelection campaign. The Bretton Woods system, where currencies had fixed values in terms of gold, inevitably collapsed. Thus the last links between gold and money were broken and a completely fiat monetary system was established.

The bubble of the 1960s and the subsequent collapse have been well chronicled by John Brooks in his book *The Go-Go Years*. The "go-go '60s" refers to the market for technology stocks during the 1960s, when the "Nifty Fifty" emerged as a list of "one decision" stocks that could be bought and held forever. This list of stocks included Coca-Cola and IBM as well as troubled companies of the future, such as Kodak and Polaroid. Like the investment trusts of the 1920s, mutual funds were touted as the fastest path to riches for the common man. As the bubble expanded, investment gurus such as Gerald Tsai used aggressive investment techniques to generate huge increases in the value of their mutual fund shares, while others made millions building the conglomerate corporations that spanned many industries and nations.

John Brooks[7] well captured the euphoria that emanated from this new-era stock market: "As mutual-fund asset values went up, new money poured in. Tsai and others like him seemed to have invented a money-making machine for anyone with a few hundred or several thousands of dollars to invest." He even labeled Tsai "the first big-name star of the new era." Unfortunately, Brooks was unable to properly diagnose the cause of the mania, attributing it largely to greed and irrationality:

> Where were the counsels of restraint, not to say common sense, in both Washington and on Wall Street? The answer seems to lie in the conclusion that in America, with its deeply imprinted business ethic, no inherent stabilizer, moral or practical, is sufficiently strong in and of itself to support the turning away of new business when competitors are taking it on. As a people, we would rather face chaos making potsfull of short-term money than maintain long-term order and sanity by profiting less.[8]

Brooks noted that "man's apparent capacity to learn from experience is an illusion." Man is able to benefit from experience, but our collective ability to learn and pass knowledge on to future generations depends on our ability to formulate correct theories regarding our experiences. Like many others, Brooks seems oblivious to the usefulness of economic theory in this regard, although his analysis regarding experience and lack of a stabilizer does reflect favorably on Austrian business cycle theory.

However, Brooks is correct and quite methodical in showing the similarities between the 1920s and the 1960s. In each case there was a new era and a new way of economic thinking. Both episodes had their investment stars that fell into disgrace. In both cases there were charges of corruption and malfeasance that led, after the fact, to attempts at reform via legislation. At the heart of both eras — the vehicle of mania and deception — was technology. By the history of Wall Street, Brooks was able to show that the collapse in the stock market was actually much worse than the Dow Jones stock index indicated. Many of the best-performing stocks of the decade turned into the worst-performing stocks of the next decade, but were not in the Dow index. This spelled trouble for many investors for years to come.

---

[7]John Brooks, *The Go-Go Years: The Drama and Crashing Finale of Wall Street's Bullish 60s* (New York: Allworth Press, 1973), pp. 137–39.

[8]Ibid., p. 187.

An even better indicator of trouble in the stock market can be found in the fact that in May 1970, a portfolio consisting of one share of every stock listed on "the Big Board" was worth just about half of what it would have been worth at the start of 1969. The highfliers that had led the markets of 1967 and 1968 — conglomerates, computer leasers, far-out electronics companies, franchisers — were down precipitously from their peaks. Nor were they down 25 percent, like the Dow, but 80, 90, or 95 percent. This was vintage 1929 stuff, another economic depression, with all the economic pain and emotional hardship that mired both stock markets and the economy for years to come.[9]

The stock market as measured by the Dow did decrease 25 percent between 1969 and 1971 and then, after the publication of Brooks's book, lost another 20 percent by mid-1975. However, the inflation-adjusted losses in the stock market were larger and longer lasting than an ordinary price chart of the Dow might suggest. The inflation-adjusted or "real" purchasing-power measure of the Dow indicates that it lost nearly 80 percent of its peak value during this time period. When Brooks drew out the similarities between 1929 and 1969, he stopped short of declaring a second Great Depression. However, while the economic pain of the 1970s and early 1980s may not have matched the Great Depression of the 1930s, it could easily qualify as an economic depression.

The decade began with recession and the abandoning of the gold monetary system and saw the emergence of "stagflation" — that is, stagnation and inflation. It ended with the highest monthly misery index in 1980. The index is calculated by adding the inflation rate to the unemployment rate. The 1970s is not generally recognized as a depression by economists. However, it certainly was part of a twelve-year period of economic pain and uncertainty compounded by price controls, the gasoline shortages, Watergate, and defeat in the Vietnam War. It should also be noted that mainstream economists have changed the meaning or application of terms such as depression, panic, and crisis, substituting milder-sounding terms such as recession and correction.

Statistical evidence clearly demonstrates that the 1970s was a turning point in the wrong direction for the American economy. The Bretton Woods gold standard was abandoned, prices increased, and the dollar rapidly depreciated. Unemployment and underemployment increased, and they set

---

[9]Ibid., p. 4.

post-WWII highs in the early 1980s. The federal government abandoned a longstanding tradition of balanced budgets for the current regime of ever-increasing deficits and a skyrocketing national debt. The personal saving rate of Americans — which had been on an increasing trend until 1971 — flattened out and began its current declining trend toward a zero savings rate.

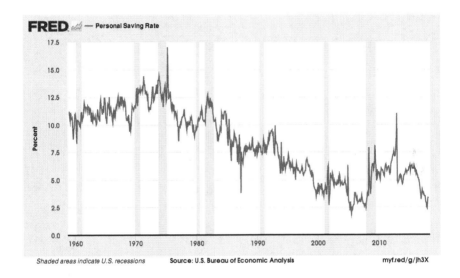

Shaded areas indicate U.S. recessions   Source: U.S. Bureau of Economic Analysis   myf.red/g/jh3X

It was the 1970s when the trade balance first destabilized, and then began the trend of escalating trade deficits. Naturally when the people are saving less and the government is borrowing more, the new loans have to come from foreigners. Going back to the 1930s, net exports of goods and services hugged the zero line. Then in the 1970s it broke below the zero line and continued to head lower. For the fifteen years leading up to 2010, the trade deficit averaged over $500 billion. The stability of the past had been replaced with the instability and erosion that fiat paper money inevitably brings.

Another crucial factor is the impact of the monetary regime on income distribution, one of the most glaring issues of our times. Money is one important factor that is largely ignored by those both on the political left and the political right. It is also largely ignored by mainstream economists, such as Thomas Piketty (2014).[10] However, the choice of monetary system

---

[10]Thomas Piketty, *Capital in the Twenty-First Century* (Cambridge, MA: Harvard University Press, 2014).

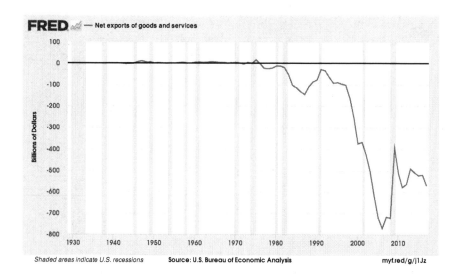

FRED — Net exports of goods and services

and monetary policy does have predictable and historically validated effects on economic inequality.

A monetary system that is dominated by a central bank, such as the Federal Reserve, and uses fiat money, as in our current monetary system, can expect to benefit certain people, such as bankers, financiers, and people with debt. Likewise, because such a system is inflationary, it tends to hurt wage workers and savers. Such a system can be expected to hurt the lower- and middle-income classes and enrich those in the financial industry and the upper-income class.

A gold standard has historically had a tendency for prices to be stable or slightly deflationary. This means that wage rates, cash balances, savings, and bonds tend to gain purchasing power over time. This type of monetary system rewards the hard-working and frugal classes, which leads to an expansion of the middle-income class and the economy.

This graph from the Pew Research Center provides enticing evidence of the differential impact of gold versus fiat paper money.

The graph shows that economic inequality declined in the United States from 1917 to the early 1970s, when Nixon took the United States off of the Bretton Woods gold standard. The darker shaded areas of the graph represent the 99 percent, while the light area at the top represents the percentage of total income of the upper 1 percent. Economic inequality increased during the inflationary 1920s, but the lower-income classes rapidly improved versus the 1 percent when the gold standard was restored after WWII. The graph shows both marginal improvement and stability in economic inequality from the late 1940s to the early 1970s. Since going off the gold standard in 1971 the trend has been for much greater economic inequality.

All of these problems were not due to the laziness of the American people. Females moved into the workforce in record numbers, and the two-income family was established, mostly to try to maintain standards of living. Unfortunately, the 1960s and 1970s were two decades when government employment expanded the most, so that much of this increased labor effort produced little of value. Working for government can even be a net negative for the economy in the sense that government employees can do actual harm to the production of useful goods and services. The "new economists" in the service of the state are a good example of that.

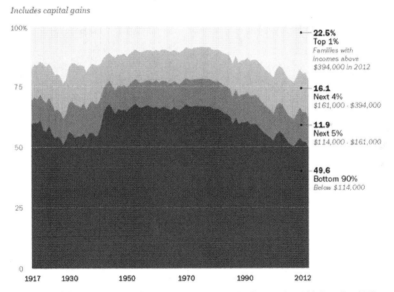

Share of Total Annual Income by Income Bracket Groups

Includes capital gains

22.5%
Top 1%
Families with incomes above $394,000 in 2012

16.1
Next 4%
$161,000 - $394,000

11.9
Next 5%
$114,000 - $161,000

49.6
Bottom 90%
Below $114,000

Source: "Striking it Richer: The Evolution of Top Incomes in the United States," by Emmanuel Saez, UC-Berkeley (Sept. 2013)
PEW RESEARCH CENTER

CHAPTER 15

The Return of the Austrians

The 1960s and 70s were precarious times for the Austrian school. Ludwig von Mises was very old, retired, and would die in 1973 at the age of ninety-two. Friedrich Hayek was also retired and ensconced at the University of Salzburg in Austria from 1969 to 1977. He called his move to Salzburg a mistake. He had not worked on business cycles and monetary policy for many decades and his research interests at this time were very different. Henry Hazlitt retired from *Newsweek* in 1966 at the age of seventy-two. Murray Rothbard was a young man and was marginalized and isolated, with little institutional support. There were precious few other Austrian economists in the entire world, and the next generation of Austrian economists had not left graduate school or had not even entered graduate school.

Mises at the age of eighty-nine continued to lecture during the critical 1968–70 period, and make public appearances. Some of his more important lectures included: "The Problems of Inflation" (April 3, 1968); "On Money" (April 3, 1969); "The Balance of Payments" (May 1, 1969); "A Seminar on Money" (November 8, 1969); "The Free Market Society" (February 21, 1970), where he discussed the problems arising from increasing the supply of money; and "Monetary Problems" (June 23, 1970), where he discussed why the return to the true gold standard was so important and essential for economic growth and stability and why the Bretton Woods system was so problematic. Sampling these lectures makes it obvious that

Mises in his elder years was completely attuned to the monetary-policy problems and their potential consequences and was doing his best to alert others of the looming dangerous outcomes.

Henry Hazlitt was hardly retired either. After leaving *Newsweek* in the fall of 1966 he began writing for the *Los Angeles Times*, and between the fall of 1966 and June 1969 Hazlitt published 177 articles in the *Times*.[1] Almost all of the articles discussed the dangers looming because of current monetary and fiscal policy. He clearly saw that the Bretton Woods gold standard was the core problem because it led to too much government spending and a loose monetary policy. For example, he wrote articles such as "Budget Out of Control" (February 12, 1967), "People Want Gold" (February 22, 1967), and "Currency Crisis Ahead" (March 29, 1967) in early 1967. In 1968 he wrote "What a Gold Reserve Is For" (February 3, 1968), "The Most Irresponsible Budget" (February 11, 1968), and "The Dollar Crisis: A Way Out" (March 17, 1968). Hazlitt wrote in 1969 on topics like "The Coming Monetary Collapse" (March 23, 1969), "Pretending That Paper Is Gold" (May 4, 1969), and "Good-Bye to the 'New Economics'" (June 8, 1969). Hazlitt clearly saw the critical fault in the Bretton Woods System: that the US government would overspend — for example, spending on the Vietnam War, the space mission to the moon, and the War on Poverty — and pay for it by printing dollars. He clearly saw early on that the Bretton Woods–style gold standard would collapse, which it did in 1971.

Murray Rothbard was also keenly aware of what was happening to the US economy in the late 1960s. He published a small pamphlet on the subject of business cycles in 1969 — *Economic Depressions: Their Cause and Cure*. This was just prior to the end of the longest expansion in US history and the beginning of thirteen years of stagflation and depression. It is very similar to Mises's book *The Causes of the Economic Crisis* published the year before the stock market crashed in 1929. Rothbard would continue writing about the looming crisis and the role of the Austrian business cycle theory:

> In the sphere of economics the Nixon Administration had been highly touted among conservatives. It was supposed to herald a return to the free-market and a check upon galloping inflation through monetary restriction. Again, nothing has happened. The much publicized monetary

---

[1]Jeffrey A. Tucker, *Henry Hazlitt: A Giant of Liberty* (Auburn, AL: Mises Institute, 1994).

tightening has been half-hearted at best, and provides no real test of the effectiveness of monetary policy. For the Administration has been doing precisely what its spokesmen had been deriding the Democrats for doing: trying to "fine-tune" the economy, trying to cut back ever so gently on inflation so as not to precipitate any recession. But it can't be done. If restrictionist measures were ever sharp enough to check the inflationary boom, they would also be strong enough to generate a temporary recession.[2]

Rothbard continued his assault on Nixon's economic policies:

> The phenomenon of inflationary recession cannot be understood by Establishment economists, whether of the Keynesian or the Milton Friedman variety. Neither of these prominent groups has any tools to understand what is going on. Both Keynesians and Friedmanites see business cycles in a very simple-minded way; business fluctuations are basically considered inexplicable, causeless, due to arcane changes within the economy, although Friedman believes that these cycles can be aggravated by unwise monetary policies of government.[3]

In contrast, Rothbard was keenly aware of this political dilemma, the "inflationary recession," because he attended some lectures by his then thesis advisor Dr. Arthur F. Burns[4] at Columbia University in 1958. Rothbard recalled the incident with his professor and later chairman of the Federal Reserve:

> I remember vividly a prophetic incident during the 1958 recession, when the phenomenon of inflation-during-recession hit the country for the first time. I attended a series of lectures by Dr. Arthur F. Burns, former head of the Council of Economic Advisers, now head of the Federal Reserve Board, and someone curiously beloved by

---

[2]Murray N. Rothbard, "Nixon's Decisions," *Libertarian Forum* 1, no. 8 (July 15, 1969): 1.

[3]Ibid., p. 4.

[4]Doug French, "Arthur Burns: The Ph.D. Standard Begins and the End of Independence," in *The Fed at One Hundred: A Critical Review on the Federal Reserve System*, edited by David Howden and Joseph T. Salerno (Heidelberg, New York, London: Springer, 2014), pp. 91–102.

many free-market adherents. I asked him what policies he would advocate if the inflationary recession continued. He assured me that it wouldn't, that prices were soon leveling off, and the recession would soon be approaching an end; I conceded this, but pressed him to say what he would do in a future recession of this kind. "Then," he said, "we would all have to resign." It is high time that we all took Burns and his colleagues up on that promise.[5]

Rothbard is directly confronting the "new economists" and their beloved Phillips Curve analysis with the phenomenon we now call stagflation, which Rothbard called an "inflationary recession."

Rothbard also attacked the Nixon administration's labor guidelines and income policy. He correctly predicted that such policies would likely lead to wage and price controls, which they did the following year:

While we can firmly predict accelerating inflation, and dislocations stemming from direct controls, we cannot so readily predict whether the Nixonite expansionism will lead to a prompt business recovery. That is problematic; surely, in any case we cannot expect any sort of rampant boom in the stock market, which will inevitably be held back by interest rates which, despite the Administration propaganda, must remain high so long as inflation continues.[6]

Rothbard went on to show that Keynesian and Friedmanite economists cannot understand this phenomenon and have no way to address such problems. In contrast, he showed how Austrian economists can understand this phenomenon through price theory and capital theory and that they do have policy recommendations on how best to address the problems of stagflation. Interest rates must be raised in order to flush out malinvestments and price inflation from the economy.

F. A. Hayek was awarded the Nobel Prize in economics in 1974 for his work building on Mises's writings on business cycle theory. Hayek had been working in isolation in Austria and concentrating on his research in entirely different directions for some years. However, when the crisis hit

---

[5]Murray N. Rothbard, "The Nixon Mess," *Libertarian Forum* 2, no. 12 (June 15, 1970): 1–3.
[6]Murray N. Rothbard, "Nixonite Socialism," *Libertarian Forum* 3, no. 1 (January 1971): 1–2.

in the early 1970s he rushed back into action. Hayek's[7] first publication on this issue was put together by Sudha R. Shenoy, the daughter of the great Indian economist B. R. Shenoy. She seamlessly strung together materials from Hayek's early writings on money and business cycles into a coherent monograph. To this 1972 book, Hayek contributed the essay "The Outlook for the 1970s: Open or Repressed Inflation?" He also published three monographs — *Choice in Currency: A Way to Stop Inflation* (1976), *Denationalization of Money: The Argument Refined* (1977), and *Unemployment and Monetary Policy: Government as Generator of the "Business Cycle"* (1979) — that sought to address the problem of the monetary crisis and economic depression.

The Austrians of the time were few but they turned out to be very vocal and correct about the threat of economic crisis. In fact their emphasis on raising interest rates and stopping the money printing might have been very influential in the form of the interest rate policy adopted by Fed chairman Paul Volcker (1979–87). It did cause a severe contraction, but it did end the monetary and price inflation and set the stage for a robust recovery.

It should also be noted that Dr. Ron Paul, an advocate of Austrian economics, decided in 1971 to run for a seat in the House of Representatives because Nixon had taken the United States off the gold standard. He has helped build a worldwide movement for Austrian economics. Also, the Cato Institute was founded in 1974 by Ed Crane, Murray Rothbard, and Charles Koch. The Cato Institute in 1982 published the monographs by F. A. Hayek, as well as *The Case for Gold: A Minority Report of the U.S. Gold Commission*, by Ron Paul and Lewis Lehrman.[8] Finally, the Ludwig von Mises Institute was founded in 1982 by Llewellyn H. Rockwell, Jr.; its premier mission is to educate people about the benefits of a true gold standard as described in the Gold Commission's minority report. The monetarist-packed US Gold Commission won the battle to maintain fiat money, but Ron Paul, the Cato Institute, the Mises Institute, and the Austrian school have all grown enormously in influence since then.

---

[7] F. A. Hayek, "The Outlook for the 1970s: Open or Repressed Inflation?" in *Tiger by the Tail: The Keynesian Legacy of Inflation*, edited by Sudha R. Shenoy (Washington, DC: Cato Institute, 1972).

[8] Ron Paul and Lewis Lehrman, *The Case for Gold: A Minority Report of the U.S. Gold Commission* (Washington, DC: Cato Institute, 1982), which was based on the research of Murray Rothbard.

CHAPTER 16

Bubble-Bust in Japan

PREFACE

During the 1980s Japan was feared as an economic and technological powerhouse. Most observers attributed their stock market bubble and high growth rates to easy monetary policy, management style, and government managed technological development. Since 1990, the Japanese government has been fighting price deflation with monetary inflation and trying to increase growth by government deficit spending. By all accounts it has not worked. Their economy remains mired in low growth, they have by far the highest ratio of government debt to GDP in the world, and they face a dramatic demographic crisis as their population continues to age. This chapter is the lesson of what NOT to do and who not to listen to for advice.

Business cycles and bubbles differ from one another, but the technical similarities between the Japanese and US bubbles are striking. The Japanese bubble began in the early 1970s, the US bubble started in the early 1980s. Both stock markets grew rapidly for thirteen years and then went parabolic to form bubbles, which peaked in Japan at the end of 1989 and in the United States during early 2000. Both stock markets lost about a third of their value eighteen months after their peaks. The Nikkei Stock Index has since lost as much as three-quarters of its peak value, while the Dow Jones

Industrial Average has been down 40 percent and the NASDAQ Composite down by 75 percent of its peak value. The real estate bubble continued in Japan for some time after the stock market began its meltdown, and likewise, real estate — particularly housing — experienced (two) bubbles since the initial breakdown of the US stock market in 2000.

The surprising thing is that in the United States the lessons of the Japanese bubble seem to have almost gone unnoticed. Japan experienced fourteen years (now more than twenty-five years) of economic stagnation since its bubble popped. Most troubling, the United States not only failed to heed the warnings of the Japanese bubble, it has thus far mimicked Japan's failed attempts to stimulate its economy with extremely low interest rates and large government budget deficits. Both countries have opted for a slow, agonizing "recovery," rather than a sharp correction of past errors that would quickly reallocate resources and return the economy to sustainable growth. Experts tell us that the Japanese and their economy are very different from the Americans and their economy and that the Japanese bubble and Japan's policy response to its crash were likewise different, but while there certainly are many important differences between the US and Japanese bubbles, the technical features and new-age thinking are strikingly similar in both bubbles.

For example, there is no doubt that technology and new-era thinking played a major role in the Japanese bubble. During the bubble, Japan took over leadership of high technology in the areas of consumer electronics, the automobile industry, manufacturing, and even robotics, and was perceived as a major threat to dominate all technological development around the globe — just as the United States is today. The threat posed by Japan's growing technological prowess can be seen in the titles of books published during the bubble era: *Japan's High Technology Industries*, edited by Hugh Patrick and Larry Meissner (1986); *The Technopolis Strategy: Japan, High Technology, and the Control of the Twenty-First Century*, by Sheridan Tatsuno (1986); *A High Technology Gap?: Europe, America, and Japan*, edited by Andrew J. Pierre (1987); *The Science and Technology Resources of Japan: A Comparison with the United States*, by Maria Papadakis (1988); *Created in Japan: From Imitators to World-Class Innovators*, by Sheridan M. Tatsuno (1990); *Japan as a Scientific and Technological Superpower*, by Justin L. Bloom (1990); *Japanese Technology Policy: What's the Secret?* by David W. Cheney and William W. Grimes (1991); and *Japan's Growing Technological Capability: Implications for the U.S. Economy*, edited by Thomas S. Arrison et al. (1992).

Writing near the pinnacle of the bubble in the stock market, Fumio Kodama[1] explained that the Japanese takeover of technological progress was a result of a new Japanese paradigm that was ushering in a new era:

> Japan is becoming one of the frontrunners in industrial technology, which means that prominent science and technology policy researchers all over the world now pay more attention to Japan. Considering this change more deeply, one can understand the reason for the researcher's academic interest: the paradigm of technological innovation is shifting.

Kodama[2] found that in Japan the innovation of high technology "seems to be different from that for conventional technologies," and therefore studies focused on Europe and the United States would not lead to a "new scientific framework for analyzing innovation of high technologies." He suggested that we break away from the inadequate linear model of the past to the unlimited model experienced under the unique "social and cultural context" of Japan. Kodama[3] even ended his book with the suggestion that it was the Japanese cassette-tape recorder, VCR, and fax machine that made the Iranian revolution, Philippine revolution, and Tiananmen uprising possible. This is classic new-era bubble thinking.

Another component of modern new-era thinking is the belief that the so-called scientific management of the economy creates perpetual prosperity. Here the Japanese experience epitomizes this phenomenon because the Japanese economy was said to represent a new "third way," positioned between the free market economy and that of the centrally planned economy. In Japan, government and corporations act cooperatively in both their self-interest and the general interest of the nation. Bureaucracies help plan and coordinate the economy. They provide incentives, such as financing and tax breaks, in order to channel investment in profitable directions. Corporations, in turn, participate in joint research programs with their competitors, but share the results among participating firms, with each choosing what technological advances to employ in their firms. Production planning is facilitated by an overlap of ownership between

---

[1] Fumio Kodama, *Analyzing Japanese High Technologies: The Techno-Paradigm Shift* (London: Pinter Publisher, 1991), p. 171.

[2] Ibid., p. 172.

[3] Ibid., pp. 173–74.

final-good producers and their input suppliers. Japanese management, especially during the bubble, was said to spur innovation, enhance product quality and reliability, and create large market shares in export markets for Japanese industries. Alas, none of this could prevent a meltdown of the Japanese stock market and well more than a decade (now more than a quarter century) of stagnation in the Japanese economy.

New-era thinking about the scientific management of the economy was never more prominent and bold than during the Japanese bubble of the 1980s. It was often said that the Japanese system would lead to economic dominance and threaten the preeminence of the US economy. Laura D'Andrea Tyson, who would later become chairman of President Clinton's Council of Economic Advisors, outlined (at the apex of the bubble) the "threat" of Japan's technological superiority:

> Certainly Japan continues to obtain technology wherever it is available and to translate it into commercial advance, as the United States itself did for so long. However, now talk has begun of a new, "technoeconomic" paradigm emerging in Japan, a new trajectory of technological development. That trajectory emerged from a pattern of industrial catch-up shaped by policies of import substitution and export promotion. As Japan reaches industrial maturity in a broad range of industries, its government is exerting substantial efforts to build a Japanese position in advancing technologies. Agencies such as the Ministry of Trade and Industries (MITI), which have become familiar names in policy discussions in the United States, are involved.[4]

In Japan, the government channeled research and development efforts, directed financing, and protected markets for business. This new, third way of government management of the economy was thought to be Japan's source of economic strength and was to inevitably place it in a position of economic preeminence. As Tyson and Zysman[5] confidently asserted:

---

[4]Laura D'Andrea Tyson, John Zysman, and Giovanni Dosi, "Trade, Technologies, and Development: A Framework for Discussing Japan," in *Politics and Productivity: The Real Story of Why Japan Works*, edited by Chalmers Johnson, Laura D'Andrea Tyson, and John Zysman (Cambridge, MA: Ballinger Publishing, 1989), p. xiv.

[5]Laura D'Andrea Tyson, and John Zysman, "Preface: The Argument Refined," in ibid., p. xiv.

A generation from now, Japan will almost certainly have created its own mechanism for advancing the technological frontiers in a range of domains. Now the continuing pace of productivity increase suggests that Japan may indeed be on a growth trajectory different from that of the United States. As Japan ascends, America frets about its decline.

Tyson and her coauthors, Dosi and Zysman,[6] questioned the validity of traditional economic thought, as all new-era thinkers must. They justified Japan's "often flagrant and self-aware violations of the nostrums of traditional economic thinking" because when "technological change is a key determinant of market outcomes, standard economic models that treat such change as exogenous are a poor guide to understanding the dynamics of market competition and the effects of policy on such competition." They argued that the "nostrum" of economic efficiency should be abandoned in favor of the less constraining and poorly defined notions of growth efficiency and technological efficiency.

Leaving the anchor of economic efficiency and traditional economic thinking behind, Tyson, Zysman, and Dosi[7] were able to justify a variety of noneconomic policies such as "beggar thy neighbor" protectionism. She heralded the concept of growth efficiency, which is essentially a Keynesian idea that rests on the assumption "that there are always unutilized resources that can be mobilized to meet growing demand. ... It is exactly this kind of thinking that led the Japanese to target industries whose products were perceived to have high income elasticities as a foundation for rapid economic growth." Ignoring the economic condition of scarcity and grasping at the concept of an economy of perpetually unutilized resources is a precondition for new-era thinking, as well as a quintessential mistake of freshman college students taking their first course in economics. If resources are perpetually available then an unlimited amount of all goods and services can be produced and there are no economic problems to solve. This would seem to be the most basic of economic errors and a particularly grievous one to make in analyzing resource- and land-poor Japan.

---

[6]Ibid., pp. 4–5.

[7]Ibid., pp. 14–15.

Naturally Tyson also had to offer a rationale for why markets do not work, and she concluded that entrepreneurs will pass up more profitable long-run investments in order to pursue short-run profits under certain conditions. Tyson, Zysman, and Dosi[8] even admitted that their argument was simply a variation of the long-discredited infant-industry argument for protectionism:

> Under conditions of nondecreasing returns there is simply no way that markets can relate the varying future growth efficiencies of various industries to relative profitability signals facing individual producers. Basically, this argument is a variant of the infant-industry argument. Because of increasing returns, current market signals can be misleading indicators of future profitability. Consequently, government policies to promote a domestic industry with high future growth potential can improve economic welfare in the long run.

It would seem from the perspective of Tyson, Zysman, and Dosi that modern-day entrepreneurs might invest in the production of black-and-white television sets or mechanical typewriters made out of jute if not for the prodding and oversight of government bureaucrats.

In their justification of Japan's new-era thinking, Tyson, Zysman, and Dosi viewed technology from the historical rather than economic perspective. In an age of information and communication technology, their "path dependent" and "sticky" processes of technological development seem odd and not entirely appropriate for new-age theorists, who often view technology as "spontaneous," perfectly flexible, and ever present. Nevertheless, they clearly are new-era philosophers of the Japanese bubble and its new technological paradigm:

> The expression *technological paradigm* ... involves a new set of best practice rules and customs, new approaches to how to relate technology to market problems, new solutions to established problems. The notion of a major industrial transition, of a second industrial divide, of a shift from "Fordist to flexible" manufacturing that has

---

[8]Ibid., p. 17.

become a fad in some debates points to just such a shift in technological paradigm.[9]

In retrospect, the new-era thinkers of the Japanese bubble economy seem conceited and hopelessly naïve, but that is the power of bubbles to deceive. One of the few observers to correctly identify and characterize the bubble was Christopher Wood,[10] who wrote that Japan "became so arrogant in the late 1980s because it really believed it was immune from the natural laws of the marketplace. This really was one of the most astonishing acts of mass delusion ever, and future historians … will marvel at it." The Japanese people might be particularly susceptible to the delusions of a stock market bubble because their culture has so long emphasized honesty and respect for authority, and the government has carefully maintained the isolation of its people, both of which could contribute to herd-like behavior and which make them ripe for what Charles Mackay famously called "the madness of crowds." The Japanese also have characteristics in their social psychology, as well as their well-known emphasis on precision and details, that might make them more susceptible to new-era delusions. The truth is that all these psychological characteristics are unimportant in terms of the cause of bubbles.

In the wake of the bubble and bust, Japan experienced a long series of corruption scandals, a procession of failed prime ministers, the ousting of financial ministers, the conviction of bureaucrats for corruption, and the breakup of its one-party system. However, the Japanese have failed to truly recognize the cause of their bubble and to liquidate their economic mistakes. Instead they embarked on a post-bubble course of easy credit, public works, and deficit spending that has only served to condemn the Japanese economy to continuing economic doldrums.

POSTSCRIPT

The success of Japan after WWII was due entirely to the free market economy, small government, low taxes, an appreciating currency, and a very high personal savings rate. That all changed when the bubble was born in the late 1980s because of overly stimulating monetary policy. A quarter

---

[9]Ibid., p. 31.

[10]Christopher Wood, *The Bubble Economy: Japan's Extraordinary Speculative Boom of the '80s and the Dramatic Bust of the '90s* (New York: Atlantic Monthly Press, 1992), p. 255.

century after the stock market meltdown Japan is still mired in an economic slump. At the prodding of mainstream economists, such as Paul Krugman, Japan has embarked on massive amounts of public works projects, enormous amounts of government borrowing, and extreme levels of monetary stimulus and quantitative easing. None of this has worked. It has left the country with the largest national debt relative to GDP in the world. It has also diverted the attention of the Japanese people and thus prevented the country from addressing its demographic crisis. In fact, it might have made the demographic crisis worse. After all, why get married and have children when the children will have to bear the enormous burden of the national debt?

CHAPTER 17

Who Predicted the Bubble?
Who Predicted the Crash?

Science is prediction.
— Motto of the Econometrics Society

Those who have knowledge, don't predict. Those who predict, don't have knowledge.
— Lao Tzu

Predicting economic behavior is inherently difficult. As Niels Bohr joked, "Prediction is very difficult, especially if it's about the future."[1] People's economic actions are subject to choice and change, unlike the subject matter of the physical sciences, which has fixed properties. Therefore, the future must remain uncertain. Predicting the economy as a whole is fraught with additional dangers and complications, and all leading indicators of economy-wide change either do not have or eventually lose the capacity to predict the future accurately. As Paul Samuelson once quipped, "Wall Street indices predicted nine out of the last five recessions."[2] In light of these difficulties, economists have taken widely divergent positions on prediction.

Originally published "Who Predicted the Bubble and Who Predicted the Bust?" *Independent Review* 4, no. 1 (Summer 2004): 5–30. Excerpted here and reprinted with permission.

[1]Quotation at http://www.brainyquote.com/quotes/quotes/n/q130288.html

[2]Paul A. Samuelson, "Science and Stocks," *Newsweek*, September 19, 1966, p. 92.

Many modern mainstream economists, like their colleagues in the physical sciences, view prediction as the essence of science. If you cannot predict with a high degree of accuracy, then you are not being scientific. You must put your science to the empirical test and pass that test. The dominance of positivism in economic methodology encourages economists to worry less about the logical consistency of their models and to concentrate more on the development of models that exploit historical data in making predictions. Government and business economists then use the models to forecast variables such as gross domestic product, interest rates, unemployment, company sales, stock prices, housing starts, and demographic changes.

There is also substantial support for the position that we cannot predict and that economists have a terrible forecasting record. With respect to the technology bust in 2001, Mike Norman put this view of economists in perspective:

> I'm an economist. Big deal, right? Until last year, economists got even less respect than Wall Street analysts; now, we're just a notch above. Admittedly, this reputation is well-deserved, because it comes from our less-than-stellar ability to get economic forecasts right. With all of that data and plenty of powerful computing ability, you'd think we could produce better forecasts. Heck, even the local weatherman puts us to shame.[3]

"The Street," having witnessed countless forecasts go wrong, is naturally suspect. As Lindley Clark once noted in the *Wall Street Journal*, "Economists have a great deal of trouble predicting the future, and it's unlikely that this unhappy situation ever will change."[4] Indeed, some economists think that forecasts are akin to "magic" and that such magic is contradicted by the very essence of economic science. Deirdre McCloskey has expounded on this view of economic forecasts:

> Economics is the science of the postmagical age. Far from being unscientific hoobla-hoo, economics is deeply anti-magical. It keeps telling us that we cannot do it, that magic

---

[3]Mike Norman, "Dismal Science May Get a Little Sunnier," *Special to the Street*, April 21, 2003.

[4]Lindley H. Clark, Jr., "Housing May Be in for a Long Dry Spell," *Wall Street Journal*, January 19, 1990.

will not help. Only the superstitious think that profitable forecasts about human action are easily obtainable. That is why economics, contrary to common sneer, is not mere magic and hooblahoo. Economics says that forecasts, like many other desirable things, are scarce. It cannot be easy to know what great empire will fall or when the market will turn. "Doctor Friedman, what's going to happen to interest rates next year?" Hoobla-hoo. Some economists allow themselves to be paid cash money to answer such questions, but they know they cannot. Their very science says so.[5]

Though agreeing in the main that forecasting has questionable value, Michael Bordo[6] claims that forecasting has some scientific and practical value and is not all just snake oil and magic. He notes that not all economists have been such dismal failures as forecasters: Richard Cantillon made correct predictions about John Law's Mississippi Bubble system based on economic theory, and he made a fortune as a result.

Others, following the famous Chinese philosopher Lao Tzu, are skeptical about the prospects for prediction but do not altogether reject the possibility of accurate prediction. They merely restrict themselves to hypothetical and qualitative prediction. Foremost among this group are the Austrian-school economists, who reject the notion of fixed relations between human-controlled variables and even the idea that data can be used to "test" an economic theory. Austrian economist Ludwig von Mises rejected the general notion of forecasting and claimed that economics can provide only qualitative predictions about particular policies:

Economics can predict the effects to be expected from resorting to definite measures of economic policies. It can answer the question whether a definite policy is able to attain the ends aimed at and, if the answer is in the negative, what its real effects will be. But, of course, this prediction can be only "qualitative." It cannot be "quantitative" as there are no constant relations between the factors and effects concerned. The practical value of economics is

---

[5]Donald McCloskey, "The Art of Forecasting: From Ancient to Modern Times," *Cato Journal* 12 (Spring–Summer 1992): 40.

[6]Michael Bordo, "The Limits of Economic Forecasting," *Cato Journal* 12 (Spring–Summer 1992): 47.

to be seen in this neatly circumscribed power of predicting the outcome of definite measures.[7]

The problem of predicting (with the goal of preventing) stock market
bubbles and crashes is especially important, not just because busts result in
huge financial loses for some investors, but because many of these extreme
financial cycles can disrupt the financial system and lead to real economic
contractions.[8] Unfortunately, economists have yet to develop a generally
accepted view of bubbles and have little to offer in predicting them.

BUBBLE PREDICTIONS

*If you can look into the seeds of time, and say which grain
will grow and which will not, speak then unto me.*

— William Shakespeare, *Macbeth*

*Responsible economists and economic analysts should have
been warning the public about the prospects of a market
crash and its implications for both the economy as a whole
and their personal fortunes. However, few economists were
issuing such warnings.*

— Dean Baker, "Dangerous Minds? The Track Record of
Economic and Financial Analysts"

One person who did issue warnings regarding the stock market bubble
and the problems a stock market crash might generate was Dean Baker
of the Center for Economic and Policy Research. In the aftermath of the
technology bust in 2001, he made the following observations:

> 1. It should have been very simple for any competent ana-
> lyst to recognize the bubble as the ratio of stock prices to
> corporate earnings hit levels that clearly were not sustain-
> able in the late nineties. ... The failure to recognize the
> bubble and warn of its consequences stems in part from a

---

[7]Ludwig von Mises, *The Ultimate Foundations of Economic Science: An Essay on Method*
(Princeton, NJ: D. Van Nostrand, 1962), p. 67.

[8]Frederic S. Mishkin, and Eugene N. White, "Stock Market Bubbles: When Does Intervention Work?" *Milken Institute Review: A Journal of Economic Policy* 5 (2nd quart. 2003).

misunderstanding of the stock market and its role in the economy. ...

2. While there were some economic analysts who did warn of the market bubble, their views were almost completely excluded from the media. ...

3. Due to their failure to recognize the stock market bubble, official forecasters, like the Congressional Budget Office (CBO) and the Social Security Administration (SSA), made projections that were implausible on their face. ...

4. Most managers of large investment funds, including public and private pensions, and university and foundation endowments, failed to see the bubble and its inevitable collapse. ... While the failure to recognize and warn of the stock bubble amounted to an enormous professional lapse, few economic or financial analysts seem to have paid much of [a] price for their mistake.[9]

I myself presented such warnings and analysis in public lectures, radio broadcasts, and newspaper articles and on the internet, but with little or no effect. In a public lecture in Houston on July 15, 1999, I addressed an audience about Alan Greenspan's "luck" in increasing the money stock without price inflation, and I warned that the Fed's actions inevitably would have negative economic consequences, especially for stocks and the dollar. I appeared on the *Financial Sense News Hour* on April 3, 2000, and April 4, 2001, and on a radio show called *Credit Bubble*.[10] On the Barstool Economist list on January 5, 2001, and January 7, 2001, I issued warnings that the dollar (then near its peak) would probably weaken over time. I also wrote several letters to newspapers, such as *Investor's Business Daily*, during this period, none of which was printed.

The *Wall Street Journal*'s semiannual survey of economic predictions indicates that forecasters have had difficulties in understanding the stock market bubble. The survey released on January 4, 1999, found forecasters to be concerned about the economy and forecasting low rates of economic

---

[9]Dean Baker, *Dangerous Minds? The Track Record of Economic and Financial Analysts* (Washington, DC: Center for Economic and Policy Research, 2002), p. 3.

[10]See http://www.financialsense.com/Experts/Thornton.htm

growth, the majority expecting higher inflation and a 30 percent chance of entering a bear market in stocks. The survey released July 2, 1999, found those same economists raising their forecasts of the GDP growth rate by 50 percent for the remainder of 1999 in response to higher-than-predicted growth rates in early 1999. Even though they remained personally bullish on the stock market, they expressed greater concern about a bear market beginning in 1999. After the Y2K crisis passed, the survey released on January 3, 2000, found economists to be euphoric about the prospects for 2000. "There is no end in sight to the expansion," said Allen Sinai, an economist at Primark Corporation. The group remained bullish on stocks, and 95 percent of the forecasters attached a probability of less than 30 percent to the onset of a recession. Only longtime bear Gary Shilling forecast a recession based on the stock market's crashing. After a decline of more than 30 percent in the NASDAQ index, the survey released on July 3, 2000, found economists confident that the Federal Reserve (the Fed) would engineer a "soft landing"; the optimists believed in the Fed's perfect soft landing, whereas the pessimists foresaw a soft landing but worried that the Fed would not do enough to fight inflation. However, the group finally was starting to express more concern about the future of the economy and the stock market. These forecasters' record seems extremely weak. Even as reported by the *Wall Street Journal*, their record is poor: they seemed to have no clue about changes in the economy's short-term outlook, instead simply projecting the historical trends forward.

The record of government economists mirrors that of Wall Street analysts. I compare forecasts from the Congressional Budget Office (CBO) and the White House with those from Wall Street in table 1. Under each group's heading, its annual forecasts for the period 1992–2002 are compared with actual economic growth rates. From 1992 through 1996, the forecasts were accurate as the economy followed the trend line. From 1996 through 2000, forecasters from all three groups underestimated economic growth rates as the economy and the stock market went into the bubble phase. Then, from 2000 to 2002, they all overestimated economic growth rates, following the trend and failing to anticipate the meltdown in the stock market and the economy. The mean absolute error for all three groups was approximately one percentage point, so their average forecast for growth rates was off by approximately 20 percent.

Two of the most famous predictions concerning the stock market came from James K. Glassman and Kevin A. Hassett in their 1999 book

Table 1
CBO, Administration, and *Blue Chip* Forecasts of Two-Year
Average Growth Rates for Nominal Output (by Calendar Year, in Percent)

	Actual	CBO Forecast	Error	Administration Forecast	Error	Blue Chip Forecast	Error
GDP							
1992–1993	5.3	5.7	0.4	5.4	0.1	5.5	0.2
1993–1994	5.7	5.3	−0.3	5.3	−0.3	6.0	0.4
1994–1995	5.6	5.6	0	5.7	0.1	5.6	0.1
1995–1996	5.2	5.2	0	5.6	0.3	5.7	0.5
1996–1997	6.0	4.7	−1.3	5.1	−1.0	4.5	−1.5
1997–1998	6.0	4.6	−1.5	4.7	−1.3	4.6	−1.4
1998–1999	5.6	4.5	−1.1	4.2	−1.4	4.5	−1.0
1999–2000	5.8	3.9	−1.8	4.0	−1.7	4.1	−1.7
2000–2001	4.3	4.9	0.6	4.9	0.6	5.1	0.8
2001–2002	3.1	5.2	2.0	5.4	2.3	5.1	2.0
Statistics for 1982–2001							
Mean error	*	*	0.2	*	0.4	*	0.2
Mean absolute error	*	*	1.1	*	1.2	*	1.1

Source: U.S. Congressional Budget Office 2003.

Dow 36,000: The New Strategy for Profiting from the Coming Rise in the Stock Market[11] and from Robert J. Shiller's *Irrational Exuberance*[12] in 2000.

Some traditional investment advisors were quick to warn against Glassman and Hassett's recommendations. In particular, Charles Murray of the American Institute for Economic Research noted that such books are often a harbinger of disaster:

> At the time (October 25, 1999), we said that books such as Dow 36,000 seem mainly to make their appearance at or near market tops. In fact, investors had their choice among Dow titles in the past year: David Elias explained why the Dow will reach 40,000 in *Dow 40,000*; whereas Charles W. Kadlec and Ralph J. Acampora predicted (although wouldn't guarantee) that the Dow will eclipse 100,000 in — you guessed it — *Dow 100,000*.[13]

[11]New York: Random House.

[12]Princeton, N.J.: Princeton University Press.

[13]Charles Murray, "Bubble Trouble," *Research Reports* 67, no. 11 (June 12, 2000): 63.

Murray's traditional approach led to the conclusion that the market was in a bubble and to a prediction that a crash or bear market was imminent. Readers could have protected themselves against the crash by acting on Murray's advice:

> Readers of these Reports know that for some time we have noted that the market's valuation of common stocks has been markedly high in relation to most measures used in security analysis — cash flow, book value, earnings, etc. However, the historical record does not tell us what the "right" valuation is, only that the current valuations are exceptional. We have also observed that the current bull market is of unprecedented duration and magnitude and that at some point a genuine bear market or even crash can be expected. Again, at what point this valuation becomes unsustainable is far from clear.[14]

Murray noted that the traditional valuation methods have shortcomings and that for larger purposes, such as the prevention of bubbles, valuation techniques do not tell us what causes bubbles in the first place.

Another good foil to Glassman and Hassett is economics and financial writer Christopher Mayer,[15] who investigated and wrote about their book during its heyday. He concentrated on the meaning of the term *overvalued* — not so much on how to determine when something is overvalued numerically, but on the cause, meaning, and effect of overvalued stocks. Specifically, he criticized the notion of perfectly rational and efficient markets and showed how markets can, in a sense, lose their rationality. First, Mayer introduced the general mindset of the new paradigm that dominated the view of the market during the bubble, and he linked Glassman and Hassett to this mindset:

> Are stocks overvalued? One answer is that it depends on whom you ask. Those who are buying and holding apparently think that they will be able to sell them at higher prices. Maybe they believe in a new paradigm where the old yardsticks of value are useless. James Glassman and Kevin Hassett recently wrote a book called *Dow 36,000*

---

[14]Ibid., p. 64.

[15]Christopher Mayer, "The Meaning of Over-valued," *Mises Daily*, March 30, 2000.

in which they maintain that the stock market is currently undervalued.[16]

Next, he made his own prediction, linking Glassman and Hassett with the hapless Irving Fisher. More important, he explained specifically why a bubble existed, rather than arguing simply that the market was overvalued by some historical yardstick:

> Looking back, future financial historians will likely relate the Glassman/Hassett thesis to Irving Fisher's famous proclamation in 1929 that "stock prices have reached a permanent and high plateau." James Grant likes to say that there are three common features of a bubble: one part fundamental (i.e., a technological revolution), one part financial (i.e., a surge in money and credit) and one part psychological (i.e., a suspension of belief in traditional valuation measures). All the ingredients would appear to exist in the current bull market.
>
> As is often said, only time will tell. Unfortunately, no theory of cycles or bubbles can tell us precisely when it will all end. Maybe twenty years from now, we will be able to definitively state whether these prices were reasonable or whether the boom time of the 1990s ended in a bust. From where I sit, heeding the teachings of the Austrians, I'll place my bet on the latter.[17]

One of the earliest prognostications regarding the boom and bust was certainly the one mentioned by analyst James Grant, the editor of *Grant's Interest Rate Observer*. Grant closed his book *The Trouble with Prosperity*, written in May 1996 "at what may or may not prove to be the ultimate peak of the speculative frenzy," with the following conclusions:

> Predictably, the risks to saving are the greatest just when they appear to be the smallest. By suppressing crises, the modern financial welfare state has inadvertently promoted speculation. Never before has a boom ended except in crisis. In anticipation of just such an outcome, a skeptical Seattle investor, William A. Fleckenstein, founded a hedge fund in 1995 to buy cheap stocks and to sell dear

---

[16]Ibid.

[17]Ibid.

ones. He named it The RTM Fund, the initials signifying "reversion to the mean." They may be the financial watchwords for the millennium.[18]

Grant continued to warn investors about the stock market bubble in his investment newsletter, to provide detailed explanations of the cause of the bubble, and to chronicle the relevant statistics.

Another early analysis came from Tony Deden (1999) at Sage Capital Management, who identified the bubble and its causes and predicted a crash:

> We fully expect a decline in securities prices and the almighty dollar over the next years. … There is no new paradigm. Economic sins have consequences. Hopefully, perhaps even economists will learn that inflation is measured by the growth in money and credit rather than in an idiotic index of consumer prices. They might even learn that growth achieved with smoke and mirrors ultimately leads to ruin.
>
> Is the incredible rise in securities prices since 1995 a reflection of real value created or is it merely a bubble? Is this really a second Industrial Revolution that changes our very basic economic assumptions or is it not? Is it a "new paradigm"? A world of fast growth, record (low) unemployment and no apparent inflation? Have economic laws been suspended? And if not, how could so many people be so wrong?[19]

Writing near the peak in the bubble, Deden declared with regard to the size and magnitude of the distortions:

> Let there be no doubt, that what we are witnessing is, indeed, history's greatest financial bubble. The indescribable financial excesses, the massive increase in debt, the monstrous use of leverage upon leverage, the collapse in private savings, the incredulous current account deficits, and the ballooning central bank assets all describe the

[18]James Grant, *The Trouble with Prosperity: The Loss of Fear, the Rise of Speculation, and the Risk to American Savings* (New York: Random House, 1996), pp. 314–15.

[19]Anthony Deden, "Reflections on Prosperity," *Sage Chronicle*, December 29, 1999.

very severe financial imbalances which no amount of statistical revision nor hype from CNBC can erase.[20]

He was equally clear and unequivocal about the cause of the bubble and related distortions in the economy:

> Their cause is not the fault of capitalism as it has been suggested, but an excessive amount of money and credit created by central banks. Yet, this seems to escape the understanding of those who will, in one day, convene congressional hearings to determine what caused this destruction. The culprit is, as it always has been, the same organization, which professes interest in bringing about price stability and low inflation: The Federal Reserve Bank and its policies of money market intervention, credit creation and loose money.[21]

Economist Jörg G. Hülsmann, writing in August 1999, provided an analysis and prediction of the stock market bubble based on the post-1980 monetary regime in the United States. He concluded that the market boom had been created artificially and that it was doomed to fail:

> You do not need a rocket scientist to predict the bitter end of this evolution. ... Just as any other state of affairs that has been artificially created and maintained by inflation, the present system bears in itself the germs if its own destruction. It will experience a flat landing of which even the most recent crises in South-East Asia, Russia, and Latin-America only give a weak foretaste.[22]

Hülsmann discussed the alternative courses of action that the Fed might take to deal with the boom and bust in the stock market. The first is to continue inflating money and credit, the second to stop that inflation. However, he concluded: "In any case the crisis is therefore inevitable. It breaks out as soon as the price-enhancing effect of the inflation is no longer neutralized through currency exports or other factors. (And of course the crisis accelerates when the inflationary currency streams back from

---

[20]Ibid.

[21]Ibid.

[22]Jörg Guido Hülsmann, *Scöne neue Zeichengeldwelt* (Brave New World of Fiat Monies). Postface to Murray Rothbard, *Das Schein-Geld-System* (Gräfelfing), p. 140.

abroad)."[23] From these arguments, he concluded that the system of boom and bust based on national fiat currencies must eventually come to an end and that either path of economic policy will entail extreme changes in our political economy:

> It is but a question of time until North-America and Europe also reach the dead end of an economy built on fiat money. At that point, however, there will be nobody to extend the life span of this shallow game through further credits and further inflation. Either the western economies will then be under total government control, as it has already been the case in German National Socialism, or we are expecting a hyperinflation. It may take some more years or even decades until we reach this point of time. It can be further delayed through a currency union between Dollar and Euro (and Yen?). But it is and remains a dead end street, at the end of which there is either socialism or hyperinflation. Only radical free-market reforms — in Rothbard's words: return to a commodity money such as gold on a free currency market and a complete ban of government from monetary affairs — lead us out of this.[24]

If Hülsmann is correct, not just about the end of the bull market but about the economic and political consequences of the bust, then the issue of stock market bubbles, their cause, and their consequences takes on a critical importance for our understanding of the future course of the overall political economy.

Hülsmann is not the only economist who traced this business cycle back to the post-1980 monetary regime of deregulation. At the height of the bull market, allies of the Austrian school of economics held a conference at which most participants emphasized the role of the Fed in creating the boom. In particular, Frank Shostak highlighted the impact of the central bank's policies:

> Today's prevailing view is that central banks and other policy makers are knowledgeable enough to pre-empt severe economic slump. ... Notwithstanding the popular view, the US economy is severely out of balance. The reason for this is the prolonged loose monetary policies of

---

[23]Ibid., p. 147.

[24]Ibid., p. 154.

the US central bank. The federal-funds rate which stood at 17.6% in April 1980 fell to the current level of 5%. At one stage in 1992 the rate stood at 3%. The money stock M3 climbed from $1824 billion in January 1980 to $6152 billion at the end of June 1999. In a time span of less than a decade it grew by over 200%. Another indicator of the magnitude of monetary pumping is the Federal debt held by the US central bank. It jumped to $465 billion in the first quarter of 1999 from $117 billion in the first quarter 1980, a 300% rise. Obviously the sheer dimension of the monetary pumping and the accompanied artificial lowering of interest rates has caused a massive misallocation of resources which ultimately will culminate in a severe economic slump.

The intensity of the misallocation of resources was further strengthened with the early 1980's financial deregulation. The idea of financial deregulation was to free the financial system from the excessive controls of the central bank. It is held that freeing financial markets will permit a more efficient allocation of economy's scarce resources, thereby raising individual well being. It was argued that the overly controlled monetary system leads to more rather than less instability. Nonetheless, rather than producing more stability, the "liberated" system gave rise to more shocks.

The 1980's financial de-regulation resulted in a reduction of the central bank supervisory powers. The weakening in the central bank controls gave impetus to a greater competition in the financial sector. This in turn through the fractional reserve banking sparked the unrestrained creation of credit and money out of "thin air." The money out of "thin air" in turn has been further processed by creative entrepreneurs, who have converted this money into a great variety of financial products, thereby contributing to a wider dissemination of the monetary pollution.[25]

On the basis of his analysis of the then-current economic utopia, Shostak concluded that the economy was poised for bad times ahead: "It seems therefore that the chaotic state of world financial markets will

---

[25]Frank Shostak, "Inflation, Deflation, and the Future," *Mises Daily*, October 5, 1999.

continue to get worse, unless gold is allowed to assume its monetary role. Notwithstanding that[,] there is very little reason for being optimistic in the current economic climate."[26]

The most forceful prediction of both a stock market bubble and a stock market bust came from bearish economist George Reisman in an article published on August 18, 1999, at the height of the stock market bubble. He began with the observation that the conditions of reality were clearly askew, an observation that most market commentators made only in hindsight:

> Clearly, something is wrong. It simply cannot be that we can have a society in which everybody lives by day trading in the stock market. While the stock market does make an important contribution to capital accumulation and the production of wealth, it is far from an unlimited one, and its contribution is not enlarged by hordes of essentially ignorant people dabbling in it on the basis of tips and hunches. Yet such an absurd outcome of practically everyone being able to live by means of buying stocks cheap and selling them dear is what is implied by an indefinite continuation of the bull market. As a result, it is inescapable that the bull market must end.[27]

For Reisman, predicting stock market bubbles and crashes is not a matter of measurement, but of cause and effect. He made the common sense observation that to understand the cause of a stock market bubble is to understand its ultimate effect: "To understand precisely how and when this will come about, one needs to understand what has been feeding the current bull market. Then one can understand what will put an end to it — what will constitute pulling its foundation out from under it." He found the ultimate cause of extreme movements in the economy in general and in the stock market bubble in particular to be government intervention in connection with the money supply and interest rates: "The only thing that explains the current stock market boom is the creation of new and additional money. New and additional money, created virtually out of thin air, has been entering the stock market in the financing of corpo-

---

[26]Ibid.

[27]George Reisman, "When Will the Bubble Burst?" *Mises Daily*, August 18, 1999.

rate mergers and acquisitions and of stock repurchases by corporations."[28] Shunning issues of technological change and psychology, Reisman concluded not only that excess financing for the stock market was the cause of the bubble, but that this money ultimately finds its way throughout the economy, spreading higher prices and bringing the stock market back to reality. He therefore separates technology and normal economic growth from inflation-financed bubbles in stock prices. Obviously, both phenomena occurred simultaneously and mingled during the 1990s:

> The increase in the quantity of money exerts its favorable effect on stock prices only when, as in the last few years, the increase is concentrated in the stock market and has not yet sufficiently spread throughout the rest of the economic system. When it does spread throughout the economic system and begins substantially to raise commodity prices, the effect on the stock market becomes negative.
>
> The application to the stock market is that the market will stop rising as soon as the Federal Reserve becomes sufficiently alarmed about the inflationary flooding of the economy as a whole that emanates from the stock market bathtub so to speak. When the Federal Reserve is finally moved to turn off the water — the new and additional money — flowing into the stock market, its rise will be at an end. Indeed, not only will the stock market stop rising, it will necessarily suffer a sharp fall.
>
> The inescapable implication is that sooner or later, the stock-market boom must end. The bubble must break.[29]

Reisman, it appears, made an accurate analysis of the stock market, identified the cause of the bubble, and accurately predicted that the stock market would crash.[30]

Economic and stock analyst Sean Corrigan also provided well-timed prognostication of the bubble and deep insight into its cause. He compared conditions during the fall of 1999 to those during the late summer of 1987, the Japanese bubble of the late 1980s, and the Roaring Twenties in the

---

[28]Ibid.

[29]Ibid.

[30]For an updated analysis, see George Reisman, "It May Be Bursting Now, and Faulty Economic Analysis May Cost Investors Dearly, Capitalism.net, February 26, 2000.

United States. He dismissed the idea that technology and a "new paradigm" could have been responsible for the run-up in stock prices in the late 1990s. In his view, debt of all kinds was expanding at high rates at a time when the saving rate was plummeting. The solution to this economic paradox was straightforward for Corrigan. He blamed Alan Greenspan for overly generous provision of high-powered money, and he then proceeded to explain the impact of this highly expansionary monetary policy:

> Monetary pumping on this order, as the Austrians will tell you, leads to serious distortions in the price structure of an economy which cannot be captured in crude, aggregate, index numbers. These distortions between the value of goods, present and future, lead to mal-investments and a clustering of false decisions. Factories built and productive processes put in train based on a market rate of interest artificially lowered by the effulgence of fiduciary media are not backed up by real savings and thus become misaligned with a propensity for consumption which has, if anything, intensified.[31]

What effect do these distorted prices and investments have? Corrigan went on to make a bold and far-reaching prediction:

> A raft of "entrepreneurial errors" lies ahead. This means not only the prospect of half-finished malls, hotels and offices, but also completed, now distinctly sub-par undertakings: businesses and plants which cannot possibly earn the returns projected at inception. Less visible, though more widespread, such an overhang will depress returns on capital where they do not wipe it out completely. The credit expansion, once it draws to its inevitable end, will impoverish everyone, everywhere.[32]

Writing at the end of the boom, bearish economist Hans Sennholz described both the direct cause (credit creation by the Fed) and its effects in creating the boom in both the stock market and the general economy, taking special note of the explosion in the use of derivatives:

> Surely, the American economy looks very dynamic and the value of the stock market is the highest in U.S. history,

---

[31]Sean Corrigan, "Will the Bubble Pop?" *Mises Daily*, October 18, 1999.
[32]Ibid.

but the private economy is incurring the biggest financial deficits since the Second World War. The country is suffering record current account deficits with net external liabilities now exceeding 20 percent of GDP and rising.

Wall Street may be celebrating the decline in government deficits, but other debts continue to grow by leaps and bounds. According to the Fed's Flow of Funds, household debt (mainly home mortgages) is growing at an annual rate of 9.25 percent, total household debt as a share of personal income now exceeds 103 percent. Business debt is soaring at a 10.5 percent rate. Corporate debt of non-financial firms is rising at a 12 percent rate, the fastest in more than a decade.

While some of these debts are going into new investments, much is spent on share buybacks. In short, corporations are going into debt to boost their share prices. Margin debt in the stock market is growing faster than any other type of credit. In 1999 it soared by 46 percent, now exceeding $206 billion, which is the highest in U.S. history. Unfortunately, if this growth of debt should come to a halt, or merely slow down, it may break the fever of the boom and usher in the readjustment.[33]

Sennholz went on to describe the precarious position of the economy and the stock market. He described the contraction in the market as an inevitable consequence of the credit-induced boom and as something the Fed had no power to fix:

The American economy is in its 10th year of cyclical expansion, which is the longest on record. A grave risk in this setting is a sudden fall in share prices, a bear market, which would evoke a dramatic fall in consumer confidence and demand. Since consumption is driving more than two-thirds of American production and growth, a sharp decline of consumer demand would soon lead to a decline in production, which may trigger an international run from the dollar. In order to stem such a run and attract enough foreign capital to cover the current account deficit of more than 4 percent of GDP and carry external liabilities of more than 20 percent of GDP, the

---

[33]Hans Sennholz, "Can the Boom Last?" *Mises Daily*, July 31, 2000.

Federal Reserve would have to raise its rates. But such a raise at a time of falling stock prices and falling output would soon aggravate the decline and lead to a painful recession. The present pleasant scenario of rising productivity and income, high stock prices and a strong dollar would soon turn into the opposite — falling productivity and income, falling stock prices and a weak dollar, declining imports, rising inflation, rising interest rates, and rising unemployment. The longest economic boom in history would give way to a long recession.[34]

Just as clearly, the cause of the credit creation and therefore the boom is the Fed and the policy of central bankers:

The economic maladjustments due to many years of monetary manipulations by the Federal Reserve System are the prime source and mover of the inevitable readjustment. Once the market structure no longer reflects the unhampered choices of all participants, the readjustment is unavoidable. In the end, the laws of the market always prevail over the edicts of political controllers and regulators. They even reign over the wishes of a few central bankers. Surely, government officials and central bankers have the power to lessen or aggravate the stresses of readjustment as they have the power to interfere with the economic lives of their nationals.[35]

At a time when many were still unsure about the causes and consequences of the initial features of the bust, others such as William Anderson clearly saw the "beginnings of the end" and emphasized that this big cycle of boom and bust was nothing new to US economic history:

We have, supposedly, learned our lessons since the 1970s. Alan Greenspan knows more than previous Federal Reserve chairmen, Robert Rubin was a brilliant Secretary of the Treasury, the internet is providing new ways of doing business, and Bill Clinton has marvelously orchestrated the whole thing. The stock market is rising, and the government (or at least the current regime, according to Al Gore in his stump speeches) knows how to continue

---

[34]Ibid.

[35]Ibid.

the prosperity. This time, we really are experiencing the New Economy.

Pardon me if I dissent. If history tells us correctly, we are in our third "New Economy" in the last 80 years. The first episode of "prosperity forever" came in the late 1920s, as the bull market, low unemployment numbers, and general good times led newly-elected President Herbert Hoover to declare, "In no nation are the fruits of accomplishment more secure." We know the rest of that sorry story.[36]

Anderson was careful to distinguish the cause of the boom from the normal or natural features of economic growth. He also distinguished between a potential catalyst of the bust (the Microsoft trial) and its underlying causes:

But for all of the high-technology wonders and the gains made from deregulation, the one substantial part of the New Economy consists simply of an economic boom in all that the phrase implies. The engine behind the boom is also the locomotive behind the inevitable bust: the Federal Reserve and its inflationary policies.

As things stand currently, the once-vaunted bull market is in flux. This is partly due to the government's arrogance in believing it could attack Microsoft without harming other high-technology firms that have been the most visible in the current economic expansion. That the NASDAQ has lost much of its value since Janet Reno's Department of Justice [DOJ] won the first round of its attempt to dismember Microsoft bears testament to this administration's foolishness regarding economic matters.

But even without the DOJ's Microsoft follies, the high-technology sector of the economy faces real problems. First, the bubble that pushed so many of the "dot-com" initial offerings into the stratosphere had burst even before Reno's pyrrhic victory. Second, the malinvestments as described by Ludwig von Mises and Murray Rothbard that occur as the result of wildly expansive monetary policies by the Fed have been centered in the high technology sector. The growth of new money that is the signature of

---

[36]William Anderson, "New Economy, Old Delusion, *Free Market* 18, no. 8 (2000): 5.

inflation can come only through the fractional-reserve banking system in the form of loans, which, as noted earlier, have found their way into high technologies, real estate, and the stock market.

Should a large number of high technology investments go bust, or if profit rates disappoint potential investors, the new money will stop pouring into that sector. By that time, we will be seeing an increase of commodity prices, and inflation will be recognized as a serious problem. The next stage will be the beginning of the recession, as the malinvestments that grew willynilly during the period of monetary expansion will have to be liquidated.

The US economy the past five years has been able to absorb a large amount of new money, much more so than it could have done two decades ago. That does not mean, however, that it is inflation-proof or is impervious to malinvestments. The Misesian theory of the business cycle is a comprehensive theory. It has not lost its explanatory power in 2000 any more than it was irrelevant in 1969 or 1929.

While we may be currently celebrating a record boom, we have not overturned the laws of economics. No doubt when it happens, the usual Keynesians in the halls of academe and in the media will blame high interest rates and the Fed's refusal to expand credit. In truth, there will be another explanation, one that people are ignoring now and will ignore then.[37]

Supply-side economist Jude Wanniski (2000) attributed the bust in the stock market during April 2000 to tax liabilities accrued from capital gains in the late 1990s. Investors who had capital gains in 1999 had to pay taxes on those gains on April 15, and Wanniski suggested that investors selling shares in order to pay their taxes ignited the decline in the prices of the stocks composing the NASDAQ index. Although this observation provides insight into what might have initiated the bursting of the bubble, Wanniski himself did not believe in financial bubbles and encouraged his clients to jump back into the market after tax season was over.[38]

---

[37]Ibid., p. 6.

[38]Jude Wanniski, "Letters to Clients," March 30 to April 19, 2000.

Another important prediction came from economists Stan Liebowitz and Stephen Margolis, who were considering questions of competition and antitrust policy in high-technology markets. They correctly described these markets as displaying a speculative bubble near the apex of the bubble: "This is not to imply that a speculative bubble, which seems the proper description for Internet stocks as this book is being written [spring 1999], is required to assure sufficient financing."[39] Liebowitz later provided a more detailed examination (published after the bubble had burst) of why the bubble happened:

> The book ... focuses on understanding why financial events went so awry. ... Many of the prognostications about the internet — rapidly increasing number of users, rapidly increasing advertising revenues, rapidly increasing sales — fertilized wildly optimistic prognostications for the performance of Internet firms, as if a virtual cornucopia of wealth would come streaming down upon investors in those companies [and it did for those lucky enough to get in early]. ... But even if all the prognostications of users and revenue growth had been true, as some of them were, that would not have assured the rosy financial scenario that so many investors and analysts anticipated.[40]

CONCLUSIONS

Such is the exuberance on Wall Street that only a brave man insists that the American stock market is overdue for a crash. Down the long history of bubbles ready to burst, it was ever thus.
— *Economist*, March 25, 2000

The foregoing survey of predictions regarding the stock market bubble of the 1990s was conducted against a background condition that economists do not agree on either the role of prediction in economic science or the causes of stock market bubbles. The purpose was to identify

---

[39]Stan J. Liebowitz, and Stephen E. Margolis, *Winners, Losers, & Microsoft: Competition and Antitrust in High Technology* (Oakland, CA: Independent Institute, 1999), p. 115.

[40]Stan J. Liebowitz, *Rethinking the Network Economy: The Real Forces That Drive the Digital Marketplace* (New York: Amacom, 2002), p. 2.

who correctly ascertained the existence of a stock market bubble and who correctly predicted a stock market crash. The appendix at the end of this article provides a timeline of additional quotes reflecting insight, unawareness, or confusion regarding the macroeconomic contours of the bubble and the crash. More important, however, this survey has examined how the boom was identified and what its cause was. These issues are important because stock market booms and busts entail massive transfers and financial losses in the economy, and when associated with severe downturns in the business cycle, they can cause significant economic costs, distortions, and inefficiencies. Economic crises have often provided the occasion for a ratcheting upward of the size, scope, and power of government (Higgs 1987). In extreme cases, such radical changes in financial and economic conditions may give rise to social upheaval and political instability.

In general, the correct predictions fall into two categories. Those in the first group were based on the analysis of valuation. Using standard measures of stock market value, such as the price-to-earnings ratio, economists such as Robert Shiller and a small number of market analysts who were bearish in 1999 concluded that the stock market had become extremely overvalued and therefore was experiencing bubble-like conditions and was fated to decline steeply. Unfortunately, most of these forecasters did not provide detailed economic analysis of their predictions. The use of valuation measures is indeed helpful, but such measures are essentially only tools of historical analysis for comparing ratios and percentages from one time period to those from another period or to historical averages. In the recent bubble, most bulls always found a way to adjust the valuation measures to account for modern conditions and to make the stock market appear undervalued.

The second group of correct predictions came from outside the mainstream of the economics profession. Most came from economists associated with the Austrian school of economics, including academic economists, financial economists, and fellow travelers of the school. These predictions began to come forth in 1996 and continued until after the downturn in the stock market, but most of them occurred close to the peak in the stock markets. Austrians tend to have a negative view in general, and they are quick to emphasize the negative aspects of economic conditions, but they also distinguish bubbles and business cycles clearly from other economic phenomena and trends. Given that the Austrian economists are both relatively few in number and marginalized in the profession, their dominance in making correct predictions seems to be something of an elephant in the soup bowl, especially in light of their general disdain for forecasting and for the mainstream's requirement of accurate prediction. In my survey, I tried to avoid the inclusion of "permabears," or analysts who are perpetually bearish on the stock market. It should be noted, however, that James Grant is a self-admitted permabear and that his prediction came too early in terms of market timing. The predictions are summarized in table 2.

It is especially noteworthy that all the Austrian predictions provided an economic explanation of the bubble and that their explanations were relatively consistent across the group. To generalize, the Austrians perceived the Fed to be following a loose monetary policy that kept interest rates below the rates that would have prevailed in the absence of that policy.

Table 2
Forecasts and Schools of Economic Thought

Name	Forecast	Date	School of Thought
Dean Baker	Bubble	1999–2000	Post-Keynesian
James Glassman	Dow 36,000	1999	Supply-sider
Kevin Hassett	Dow 36,000	1999	Supply-sider
David Elias	Dow 40,000	1999	Unknown
Charles Kadlec	Dow 100,000	1999	Unknown
Robert Shiller	Bubble/Bust	1999	Behavioral finance
Charles Murray	Bubble/Bust	2000	Valuation measures
Christopher Mayer	Bubble/Bust	2000	Austrian
James Grant	Bubble/Bust	1996	Austrian
Tony Deden	Bubble/Bust	1999–2000	Austrian
Jörg Hülsmann	Bubble/Crisis	1999	Austrian
Frank Shostak	Bubble/Bust	1999	Austrian/technical
George Reisman	Bubble/Bust	1999	Austrian
Sean Corrigan	Bubble/Bust	1999	Austrian
Hans Sennholz	Bubble/Bust	2000	Austrian
William Anderson	Bubble/Bust	2000	Austrian
Jude Wanniski	Market Crash	2000	Supply-sider
Jerry Jordan	Bubble	1997	Monetarist
Llewellyn Rockwell	Bubble/Bust	1999	Austrian
Greg Kaza	Boom/Bust	1999	Austrian
Holman Jenkins	Buy and Hold	1999–2000	Business
William McDonough	Financial Stability	1999	Pres. of N.Y. Fed
Economist magazine	Bubble/Crash	2000	Keynesian/Hayekian

Individual writers emphasized the Fed's willingness to bail out investors consistently during the 1990s, thereby desensitizing investors to risk. As a result, a period of "exuberance" and wild speculation took place, culminating in the hysteria of a stock market bubble. If the Austrian analysis is correct, the Fed has been a significant source of financial and economic instability. This analysis also suggests that the Fed's bias toward keeping rates as low as possible may cause significant economic losses and that a better policy might be to let market forces determine interest rates without intervention.

Those who discovered the "boom" in the economy and the "bubble" in the stock market and who predicted either a "bust" in the economy or a crash in the stock market work within an analytical tradition dating back to Richard Cantillon, whose *Essay on the Nature of Commerce in General* was published in 1755. The Cantillon tradition was carried forward and extended in the works of Turgot, Say, Bastiat, Menger, Wicksell, Böhm-Bawerk, Mises, Röpke, Hayek, and Rothbard, and it is now a hallmark of the modern Austrian school of economics.

At the core of this mode of analysis is an emphasis on entrepreneurship and the study of what causes prices to rise and fall, encompassing wages, rents, profits, interest, and the purchasing power of money. With respect to the business cycle, the Cantillon tradition shows that disturbances in the supply of money and credit, especially when a monetary authority expands the supply of paper money, changes relative prices. Artificial reductions in interest rates encourage investment and increase the valuation of capital assets, longer-term assets increasing in value more than shorter-term ones. The resulting changes in the structure of production (buildings, technology, and the pattern of industrial organization) are called Cantillon effects. They occur during the boom, a phase when resources are misallocated, both to malinvestments and to misdirected labor. As relative prices correct themselves in the bust, resources are reallocated by mechanisms such as bankruptcy and unemployment. Capital-asset prices are extremely volatile during this process.

Although Austrian ideas have received more notice and attention in the financial media and in academic publications in recent years, a survey of economic textbooks at the undergraduate or graduate level would find hardly a word about Austrian business cycle theory or about Cantillon effects. It may be too early for a complete revision of economics textbooks and too much to ask that economics professors rewrite their class notes, but it certainly is time at least to introduce these concepts in classrooms and textbooks so that students can consider an alternative paradigm and evaluate its merits.

APPENDIX: SOME OTHER PREDICTIONS

• Jerry Jordan: "The problem may ... be ... in asset [stock] markets, as suggested by historical episodes in this country, notably in the 1920s, and in Japan in the late 1980s."[41] As a voting member of the Federal Open Market Committee, Jordan, president of the Cleveland Fed, voted unsuccessfully five times to raise interest rates, starting in 1998.

• Victor Zarnowitz: "The arguments in favor a [sic] new Golden Age are generally not persuasive."[42] Zarnowitz is aware of the Austrian theory of the business cycle and considers it in his analysis.

• Lew Rockwell: "At some point, and nobody knows when, the stock market is going to reverse its climb. It may even collapse."[43]

• Greg Kaza: "There is talk on Wall Street of a 'New Economic Paradigm,' that has repealed the business cycle. But surface appearances can be deceiving. ... Eventually a recession will occur."[44]

• Holman Jenkins: "The claim by Glassman and Hassett to have found a new value for the Dow is a wonderful marketing gimmick, but it is the least important part of their book. The authors are certainly right that Americans have gotten over their fear of the stock market — because the stock market works better than it used to. For investors, it has become safe to buy, hold, and forget."[45]

• Alan Greenspan: "I recognize there is a stock market bubble problem at this point," and "I guarantee if you want to get rid of the bubble, whatever it is, [increasing margin requirements] will do it".[46]

---

[41]Jerry J. Jordan, president of the Federal Reserve Bank of Cleveland in the minutes of the Federal Open Market Committee meeting, November 11, 1997.

[42]Victor Zarnowitz, "Theory and History Behind Business Cycles: Are the 1990s the Onset of a Golden Age?" NBER Working Paper 7010 (Cambridge, MA: National Bureau of Economic Research), abstract.

[43]Llewellyn H. Rockwell, Jr. "Stock Market Bailout," *Free Market* (November 1999): 4.

[44]Greg Kaza, Greg, "Downsizing Detroit: Motown's Lament," *Chronicles: A Magazine of American Culture* (November 20, 1999), p. 20.

[45]Holman W. Jenkins, Jr., 1999–2000. "Of Bulls and Bubbles," *Policy Review* 98 (1999–2000).

[46]Alan Greenspan, minutes of the Federal Open Market Committee meeting, September 24, 1996.

• William McDonough: "I think the banking system is functioning just about where I would like it to be — that is, appropriate willingness to take risk but with good, sensible judgments in general being demonstrated."[47]

• *The Economist*: "Such is the exuberance on Wall Street that only a brave man insists that the American stock market is overdue for a crash. Down the long history of bubbles ready to burst, it was ever thus."[48]

• Alan Greenspan: "It is very difficult to definitively identify a bubble [in US stock markets] until after the fact."[49]

• Nicholas Brady: "The present market collapse is different; it was caused by vastly overblown valuations. The stock market has been in a colossal bubble, a delusion born in the late 1990's that reached its zenith in 2000. While not uncommon, bubbles have always been a fact of market life, a byproduct of runaway human emotions."[50]

• Laurence Mayer: "There was a sense of frustration that we couldn't deal better with the asset-price bubble. ... But I don't think anybody has come up with a strategy that people felt would have gotten the job done."[51]

• Matthew Spiegel: "The difficulty with declarations claiming that large stock price moves are 'bubbles' or 'panics' is that they rely on perfect hindsight, typically generated only a few months or a year following the event. But investors do not have that luxury. They must price securities based on the information they have at the time they make their decisions."[52]

• Robert Shapiro: "If not technology shocks or market pricing failures, what's driving the current business cycle? It's not terrorism or war. Terrorism doesn't exact sufficiently large direct costs to drive the economy; and it's hard to argue that its psychological effects have slowed growth, when the economy turned around in the quarter immediately following 9/11 and turned in its best performance in years in the quarter after that.

---

[47]William McDonough, president of the New York Federal Reserve, quoted by *Reuters*, September 26, 1999.

[48]*The Economist* 2000, p. 84.

[49]Alan Greenspan, speech at the Federal Reserve Bank of Kansas City's annual conference at Jackson Hole, Wyoming, August 20, 2002.

[50]Nicholas F. Brady, "Every Market Collapse Is Different," *New York Times*, August 11, 2002.

[51]Federal Reserve governor Laurence Mayer as quoted in Carol Vinzant, "Two Schools of Thought on Economics," *Chicago Tribune*, September 3, 2002.

[52]Matthew Spiegel, "2000 A Bubble? 2002 A Panic? Maybe Nothing?" Yale School of Management (New Haven, CT, 2002), p. 5.

Nor is there hard evidence that the prospect or reality of the war with Iraq punctured business investment and consumer spending."[53]

• James Grant: "In the boom cycle, people are not so much interested in a message that says: a bust is simply a necessary part of the business cycle. In a false prosperity, good economic ideas are marginalized. That's why Austrians should prepare right now to offer the best explanation when the tide turns, as it always does. Who knows? Maybe we'll find ways to make the bust intellectually profitable. In time, Austrian economics could be again seen as the mainstream theory. It should be."[54]

---

[53]Robert Shapiro, "Spin Cycle: Why Has the Business Cycle Gone Topsy-Turvy?" Slate.com. April 15, 2004.

[54]James Grant, "The Trouble with Prosperity: An Interview with James Grant," *Austrian Economics Newsletter* 16 (1996): 8.

CHAPTER 18

"Bull" Market?

It was on a weekend during the winter of 2004 and I was getting suspicions of the coming of another Fed-induced bubble like the one of the late 1990s. Social psychology seemed to be becoming more optimistic. However, it was not perfectly clear if it was just a general boom throughout the economy, or a bubble in a particular sector. I decided to take a look for myself.

It would be hard to deny that the American stock exchanges are experiencing bull markets. Last year (2003) the NASDAQ was up over 50 percent while the Dow 30 and S&P 500 had gains of 25 percent, and it seems that everyone is bullish this year. The Dow Theory (which is not much of a theory) tells us that we are in a bull market. If you are a follower of the "January effect," where the month of January somehow determines the fate of the market for the year, you should also have a bullish outlook because all the stock market indexes ended the month in positive territory.

Only the New England Patriots' victory would seem to have spoiled the party. The Super Bowl indicator predicts a good year for the stock market if a team from the old NFC wins and a bad year when a team from the AFC wins. Then again the Super Bowl indicator has lost some of its magic

---

The original version of this chapter was published as "Bull Market," LewRockwell.com, February 9, 2004.

in recent years. Maybe we should switch to political indicators, which would suggest big gains in stocks during an election year.

But is the stock market truly showing signs of prosperity, or is it just BS?

I would like to suggest the latter and that it might not be a good time for you to obtain a home-equity loan to invest in hot tech stocks. We are going through a housing bubble, and stock valuations as measured by stock price-to-earnings ratios are at bubble levels. The buy low, sell high philosophy would lead you to sell stocks now, not buy them.

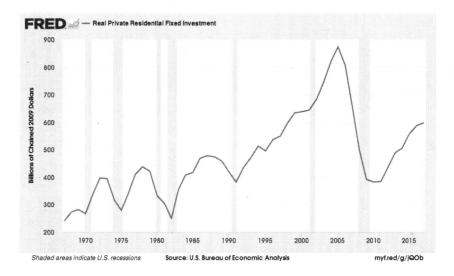

in recent years. Maybe we should switch to political indicators, which Shaded areas indicate U.S. recessions   Source: U.S. Bureau of Economic Analysis   myf.red/g/jQOb

I'm not suggesting that you sell your house or cash in your retirement funds, only that you don't throw caution to the wind and abandon traditional guidelines. Over 90 percent of stocks are now trading above their two-hundred-day moving average. I usually think of selling stocks, or at least stop buying them, when this indicator approaches 80 percent and then throw the cash back into the market when it gets down to the 20–30 percent level. At a minimum, investors should take the time to evaluate their assets and portfolio allocations between stocks, bonds, cash, and gold — between speculation and safety.

What is the case for a BS stock market based on?

First, the Federal Reserve has pushed short-term interest rates down to historically low levels. This has certainly buoyed stock prices, but it also has stymied savings and encouraged increases in consumption and debt.

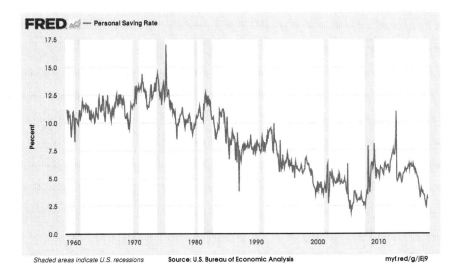

Shaded areas indicate U.S. recessions   Source: U.S. Bureau of Economic Analysis   myf.red/g/jEj9

Americans have low levels of savings and high levels of debt, and this is simply not good for the health of the economy. In fact, statistics indicate that Americans have been taking money out of saving accounts and putting it into the stock market, but are not increasing their overall savings.

Second, the federal government has increased spending and debt at a rapid rate. Both are bad for the health of the economy, but do serve to keep up the appearance of prosperity in economic statistics such as GDP and the unemployment rate. When economic recovery is fueled by government spending, combined with stimulated consumption spending and housing construction, how real can the prosperity be?

Looking backward, we should also remember the decrease in the value of the dollar. Thanks to the Federal Reserve, the US dollar index lost approximately 15 percent of its value in 2003. If you had parked your money in a foreign bank or foreign bonds you could have avoided the loss plus earned interest, making the 25 percent gains on US stocks hardly spectacular in comparison.

Looking forward, we should note that the percentage of investment advisors who are bullish on the market is near the highest level experienced over the last four years. The percentage of investment advisors who are bearish is near the lowest level over the same time period. This psychological indicator is a contrarian indicator in that the larger the number of bulls and the smaller the number of bears, the more likely is a "correction" in the stock market. It is not a perfect indicator — nothing is — but it does line up with economic analysis in finding some trouble ahead in the US stock market.

This takes me to my disclaimer. If investment advisors as a group tend to be wrong about the future of the stock market, then how good can my advice and analysis be? The answer is *caveat emptor*, and that's no BS.

CHAPTER 19

Housing:
Too Good To Be True

S igns of a "new era" in housing are everywhere in 2004. Housing construction is taking place at record rates. New records for real estate prices are being set across the country, especially on the East and West Coasts. Booming home prices and record-low interest rates are allowing homeowners to refinance their mortgages, "extract equity" to increase their spending, and lower their monthly payment! As one loan officer recently explained to me: "It's almost too good to be true."

In fact, it is too good to be true. What the prophets of the new housing paradigm don't discuss is that real estate markets have experienced similar cycles in the past and that periods described as new paradigms or new eras are often followed by periods of distress in real estate markets, including foreclosure sales, bankruptcy, and bank failures.

The case of Japan's real estate bubble is instructive. Japan had a stock market bubble in the 1980s that was very similar to the US stock market bubble in the 1990s. As the Japanese stock market started to bust, Japan's real estate market continued to bubble. One general index of Japanese real estate shows that prices rose for almost two years after the stock market crashed, with prices staying above pre-crash levels for more than five years. The boom in home construction continued for nearly six years after

---

The original version of this chapter was published as "Housing: Too Good to Be True," *Mises Daily*, June 4, 2004.

the stock market crash. Prices for commercial, industrial, and residential real estate in Japan continues to fall and are now below the levels measured in 1985 when these statistics were first collected.

It has now been three years since the US stock market crash. Chairman Greenspan has indicated that interest rates could soon reverse their course, while longer-term interest rates have already moved higher. Higher interest rates should trigger a reversal in the housing market and expose the fallacies of the new paradigm, including how the housing boom has helped cover up increases in price inflation. Unfortunately, this exposure will hurt homeowners, and the larger problem could hit the American taxpayer, who could be forced to bail out the banks and government-sponsored mortgage guarantors who have encouraged irresponsible lending practices.

MORE GREENSPAN

Once again, Fed chairman Alan Greenspan[1] has created a new-age economic panacea, and earlier this year he applauded his contribution to the economic recovery: "Very low interest rates and reduced taxes, have permitted relatively robust advances in residential construction and household expenditures. Indeed, residential construction activity moved up steadily over the year."

The key to this panacea is the process of *equity extraction* that occurs when people refinance their homes; they take equity out and spend it to increase their standard of living. However, because variable-rate mortgages are so low, their payments actually go down, so they have more of their monthly income to spend or they can upgrade to a more expensive house. As Greenspan explained:

> Other consumer outlays, financed partly by the large extraction of built-up equity in homes, have continued to trend up. Most equity extraction — reflecting the realized capital gains on home sales — usually occurs as a consequence of house turnover. But during the past year, an almost equal amount reflected the debt-financed cash-outs

---

[1]"Testimony of Chairman Alan Greenspan." Federal Reserve Board's Semiannual Monetary Policy Report to the Committee on Banking, Housing, and Urban Affairs, US Senate, February 12, 2003.

associated with an unprecedented surge in mortgage refinancings.[2]

As is the norm, Greenspan hedged his statements. He also considered some of the potential drawbacks and pitfalls on the horizon for the new paradigm in housing, but in the end he concluded that we really have nothing to worry about. Low interest rates, rising home prices, and lower financing costs mean that we actually can have our cake (i.e., our homes) and eat it too (i.e., equity extraction for consumption):

> To be sure, the mortgage debt of homeowners relative to their income is high by historical norms. But as a consequence of low interest rates, the servicing requirement for the mortgage debt of homeowners relative to the corresponding disposable income of that group is well below the high levels of the early 1990s. Moreover, owing to continued large gains in residential real estate values, equity in homes has continued to rise despite sizable debt-financed extractions. Adding in the fixed costs associated with other financial obligations, such as rental payments of tenants, consumer installment credit, and auto leases, the total servicing costs faced by households relative to their incomes are below previous peaks and do not appear to be a significant cause for concern at this time.[3]

THE HOUSING BUBBLE

I first reported on the housing bubble in the United States at the beginning of this year (2004) when the bubble was already well under way, if not in full bloom. As the chart "Real Private Residential Fixed Investment" in chapter 18 indicates, real residential investment has jumped far above both its historical trend and even its cyclical trend channel. This indicates to me that there is a bubble in residential real estate. The data for this chart originally stopped at the beginning of 2003. We now know that investment in housing increased by 8.8 percent last year. This is a historically high rate of construction, but far from a record rate increase. However, 2003 marks the ninth year in a row that housing investment was positive,

---

[2]Ibid.
[3]Ibid.

the first time that has ever occurred since the statistic has been collected. Frank Shostak[4] and Christopher Mayer[5] have also written very informative articles on the housing bubble.

Recently I came across a piece of anecdotal evidence of a housing bubble. Last Sunday afternoon, a friend of mine put a "For Sale by Owner" sign on the front lawn of a small rental house he owned on a side street. It wasn't listed with a real estate agent or in the newspaper, but he nonetheless had a couple of calls that afternoon, with many more to follow, and within a couple of days he had multiple offers before he finally accepted a bid that was substantially over his original asking price.

Mainstream economists who discount the possibility of a housing bubble would dismiss such evidence. But they also ignore all the macro evidence of the current housing boom and see it as a positive development. For example, the number of new homes being constructed is at an all-time high, despite a "soft" labor market. The annualized rate of new home construction has surpassed the two surges of the 1970s when inflation was out of control.

The prices of houses are also up circa 2004, but mainstream economists have generally ignored this development as well; and as noted above, Greenspan sees this as a positive development. Some economists can even point to the Consumer Price Index, which shows that the housing component in the CPI is steady or falling. And yet reports are coming out nearly every day saying that housing prices are up dramatically and setting records all across the country. Record prices have been recently reported in the San Francisco Bay Area, Denver, Boston, Las Vegas, the State of Washington, and even Buffalo, New York.

Nationally, the price of a median family home was up 15 percent between 2001 and 2003, with regional increases of 30 percent in the Northeast, 8.5 percent in the Midwest, 14.4 percent in the Southeast, and 20.4 percent in the West. Over the last year, increases have been reported as 18.7 percent in the Northeast, 1.9 percent in the Midwest, 3.8 percent in the Southeast, and 10.7 percent in the West, or 6.5 percent for the nation as a whole. Interestingly, the median price has actually dropped 7.2 percent in the Midwest and 7.3 percent in the South since peaking in the third quarter of 2003, while prices have been generally flat in the West. Statistics

---

[4]Frank Shostak, "Housing Bubble: Myth or Reality?" *Mises Daily*, March 4, 2003.

[5]Christopher Mayer, "The Housing Bubble," *Free Market* 23, no. 8 (August 1, 2003).

from the last couple of quarters might therefore suggest that the housing bubble may have topped out, or at least temporarily cooled down, in much of the country.

Why have home prices been increasing? David Lereah, chief economist with the National Association of Realtors, explained to *Inman News* (2004): "It's a simple matter of supply and demand. ... We continue to have more home buyers than sellers in most of the country, which results in tight housing inventories and higher rates of home price appreciation."[6] Of course the cause of higher home prices is that the Federal Reserve has kept interest rates, and thus mortgage rates, at historically low rates such that people find it easier to finance homes. In fact, despite an 18 percent increase in home prices since 2001, the median monthly payment remained the same at $789/month and the median payment as a percentage of income has actually fallen. This is the magic of monetary inflation, courtesy of Alan Greenspan.

PRICE INFLATION FOLLOWS MONETARY INFLATION

The price of just about everything I buy is going up these days. Gasoline is higher, dairy products are higher, paper products and just about everything else — higher. Mainstream economists have sounded surprised by the recent upturn in price inflation, and they have offered us every excuse to ignore signs of inflation: Ignore rising oil prices. Ignore rising food prices. Ignore rising health care costs. Ignore higher taxes and government fees. And then there is their dirty little secret about housing prices.

Higher price inflation should not have been a surprise given that the Fed has increased the money supply by 25 percent during the period 2001–3. In addition, the price of basic commodities has been rising for many months, and these higher commodity prices eventually turn up in the price of goods and services. One leading indicator of higher commodity prices is the Dow Jones Commodity Index, which represents the stock prices of major commodity producers. It has been rising since the fourth quarter of 2001 and has doubled in value since that time. This stock index is now higher than it has ever been, outside of the blip that occurred in mid-2002.

---

[6]David Lereah, "Real Estate Prices Post Double Digit Gains, *Ocala Star-Banner*, May 22, 7, 2004.

Only recently have commodity prices begun influencing government price indexes like the Producer Price Index and the Consumer Price Index. For the first four months of 2004 CPI inflation increased at an annual rate of 4 percent, which is a higher rate than we have experienced in the last few years. The Producer Price Index actually decreased in 2001, but has increased in 2002 and 2003. During the year ending June 2004, prices for finished producer goods increased 3.7 percent, while at earlier stages of production the prices for intermediate goods increased by 5.1 percent and the prices of crude materials surged 20.4 percent. This would suggest that there is potentially plenty of price inflation still in the pipeline. The experience of the 1970s would suggest that price inflation adds fuel to housing bubbles because tangible assets such as homes serve as a hedge against inflation.

THE DIRTY SECRET

While this price inflation did not surprise me, the delay in its arrival did — that is, until I came across the dirty little secret in the CPI. With prices increasing all around us, there is one thing in Auburn, Alabama, that seems to be in abundance with stable, if not declining, prices. This "good" is now being advertised on most streets throughout the town, whereas in the past it did not require much, if any, advertising over the twenty-plus years I have lived in this college town. This abundant good is housing.

It is a truly odd market when houses and apartments move in opposite directions. After all, houses and apartments are just different products in the same market for housing. In Auburn, it is nearly impossible to find the kind of house you want to buy despite frantic building by construction companies, and yet rental properties, which include many smaller houses, seem to be readily available in all shapes and sizes. Has the population changed? Have people become antirent? Or are we just in a "new housing paradigm"? Is this a "new era" of homes?

Greenspan's low interest rates have driven renters to become home-owners and knocked the market out of equilibrium. Underneath this Fed-inspired distortion rests the dirty little secret of how the cost of housing has served to limit increases in measured inflation. The Consumer Price Index has underreported price inflation because the government uses the rental value of housing, rather the actual price of houses, in its index.

In the basket of goods used to calculate CPI, the goods that have increased slower than housing include food and beverages, recreation, and education, which add up to about 30 percent of the weight in the CPI basket of goods. Housing accounts for 42 percent of the basket, with housing prices representing almost 25 percent of the entire basket. However, housing prices are calculated with "owner's equivalent rent," which is an estimate of the rent that people would have to pay for their houses. With home prices rising and rental rates stagnant, the CPI underestimates the real rate of price inflation over the last year (circa 2004) by about 50 percent.

Do Housing Bubbles Burst?

Housing prices never, or rarely, go down. That is the conventional wisdom, and the conventional wisdom is correct. Housing is always a good investment, isn't it? It's an inflation hedge and it's an investment that you get to use every day, plus you get a great tax break. And the home, after all, is a big part of the American dream, right?

Government can screw up just about anything. Given enough power and time it will screw up everything. Housing and real estate in America is just the latest example. The Federal Reserve and the Mac-Mae family of government-sponsored enterprises that facilitate various kinds of debt (i.e., Freddie, Fannie, Sallie, etc.) have conspired to create a housing bubble in the United States, and as the old saying goes, "What goes up must come down." It's only a matter of time.

Housing bubbles typically do not pop like a balloon; they don't even crash like stock markets. Rather, the air in housing bubbles tends to leak out slowly — painfully slowly — while in commercial real estate markets there is a more noticeable hiss. We really don't know the current value of our homes until we sell them. They are not traded on a daily basis, like shares of stock in Walmart. Some never get exchanged in the market, but are passed on within a family from generation to generation. The market value of a home may drop 20 percent and the owner might never realize it.

Worse yet, when the market for real estate collapses, prices are less likely to collapse because when buyers fail to make offers houses simply don't sell. Sellers often resist cutting their prices in favor of just leaving the house on the market or taking it off the market. Traditionally the market adjustment to a collapse in real estate markets has come from the quantity side, not the price side — fewer houses are sold — while price reductions tend to come gradually. This doesn't mean that housing bubbles can't exist or that the bust is any less painful, only that it doesn't make the same noise as a crash.

It is difficult to predict how long bubbles will last and when they will go bust. The best indicator is interest rates, because when the Fed forces rates down it tends to create bubbles, and when rates are forced upward bubbles tend to pop. My guess is that Greenspan will raise rates after the election.

Prior to this spike, interest rates had been falling since the early 1980s. As mentioned above, lower rates have coaxed people into refinancing their homes and extracting equity from their homes to spend on other purchases, such as cars, boats, renovations, vacations, or even investments in the stock market. As a result, owner equity as a percentage of real estate value is now at an all-time low.

Here is the unmentioned problem with Greenspan's panacea. What happens to all these "equity poor" homeowners if the return of monetary inflation establishes a new trend of higher prices and higher interest rates over the coming years?

An ever-increasing proportion of mortgage financing has come in the form of variable-rate mortgages, where the payment increases as interest rates increase. In my experience, variable-rate mortgages come with a "cap" that only allows the variable rate to increase by a certain amount. Even with the cap, however, your mortgage payment could increase by around 50 percent. I have recently learned that many variable-rate loans are now offered without a cap. If rates were to explode upward, mortgage payments for these folks could double or triple. And if this did happen, the housing market would collapse with sellers swamping buyers.

Given the government's encouragement of lax lending practices, home prices could crash, bankruptcies would increase, and financial companies, including the government-sponsored mortgage companies, might require another taxpayer bailout.

Of course inflation might not materialize. Interest rates could stay low. I reported on a new book *Deflation: What Happens When Prices Fall*[7] that even predicts that deflation will rein in our financial future. Greenspan has suggested that his economic panacea has given American homeowners greater economic "flexibility." I would suggest that it is not flexibility he offers, but the shackles to an economic nightmare. Stick with the fixed-rate mortgages, keep the equity in your homes, or go get one of those cheap apartments.

---

[7]Chris Farrell, *Deflation: What Happens When Prices Fall* (New York, 2005).

CHAPTER 20

The Economics of Housing Bubbles

Nothing better illustrates government failure and the housing crisis than the housing bubble. While the housing bubble is being created by government, homes become increasingly expensive and beyond the economic reach of first-time home buyers. Then as interest rates rise and housing prices fall, many home buyers find themselves with bad investments that they can no longer afford. What started as a grand federal-government effort to improve homeownership for all Americans through a policy of "easy money" will have unintended consequences that will leave many Americans economically scarred for the rest of their lives. An easy-money policy involves the central bank (the Fed) setting low interest rates and expanding the money supply so that it is easier to get credit (loans), and it also involves government-sponsored credit organizations such as Fannie Mae and Freddie Mac that make getting home mortgages easier.

When an economic bubble pops, many people are harmed economically. In the case of a housing bubble, this will be especially true of homeowners, particularly new homeowners who buy homes during the peak

This chapter originally appeared as "The Economics of Housing Bubbles," in *Housing America: Building Out of a Crisis*, edited by Randall G. Holcombe and Benjamin Powell (New Brunswick, NJ: Transactions Publishers, 2009), pp. 237–62. Reprinted with permission from the publisher.

phase of the housing bubble. However, the harm also consists of unemployment of labor and a loss of value to owners of capital, particularly in housing-related industries. At the individual level many people are forced into bankruptcy. On the macroeconomic level the bursting of the housing bubble can send the overall economy into recession or depression. Housing bubbles concentrate their impact in the home-building, materials and furnishings, real estate sales, and mortgage businesses.

On top of all that, people suffer psychological consequences as well. The people most involved in the bubble are confident, jubilant, and self-assured due to their apparently successful decision making. When the bubble bursts they lose confidence, go into despair and lose confidence in their decision making. In fact, they lose confidence in "the system," which means they lose confidence in capitalism, and become susceptible to new political "reforms" that offer structure and security in exchange for some of their autonomy and freedoms.

The reason economic crises create fear and concession of liberty is that people do not generally know what caused the bust or economic crisis and generally do not even know that there was even a bubble in the first place. In fact, as the bubble bursts many people deny that there is a problem and believe that the whole situation will quickly return to what they consider normal. The average citizen thinks very little about what makes the economy work, but simply accepts the system for what it is, and tries to make the most of it.

The purpose of this chapter is to show how "the system" works, how it generates bubbles, why they eventually burst, and the macroeconomic effects of bubbles. Here we apply the economic understanding of bubbles derived from Austrian business cycle theory, or ABCT, to the current 2006 case of the housing bubble and show that this aspect of the housing crisis is the result of government failure — the inevitable failure of a government bureaucracy (i.e., the Fed) to manage the money supply and interest rates in an economically rational manner. However, the same reasoning can be applied to historical bubbles, from the tulip mania in seventeenth-century Holland to the dot-com tech bubble of the late 1990s, as well as to future bubbles.

WHAT CAUSES HOUSING BUBBLES?

There are three basic views of bubbles that are held by economists and the general public. The dominant view among the general public and modern mainstream economists, including the Chicago school and proponents of supply-side economics, is to deny the existence of bubbles and to declare that what are thought to be "bubbles" are really the result of "real" factors. The second view, which is espoused by Keynesians and by proponents of behavioral finance, is that bubbles exist because of psychological factors such as those captured by the phrase "irrational exuberance." The third and final view is that of the Austrian school, which sees bubbles as consisting of real and psychological changes caused by manipulations of monetary policy. This view has the advantage of being forward looking and identifying an economic cause of bubbles. By identifying an economic cause it also directs us to policy choices that would prevent future bubbles.

Most people agree with the majority of economists that there is no such thing as a housing bubble — housing prices, they say, "never go down." Supply siders and Chicago-school economists seem to view the declaration of a bubble as an affront to *homo economicus* — economically rational man — because they view it as an assertion of some psychological flaw in people that requires government intervention.[1] They note that if there were a rational cause or causes of housing bubbles, or any type of bubble for that matter, then even if only some people believed it was a bubble, they could profit by selling homes at inflated prices and deflate the bubble long before it ever became overinflated and burst. Furthermore, if housing bubbles had irrational foundations, then certainly an economically rational man could profit enormously by shedding light on the erroneous psychological motivations that were causing the bubble.

Although there is much diversity in this camp, it is well illustrated by two economists from the Federal Reserve Bank of New York who examined concerns about the existence of a speculative bubble in the US housing market. While McCarthy and Peach did find that a housing bubble could have a severe impact on the economy — if it existed and were to burst — they ultimately concluded that such fears were unfounded:

> Our main conclusion is that the most widely cited evidence of a bubble is not persuasive because it fails to account for developments in the housing market over the

---

[1] *Homo economicus* is the model of the rational economic person that economists use to build their models and theories about the economy. This assumption asserts that people are rational and will always attempt to maximize their utility. This is a source of contention and misunderstanding among economists and between economists and other social scientists.

past decade. In particular, significant declines in nominal mortgage interest rates and demographic forces have supported housing demand, home construction, and home values during this period.[2]

Furthermore they find "no basis for concern" for any severe drop in housing prices. They found that when the United States has gone into recession or experienced periods of high nominal interest rates, any price declines have been "moderate"; and they found that significant declines can only happen regionally such that they would not have "devastating effects on the national economy."

This is essentially the view of Alan Greenspan and Ben Bernanke. In particular, Greenspan was aware of the possibility of a housing bubble, but he offered every possible reason why it did not exist, and how if one did exist it would not be a major problem. The chairman is usually difficult to interpret and at times so incomprehensible as to be almost misleading. His testimony before Congress has been labeled "Greenspam."[3] However, on the topic of the housing bubble he is clear and direct and worth quoting at length:

> The ongoing strength in the housing market has raised concerns about the possible emergence of a bubble in home prices. However, the analogy often made to the building and bursting of a stock price bubble is imperfect. First, unlike in the stock market, sales in the real estate market incur substantial transactions costs and, when most homes are sold, the seller must physically move out. Doing so often entails significant financial and emotional costs and is an obvious impediment to stimulating a bubble through speculative trading in homes. Thus, while stock market turnover is more than 100 percent annually, the turnover of home ownership is less than 10 percent annually — scarcely tinder for speculative conflagration. Second, arbitrage opportunities are much more limited in housing markets than in securities markets. A home in Portland, Oregon is not a close substitute for a home

---

[2]Jonathan McCarthy and Richard W. Peach, "Are Home Prices the Next 'Bubble'?" *FRBNY Economic Policy Review* (December 2004): 2.

[3]Mark Thornton, "Surviving GreenSpam," LewRockwell.com, February 16, 2004.

in Portland, Maine, and the "national" housing market is better understood as a collection of small, local housing markets. Even if a bubble were to develop in a local market, it would not necessarily have implications for the nation as a whole.[4]

As the bubble approached its peak, Greenspan[5] did admit that there was some "apparent froth" in some local housing markets, but overall he found that conditions in the housing market were "encouraging." In his first speech after leaving office Greenspan said that the "extraordinary boom" in the housing market was over, but that there was no danger and that home prices would not decrease.[6] The new Fed chairman, Ben Bernanke,[7] admitted the possibility of "slower growth in house prices," but confidently declared that if this did happen he would just lower interest rates. Bernanke also believed that the mortgage market is more stable than in the past. Bernanke noted in particular that "our examiners tell us that lending standards are generally sound and are not comparable to the standards that contributed to broad problems in the banking industry two decades ago. In particular, real estate appraisal practices have improved."[8]

A second view of housing bubbles and bubbles in general is that they exist, but that they are fundamentally caused by psychological factors. Many people and many important economists subscribe to this view of bubbles, including Keynesian economists and proponents of behavioral finance, such as Robert Shiller. From this perspective the business cycle is seen as the ebb and flow of mass consciousness and emotions. Real factors may play a role, but the important causal factors for deviations in the business cycle are psychological. Booms develop because people become confident and then overconfident in the economy. Investors likewise are confident and increase their tolerance for taking risk. Rising profits and asset prices lead to "speculative" behavior where economic decisions are

---

[4]Alan Greenspan, "Monetary Policy and the Economic Outlook," Testimony before the Joint Economic Committee of the US Congress, April 17, 2002.

[5]Alan Greenspan, "Mortgage Banking." Speech to the American Bankers Association Annual Convention, Palm Desert, CA, September 26, 2005.

[6]Joe B. Bruno, "Former Fed Chair Says Housing Boom Over," Associated Press, May 19, 2006.

[7]Ben Bernanke, "Reflections on the Yield Curve and Monetary Policy." Remarks before the Economic Club of New York, March 20, 2006.

[8]Ben Bernanke, Speech to the Independent Community Bankers of America National Convention and Techworld, Las Vegas, NV, March 8, 2006.

no longer based on old rules and procedures, but on the bravery instilled by a "new era."[9] As the investment mania sets in, the bubble expands. Then, for whatever reason, people begin to lose faith and new investments are exposed as disappointing. Economic reports and statistics turn sour, and stories of scandal begin to appear in the press.[10] Many investors remain determined in thinking that this turn of events is only temporary, but results grow worse, prices continue to fall, and investment projects are postponed, halted, or cancelled. The mood of the market is one of gloom or even doom. The economy enters a *depression*.

Representing the behavioral-finance camp is Professor Robert Shiller of Yale University, who is the author of *Irrational Exuberance*, the first edition of which correctly predicted the stock market bubble; the second edition predicted the housing bubble, whose "ultimate causes are mostly psychological." Like the Keynesians to follow, Shiller[11] does not deny the existence of real factors; he simply downplays them in order to emphasize psychological factors. With the case of the housing bubble he finds three important factors. First, the increased risk and chaos in the world since the technology bubble and the terrorist attacks of 9/11 have caused a flight of investment into quality and safety — your own home. Second, the explosive growth in global communications has increased the glamour appeal of living in one of the world's leading cities such as Paris, London, New York, or San Francisco. The third psychological factor is "the speculative contagion that underlies any bubble." Here one higher price begets another, and higher prices in one city lead to higher prices in another city, and the process of higher prices simply builds on itself. Shiller declared

---

[9]All of our actions involve some speculation about the future. Here "speculative" behavior refers to actions that involve great risks which are unwarranted based on the normal or known fundamentals of the economy. For example, betting on a round of golf with your friend involves some speculation and uncertainty, but past experience provides some guidance to the risks you are taking. Here, betting on a round of golf with Tiger Woods would be "speculative."

[10]It is a common misconception that corporate scandal is the source of bubbles and that it was companies like Enron and WorldCom that tricked investors during the late 1990s to bid up the stock markets to such high levels. It is true that scandal is a common feature of bubbles, but scandal could never account for more than a small percentage of bubbles, and in reality scandal is caused by the same source as the bubble itself — the existence of cheap and abundant credit that must be allocated to increasingly risky and suspect investments.

[11]Robert Shiller, "Are Housing Prices a House of Cards?" Project-Syndicate.org. September 2004.

that the first two factors will remain in effect, but the third factor cannot last forever. Once prices begin to drop, the contagion works in the downward direction and can last for years before the process is reversed again.

Representing the Keynesian camp is Paul Krugman, who is an economics professor at Princeton University and a writer for the *New York Times*. Krugman did not predict a housing bubble, but he did finally realize that we were in one and that it presented a big problem for the US economy. Commenting on the hectic pace of housing construction and the "absurd" housing prices Krugman drew parallels to previous investment manias: "In parts of the country there's a *speculative fever* among people who shouldn't be speculators that seem all too familiar from past bubbles — the shoeshine boys with stock tips in the 1920's, the beer-and-pizza joints showing CNBC, not ESPN, on the TV sets in the 1990s."[12]

It is also correct to connect the phenomenon of day traders of technology stocks in the late 1990s to the house flippers of the housing bubble. The real question is: what causes this irrational behavior? Krugman suggested that, with the housing bubble, the bubble builds on expectations of capital gains:

> So when people become willing to spend more on houses, say because of a fall in mortgage rates, some houses get built, but the prices of existing houses also go up. And if people think prices will continue to rise, they become willing to spend even more, driving prices still higher, and so on. … [P]rices will keep rising rapidly, generating big capital gains. That's pretty much the definition of a bubble.[13]

Notice that Krugman placed his emphasis on a supposedly unfounded change in taste or demand ("when people become willing to spend more on houses") but downplayed the actual cause of the change in the demand for housing ("say because of a fall in mortgage rates"), as if anything might have ignited the bubble. The more Krugman tried to provide an *economic* rationale for the bubble the more he sounded like the Austrian economists who dominate the third and final view of the housing bubble. Another possible example of this is Baker and Rosnick,[14] who demonstrate the case

---

[12]Paul Krugman, "Running Out of Bubbles," *New York Times*, May 27, 2005.

[13]Paul Krugman, "That Hissing Sound, *New York Times*, August 8, 2005.

[14]Dean Baker and David Rosnick, *Will a Bursting Bubble Trouble Bernanke? Evidence for a*

for a housing bubble and do so in a manner similar to Austrian economists; and even though they date the beginning of the bubble to 1997 they ignore the real factor that tax-law changes in that year were a catalyst to housing and higher housing prices. In fact, Krugman[15] cites fellow Keynesian Paul McCulley, who did correctly predict the housing bubble and did so in the manner typical of Austrian economists, where interest rate cuts lead to higher home prices, a construction boom, and higher consumer spending all based on increased debt — and he explicitly placed the blame for the bubble on the Fed. The problem with Keynesians such as Krugman and McCulley is that their cures — discretionary monetary and fiscal policy — usually make matters worse. Even if they could be made to work perfectly it would create a conundrum for Keynesian economists because a highly stabilized economy desensitizes investors to risk and makes them "irrationally exuberant" and thus creates the prerequisite for bubbles. Even Alan Greenspan[16] has warned, in his own convoluted way, that "history has not dealt kindly with the aftermath of protracted periods of low risk premiums."

As you can see, the first view wishes to dismiss psychological reasons for bubbles to focus only on real factors, while the second view wishes to downplay real factors in order to emphasize psychological causes. The third view believes that there are changes in both real factors and market psychology during bubbles and that both are driven by the cause of the business cycle — policy manipulations by the Federal Reserve. This view of bubbles is based on Austrian business cycle theory. This is a minority view held by Austrian-school economists and some fellow travelers of the school.[17]

According to ABCT, if the Fed does not pursue a loose monetary policy then bubbles like the technology stock bubble of the late 1990s or the one in housing that we are now experiencing would not develop. If the Fed does follow a loose monetary policy, then a bubble can develop somewhere

Housing Bubble (Washington, DC: Center for Economic and Policy Research, November, 2005).

[15]Krugman, "Running Out of Bubbles."

[16]Alan Greenspan, "Reflections on Central Banking," speech given at a symposium sponsored by the Federal Reserve Bank of Kansas City, Jackson Hole, WY, August 26, 2005.

[17]A fellow traveler is someone who sympathizes with or supports various tenets of the Austrian school without being an acknowledged member or embracing all aspects of Austrian economics.

in the economy, whether it be in tulip bulbs, stocks, or real estate. If the new money is directed toward housing, a bubble will develop in housing. Austrian economists further emphasize that the additional resources allocated to housing are resources that are not available elsewhere in an economy, so that while more resources than normal are allocated to housing construction, fewer resources are available to other areas of the economy such as manufacturing, which will experience higher costs for its inputs such as labor and materials and will produce a proportionately smaller output. It is this mismatching of resources across industries and sectors that has to be resolved — painfully — in the inevitable bust or correction.

In a real estate bubble the price of existing homes rises. The bubble also fuels the construction of new homes so that the wages of construction workers rise and labor reallocates itself into construction and related industries. The bubble also increases the price of construction materials and land. Construction and construction-related industries are also where the most unemployment occurs and where the biggest price and wage declines occur in the inevitable bust. Another unique feature of the Austrian approach is that they do not see a need for prices to increase uniformly across markets, or for prices to increase to extreme levels in all markets. Many doubters of the housing bubble point to the smaller price increases in the center of the country compared to coastal regions, but price is only one dimension of bubbles — quantity can also increase beyond sustainable levels. In fact, one could conceptualize a bubble where prices stayed the same and all the bubble adjustment occurred only in the quantity dimension. If we doubled the number of houses and prices barely budged, we would be left with too many houses for the population and all the labor and materials that went into the production of those goods (i.e., houses) would be tied up and unavailable to serve more urgent needs after the bursting of the bubble revealed that the superfluous houses were bad investments.

Among the Austrians who identified the housing bubble is economist Frank Shostak, who defined a bubble as any activity that "springs up" from loose monetary policies: "In other words, in the absence of monetary pumping these activities would not emerge." As a result of this pumping, a misallocation of resources develops whereby nonproductive activities increase relative to productive activities — something that seems to clearly characterize the US economy since he wrote in early 2003: "The magnitude of the housing price bubble is depicted ... in terms of the median price of new houses in relation to the historical trend between 1963 and 1979. In this regard the median price stood at 73 percent above the trend in December 2002."[18]

The only "problem" with his warning is that it came too soon. A year later Shostak warned that there "is a strong likelihood that the US housing market bubble has already reached dangerous dimensions."[19] While early warning maybe a problem for investors in home building stocks, the problems of predicting the timing and magnitude of bubbles and business cycles affects all forecasters, and Shostak's warning was primarily for the purpose of judging public policy. In effect he was noting that policymakers have made a mistake that they should correct immediately and not make the situation in the housing market any worse.

Also from the Austrian camp is banker Christopher Mayer, who noted that there is always a bubble in the making in a world of fractional reserve banking and fiat currency, and that housing has often been impacted by bubble conditions in the United States and elsewhere. In the summer of 2003 he identified the current housing bubble:

> The strong housing market has all the makings of being the next bubble — in particular high leverage and unsustainable price increases. While the larger economy seems to sputter along, the housing market continues to run a hot race. Low interest rates have propelled refinancing, freeing up $100 billion last year alone, according to the Wall Street Journal. Not surprisingly, the low interest rates have increased buying power and supported housing prices.[20]

In early 2004 I pointed investors to the on-going housing bubble and specifically that it might not be a good idea to increase your mortgage: "It might not be a good time for you to obtain a home equity loan to invest in hot tech stocks. We are going through a housing bubble."[21] I followed this up later that year with a more detailed examination of the housing bubble and found:

---

[18]Frank Shostak, "Housing Bubble: Myth or Reality?" *Mises Daily*, March 4, 2003.

[19]Frank Shostak, "Who Made the Fannie and Freddie Threat?" *Mises Daily*, March 5, 2004.

[20]Christopher Mayer, "The Housing Bubble," *Free Market* 23, no. 8 (August 1, 2003).

[21]Thornton, "Surviving GreenSpam."

Signs of a "new era" in housing are everywhere. Housing construction is taking place at record rates. New records for real estate prices are being set across the country, especially on the east and west coasts. Booming home prices and record low interest rates are allowing homeowners to refinance their mortgages, "extract equity" to increase their spending, and lower their monthly payment! As one loan officer explained to me: "It's almost too good to be true." In fact, it is too good to be true.[22]

The problem with the "new era" diagnosis is that it ignores the historical fact that the housing market, and the construction of structures in general, has experienced regular cycles of boom and bust, with prices rising and falling for residential, commercial, industrial, and agricultural real estate. Likewise occupancy and lease rates, new construction, and the fate of construction firms and land speculators point us to the history of real estate bubbles. In fact, statistically, housing starts are a leading indicator of the business cycle and home construction is procyclical (i.e., home construction is positively related to changes in the overall economy, but more volatile). The Skyscraper Indicator even shows that historically the building of a record-setting high skyscraper foreshadows severe negative changes in the economy.[23]

WHAT GOES UP...

ABCT demonstrates that monetary inflation has different effects depending on who receives the new money first and how it is spent. Is the new money introduced into the economy in the areas of banking and investment, consumer loans, or directly to a group of consumers or producers? Do the people who receive the money want to save it or spend it? If they save it interest rates will go down, and if they spend it interest rates will go up as entrepreneurs borrow money in order to increase production. If the money is spent, it depends on who is spending it. The economy will experience different changes if the money is given to welfare recipients instead of military generals. If the money is saved the economy will

---

[22]Thornton, "Housing: Too Good to Be True."

[23]Mark Thornton, "Skyscrapers and Business Cycles," *Quarterly Journal of Austrian Economics* 8, no. 1 (Spring 2005): 51–74.

experience different changes than if it is invested in stocks rather than housing. The point here is that monetary inflation can cause bubbles and booms in the areas of the economy where it is first introduced. This foundation of ABCT comes down to us from Richard Cantillon, the founder of economic theory, who wrote in the aftermath of the Mississippi Bubble circa 1720s. Tracking the flow of monetary inflation through the economy is very difficult, and most mainstream economists just assume away the problem and declare that money is neutral on the economy.

By the end of the eighteenth century the world had converted from free banking to central banking, with the United States being the last major nation to establish a central bank in 1913. In the first treatise on monetary theory in the modern era, Ludwig von Mises produced the foundations of ABCT.[24] With central banks established for the purpose of producing monetary inflation, Mises could now establish a general theory of business cycles rather than the case-by-case basis of Cantillon. By integrating the contributions of Carl Menger, Eugen von Böhm-Bawerk, and Knut Wicksell he was able to show that when the central bank — the Fed — increases the supply of money, it causes the market rate of interest to fall below the natural rate of interest that would have existed in the absence of Fed intervention. This would cause investors to borrow more money, to expand their investments, and to undertake riskier projects and more roundabout production processes. As these borrowers compete for assets, resources, and goods, price inflation inevitably occurs and the rate of interest will increase. This in turn will negatively affect the economy, and some of the riskier and more roundabout investment projects will be discovered to be bad investments. Bankruptcies can also impact previously existing investments and production processes that are caught in the wake of the bust. Mises student F. A. Hayek expanded ABCT to include capital theory and its integration into the structure of production.

According to ABCT, when a central bank makes loans or purchases government bonds from banks it is injecting bank reserves into the economy. Banks now have excess reserves that they can loan, but the existence of excess loanable funds means that banks must reduce the interest rate they charge, reduce the credit-quality requirements of borrowers, or both. The result is a greater quantity of borrowing and investing, particularly in projects that "pay off" over a long period of time. Lower interest rates also discourage sav-

---

[24]Ludwig von Mises, *The Theory of Money and Credit* (Indianapolis, IN: Liberty Classics [1908] 1981).

ings because the return from savings is lower. In this manner the Federal Reserve drives the market rates of interest below the natural rate of interest that would have existed in the absence of Federal Reserve intervention.

Ever since the Depository Institutions Deregulation and Monetary Control Act of 1980 and Paul Volcker's (chairman of the Fed from 1979 to 1987) war on inflation of the early 1980s, interest rates have been on a downward path. This culminated with the large reductions in the federal funds rate that followed in the aftermath of the 9/11 terrorist attack in 2001. Under Greenspan the rate was reduced from 6.5 percent in November 2000 to 1 percent in July 2003. The federal funds rate remained at 1 percent until June 2004, coinciding with the launching of the final phase of the housing bubble. The Philadelphia Housing Sector Index peaked at the end of August 2005. At this low level, interest rates were negative when price inflation is taken into account.

The federal funds rate, which is the rate that banks can borrow from other banks in order to meet their reserve requirements imposed by the Fed. The Fed "targets" this short-term rate and injects reserves into this market by purchasing government bonds from banks, thereby freeing up reserves in the banking system. This essentially is the engine of inflation because the Fed simply makes a bookkeeping entry in the bank's account with the Federal Reserve — modern inflation is essentially an electronic bookkeeping entry. The low rates of the 1960s resulted in no recession and a booming economy, but those low rates also caused the stagflation of the 1970s, where both price inflation and unemployment were very high. This culminated in Volcker's war on inflation of the early 1980s. By greatly reducing expectation of price inflation and deregulating the banking system, the Fed has been able to reduce interest rates and ignite a giant boom in financial and asset markets throughout the 1980s and 1990s, as well as the housing bubble of the early 2000s when rates were clearly pushed below their natural levels and when rates were negative, when adjusted for inflation.

When banks have access to bank reserves from the Fed at low rates they can offer their customers lower rates on loans. The impact of changes in the federal funds rate has a direct impact on mortgage rates: increasing during the 1970s and peaking during Volcker's war on inflation at 18 percent, and then generally declining throughout the 1980s and 1990s and then reaching historical lows during the early 2000s. During the housing bubble interest rates on thirty-year conventional mortgages were at their lowest levels ever during the post–gold standard era. When interest rates fall, asset prices and real estate prices tend to rise, and vice versa.

Naturally, lower rates for home mortgages have stimulated borrowing for real estate purposes. Total real estate loans first exceed $1 trillion in early 1995, reached $2 trillion in late 2002 and reached $3 trillion in early 2006 (the maximum for the bubble occurred in mid-2009 at $3.8 trillion). In addition to the Fed, there were other factors that helped direct all this new credit money into real estate. First, in 1997 homeowners were given a $250,000 exemption ($500,000 for couples) for capital gains that resulted from the sale of their house, adding greatly to the tax benefits of home-ownership. This tax break could be said to have lit the fuse of the housing bubble. Second, government-sponsored credit corporations such as Fannie Mae and Freddie Mac, which can acquire capital at a subsidized rate because of the implicit assumption that the federal government will bail them out, began to collateralize home mortgage debt on a grand scale so that lenders could quickly and easily resell the loans they make. These government-sponsored agencies have helped stimulate the flow of credit to riskier borrowers who might not otherwise have access to credit, and have therefore helped to lower the credit standards of lending institutions. The problem with these institutions is so large that even Alan Greenspan has publically scolded them.[25] In truth, the original problem lies with Alan, not Fannie or Freddie.

The artificially low rates generated by the Fed also have the effect of discouraging people from saving money and encouraging them to borrow more for consumption and speculation. The impact of monetary pumping by the Fed has driven down the personal savings rate throughout the 1980s and 1990s, and during the early 2000s it has driven the rate to zero — and even below — which means people are spending more than they earn. Contributing to the problem of the low personal savings rate are the artificially inflated asset and real estate prices which naturally make people feel wealthier and allow them to "cash out" equity from their homes when they refinance their home mortgages. During the housing bubble many Americans used their homes as a kind of giant ATM to withdraw cash from the equity in their homes. Others used the "magic checkbook" from second mortgages to spend the equity they had in their homes.[26]

[25]Kathleen Hays, "Greenspan Steps Up Criticism of Fannie: Fed Chief Says Company and Freddie Mac Have Exploited Their Relationship with the Treasury," CNN.com, May 19, 2005.

[26]Carol Lloyd, "Home Sweet Cash Cow: How Our Houses Are Financing Our Lives." SF-Gate.com, March 10, 2006.

At this point one should be wondering — how could borrowing be going up and savings going down? One answer to the question is that America was borrowing money from overseas in the form of the trade deficit, but the main answer is monetary pumping by the Fed. By artificially lowering rates via increases in the money supply the Fed created a giant gap between borrowing and saving. MZM (money of zero maturity) is a relatively new measure of the money supply and one that is close to the Austrian-school definition of money, which is that it is immediately redeemable at par. MZM includes currency, demand deposits — that is, checking accounts — traveler's checks, savings deposits, and deposits in money market mutual funds. During the period from January 1959 to August 1971 (11.7 years), when Nixon took the United States off the gold standard, the money supply grew by 82.2 percent for an average annual growth rate of 5.26 percent. Between August 1971 and 1984, when complete decontrol was established from the Depository Institutions Deregulation and Monetary Control Act of 1980 (13 years), the money supply increased by 180.4 percent for an average annual growth rate of 8.25 percent. Ever since 1984 (16.6 years) the money supply as measured by MZM grew by 390.1 percent, or an average annual growth rate of 10 percent. It would seem that all this new money first went into the New York Stock Exchange, especially during the 1980s, then the NASDAQ stock market during the late 1990s, and finally into the housing market after the dot-com bust in 2000.

A large part of the increase in the money supply found its way into the market for home mortgages. Since the recession of 2001 the increase in mortgage debt was about equal to the increase in MZM. This one stylized fact probably best illustrates the housing bubble and its cause. Another measure of the housing bubble is the amount of real private residential fixed investment. Investment in housing was low during the Great Depression and WWII, but beginning in the mid-1940s investment in housing, adjusted for price inflation, has shown a positive trend, which is based on economic and population growth over that same period. The cycle in housing investment was less severe before we went off the gold standard, more severe on the fiat standard, and even more severe after monetary deregulation in 1980. Most noteworthy is that investment in housing hit a boom high during the dot-com bubble of the late 1990s and then "jumped higher off the historical trend" during the recession of 2001, when historically it would have retreated back toward recessionary trend levels. It therefore seems clear that in terms of *investment value* there has been a housing bubble since at least the recession of 2001.

ABCT does not rely on measuring the cycle or bubble, but empirical measures do often help illustrate the approach. The next such measure is the number of homes built (apartments and other multiunit structures are not included here). Typically there are sharp downturns in the number of housing starts often coincide with the beginnings of recessions and that the sharper the drop the longer the recession. For example, in the late 1970s the number of housing starts fell from an annual rate of over 1.5 million to a rate of barely 0.5 million in the early 1980s, which was a severe recession. Since the recession of 1991 the trend in new housing starts has been steeply upward, and there was no noticeable downturn in housing starts during the recession of 2001 — the only recession on record where that did not occur. Instead housing starts continued to increase and have set several new records over the last few years. In terms of this *quantity dimension* the United States has been in a housing bubble since the early 2000s.

The final dimension of the housing bubble presented here is the price of houses. Doubters of the housing bubble claim that housing prices are rising on the East and West Coasts, but are not rising by bubble proportions in much of the center of the country. Of course housing prices have increased faster in the West and Northeast compared to the Midwest and South, but ABCT theorists would be shocked if home prices were rising uniformly across the country — after all the whole theory is based on changing relative prices, not uniform increases or decreases in a price level. There are microeconomic and public policy reasons why home prices rise more dramatically and are always at a higher level in, for example, California than they are in Alabama. These issues are explored in many of the other contributions to Powell and Holcombe.[27] However, the same could be said about stock prices during the technology bubble — rare stocks in tight supply (e.g., dot-coms) did much better than widely held stocks (e.g., stocks in the DJIA). The same was true of tulip bulbs during the tulip mania that happened in seventeenth-century Holland — rare species were affected more by monetary conditions than ordinary species, but they all went up in price.[28]

---

[27]Holcombe and Powell, *Housing America: Building Out of a Crisis.*

[28]Douglas E. French, "The Dutch Monetary Environment during Tulipmania," *Quarterly Journal of Austrian Economics* 9 (Spring 2006): 3–14.

ABCT expects prices in general to rise, but not to rise uniformly. The extent of the rise depends on both where the money is being injected and the flexibility of the supply side of the markets where the injections are taking place. However, if we look at the national price index for the typical 1996 one-family house between 1998 and 2005 we find that prices have increased by 45 percent, which is a 125 percent larger increase compared to the increase in the Consumer Price Index. According to the Bureau of the Census, the price of the average house, as opposed to the "typical" house, has been increasing even faster, which indicates that people are buying bigger, more expensive homes as well. The price dimension — while muted somewhat by the economy's ability to produce greater quantities of housing — still indicates a large increase in the real price of housing. We should also remember that new housing is generally built on lower-priced land, that house-building technology has reduced building costs, and that the large influx of labor from Mexico has also helped hold down costs.

... Must Come Down

ABCT shows that it is government failure that started the housing bubble in the first place. This is where resources are allocated in an incorrect and ultimately unsustainable fashion. In a housing bubble too many houses are built, houses of the wrong sort are built, and houses are built in the wrong locations based on the underlying fundamentals of the economy and people's real desires for housing not artificially stimulated by monetary inflation by the Fed. While most people are very happy during boom times, the Austrian economists view the boom as the real problem because this is where resources are misallocated. This is also when people become financially overextended and engage in excessive luxury spending.[29] Inflationary periods tend to be when the rich get richer and the poor get poorer.

The bubble must come to an end because it is based on an irrational allocation of resources caused by the Fed's misleading interest rate policy. Money that is tied up in an asset bubble initially prevents monetary inflation from being revealed as price inflation as measured by the Consumer Price Index. However, if the monetary pumping is used to purchase assets like stocks, bonds, or real estate then the inflation is revealed in the price

---

[29]Thomas Kostigen, "Skewed Views: If the Rich Are Doing So Well, How Much Worse Off Are the Rest of Us?" *MarketWatch*, May 23, 2006.

of those assets, which will rise even though the underlying earnings of the assets have not improved. When money begins to leak out of asset bubbles into consumption, then the price of goods that are used to determine price indexes will begin to rise. The asset bubble is popped or deflated when interest rates rise. This can occur when either the market raises rates due to rising inflation premiums on loans or when the Fed tries to curtail increases in the Consumer Price Index by preemptively raising rates.

The bursting of the bubble reveals the cluster of errors in the housing market and related industries and begins the process of reallocating resources to their best uses by changes in prices, buying and selling, relocation, bankruptcy, and unemployment. The macroeconomic effect of deflating the bubble is that it causes the economy to go into recession or depression. However, the effects of the bubble will also be concentrated as it deflates. Note that the bubble in employment in the construction industry began in 1997 when it rose above a trend level, which dates back to the end of WWII. Note too that the trend in construction employment has always been negative during recessionary periods — even the recession of 2001 — and that the negative trends often extend beyond the periods identified as recession. Given that the trends in construction employment have been so strong for so long during the housing bubble, it would not be surprising that the negative impact of the bubble would take on a similar but negative effect on construction employment and spending, and that these effects would spread beyond to the construction-materials industry, mortgage lending, real estate sales, furniture, appliances, and household-goods items.

Another natural concern about the bursting of the housing bubble is the indebtedness of the average American. As we previously have shown, the personal savings rate of Americans has been declining for many years, in part because Americans have felt wealthier due to the rising price of their real estate properties. This is then coupled with the rising debt of the average American household. Total household debt was less than $500 billion when the United States went off the gold standard in 1971. It first exceeded $5 trillion in 1996 and $10 trillion in 2004. In October 2005, the last reported period, total debt exceeded $11.5 trillion. Certainly these figures could be adjusted for inflation, population, and economic growth, but that does not negate the fact that Americans have taken on a large amount of debt, but have not set aside a similar amount of savings to offset this debt or to insulate themselves from periods of economic distress.

As the economy goes into recession and unemployment increases, homeowners with large mortgages will have a difficult time making their monthly payments and may face the possibility of bankruptcy. This "squeeze" will be compounded by the fact that many homeowners have taken equity out of their homes in recent years, increasing the size of their mortgage. Further difficulties are presented by the fact that a large percentage of borrowers have taken out variable-rate mortgages rather than fixed-rate mortgages, which means that their monthly payment will rise and will rise substantially when interest rates increase. There are variable-rate mortgages where the payment stays the same, but this entails the principal on the loan increases when rates rise, which could place these borrowers "upside down" or "underwater" on the homes, which means the mortgage would be much larger than the value of the home. Lenders have also been providing mortgage loans based on much smaller down payments, in percentage terms, with some lenders even providing loans that exceed 100 percent of the price of the house. All of this points to the likelihood of a large number of foreclosures and bankruptcies. This in turn points us to the stability of the banking and mortgage-lending industries and the likelihood of a taxpayer bailout of banks and government-sponsored institutions such as Freddie Mac that buy mortgage loans from lenders.

SUMMARY AND CONCLUSIONS

There are three views of the housing bubble. The mainstream view does not believe in bubbles and attributes such changes in the economy to real factors such as technology shocks, and believes there is nothing the government can do to solve such real problems. The Keynesian view is that bubbles exist because of psychological instabilities in the economy, not real factors, and that countercyclical policies of the government should be used to tame the business cycle. ABCT incorporates real and psychological changes into a view where bubbles are caused by the policy manipulation of the Federal Reserve.

The housing bubble that began in the late 1990s is a classic example of government failure as applied to the housing crisis. Inflation of the money supply that accompanied the Fed's cheap-credit policy led to a borrowing and building binge of an unprecedented scale. The number of new homes built, the price of new and existing homes, and the total amount of real estate investment all indicate that the Fed policy, combined with a favorable tax policy and taxpayer-subsidized lending practices, created the housing bubble.

The bubble is not just a bunch of hot air. Real resources are involved, which have been misdirected during the bubble and which will cause painful adjustments in the aftermath of the bubble. This will involve unemployment, foreclosure, and bankruptcy for many people, especially those in the construction and construction-related industries. The macro-economy will be sent into a recession or depression, which could be of a lengthy duration because of the slowness of the housing market as compared to the stock market, which can process very large changes in value within the period of one market day.

The lesson of the housing bubble is that what at first appeared to be the government's trying to help improve homeownership for Americans has been a giant government failure and will have the unintended effect of economically scaring many homeowners, particularly those who bought houses at the peak of the bubble. Others have been fooled into extracting equity from their homes, increasing their mortgages, and taking loans, such as variable-rate loans, that they believed were necessary to qualify to buy houses at inflated prices. Similar trends in housing have occurred in countries around the world as many of the world's central banks have been engaged in monetary pumping that has been injected into their housing sectors.

The policy lesson of the housing bubble, as provided by ABCT, is that the Fed is responsible for the housing bubble as well as the normal booms and busts in the economy, that it must be relieved of its authority to set what are in effect price controls on interest rates, and also be relieved of its control over the money supply. Furthermore, all federal policy toward housing should be guided by the principles of neutrality, laissez-faire, and do no harm.

POSTSCRIPT — AUGUST 8, 2009

The housing and financial crisis discussed in this chapter is now well underway and we may well have entered the worst global economic crisis of this generation. The question of how economic policy will address these problems has also been revealed in that the Federal Reserve and the US Treasury have initiated aggressive and unprecedented policy responses. Under the cover of preventing a financial market meltdown, these policy responses are really attempts to bailout the owners of large financial business. They will do little to help the housing market and will increase the overall economic harm of the housing bubble.

Will policy responses continue to be aggressive and unprecedented in the direction of greater government centralization and power as the economic crisis worsens? The importance of this question goes beyond any measure of economic harm because it can result in fundamental changes in society. It could of course result in correct economic reforms such as the abolition of the Federal Reserve, the restoration of the gold standard, and the abandonment of Federal government subsidies to housing, but as I wrote in the initial draft of this chapter in June of 2006, which the editors asked me to remove:

> On top of all that, people suffer psychological conse-
> quences as well. The people most involved in the bubble
> are confident, jubilant, and self-assured by their appar-
> ently successful decision making. When the bubble bursts
> they lose confidence, go into despair and lose confidence
> in their decision making. In fact, they lose confidence in
> the "system," which means they lose confidence in capi-
> talism and become susceptible to new political "reforms"
> that offer structure and security in exchange for some of
> their autonomy and freedoms.
>
> In this manner, great nations of people have given
> away their liberties in exchange for security. The Russians
> submitted to Communism and the Germans submitted
> to National Socialism because of economic chaos. In 20th
> century America, economic crises — and fear more gen-
> erally — provided the justification for the adoption of
> "reforms" such as a central bank (i.e. the Federal Reserve),
> the New Deal, the Cold War, and even fiat money during
> the economic crisis of the early 1970s.[30]
>
> Fear of terrorism after 9/11 resulted in a massive
> transfer of power to government at the expense of indi-

---

[30]Robert Higgs, *Crisis and Leviathan: Critical Episodes in the Growth of American Government* (New York: Oxford University Press, 1987) shows how crisis (such as war or depression) lead to large increases in the size of government that were only partially offset by cutbacks after the crisis was over. On the final page of the book Higgs correctly predicted that future crises would include terrorism in addition to war and depression.

vidual liberty.[31] Submission of liberty and individual autonomy in exchange for security and the "greater good" is now often referred to as choosing the dark side.[32]

The reason economic crises create fear and submission of liberty is that people do not generally know what caused the bust or economic crisis and generally do not even know that there was even a bubble in the first place. In fact, as the bubble is bursting many people will deny that there is a problem and believe that the whole situation will quickly return to what they consider normal. The average citizen thinks very little about what makes the economy work, but simply accepts the system for what it is, and tries to make the most of it.

Increased government intervention in housing markets and the virtual socialization of the Government-Sponsored Entities (GSEs such as Fannie Mae), and the risk of mortgage-backed securities indicates that this dangerous trend will continue.

---

[31]Robert Higgs, *Resurgence of the Warfare State: The Crisis Since 9/11* (Oakland, CA: Independent Institute, 2005) correctly predicted (in the days immediately after 9/11) that among other things that government would greatly expand its power "particularly surveillance of ordinary citizens."

[32]A crisis is a crossroad or turning point where the decision maker can make the correct or incorrect choice. The wrong, fear-driven choice is now often referred to as choosing the "dark side" *à la Star Wars* movies. See Mark Thornton, "What Is the 'Dark Side' and Why Do Some People Choose It?" *Mises Daily*. May 13, 2005.

CHAPTER 21

Is the Housing
Bubble Popping?

Friday, August 5, 2005, was a bad day for housing stocks and this could be a sign that the housing bubble may have sprung its first leak. This is what the Philadelphia Stock Exchange Housing Sector Index looked like this week — losing about 5 percent for the week.

Investors have made around 50 percent on their money since I first reported on the housing bubble,[1] and there could very well be more bubbling

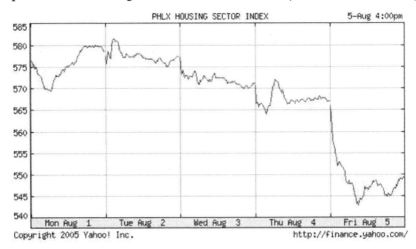

The original version of this chapter was published as "Is the Housing Bubble Popping?" LewRockwell.com, August 8, 2005.

[1]Mark Thornton, "Housing: Too Good to Be True," *Mises Daily*, June 4, 2004.

to come. In this graph of high-flying Toll Brothers (TOL), one of the largest home-building companies. The stock has increased by over 50 percent in the last year. Optimists point to the company's price-to-earnings ratio of "only" fifteen, which is below the market average.

The pessimist's case for a bursting or deflating of the housing bubble is the issue of rising interest rates. As Greenspan increases short-term interest rates it causes problems for those who have variable-rate mortgages tied to short-term interest rates. Energy prices and a slowdown in the economy can also dampen enthusiasm in the housing sector.

The larger problem may be for long-term rates because they are the foundation for fixed mortgage rates. As Greenspan increases short-term rates the thinking goes that he is reducing inflation expectations and thus reducing the likelihood of increases in long-term rates. However, if long-term rates rise, this is an indication that short-term rates are not rising fast enough to dampen inflationary price pressures.

Long-term interest rates are rising and there was a big increase in the interest rate on ten-year Treasury bonds on Friday, August 5th that coincided with the fall in home-builder stocks. Over the last summer this interest rate made a "double bottom" at about 3.9% which is almost the lowest it has been in my lifetime. It is now 4.4% and probably headed higher. [Note: it was 5.25% a year later.]

A *double bottom* is a term from technical stock analysis that is a bullish indicator, which in this case predicts higher long-term interest rates.

Higher rates spell trouble for the home builders and give some indication the housing bubble might be coming to an end.

Hopefully, Alan Greenspan will know the correct lever to pull next. He did in the 1960s.[2]

Postscript

If you look at a long-term chart of the Philadelphia Stock Exchange Housing Sector Index (symbol HGX) you will see that this was indeed the exact turning point for home-builder stocks, which typically lead the actual housing market. The Taylor rule, a guide to monetary policy, can also be said to have predicted the housing bubble/financial crisis. Woods[3] is the best analysis of the housing bubble, financial crisis, and the policy response to it.

PHLX Housing Sector

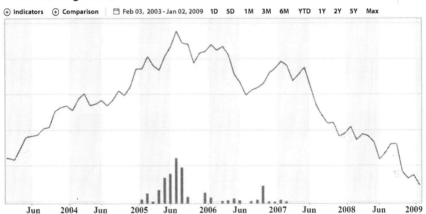

Indicators   Comparison   Feb 03, 2003 - Jan 02, 2009 1D 5D 1M 3M 6M YTD 1Y 2Y 5Y Max

Jun 2004 Jun 2005 Jun 2006 Jun 2007 Jun 2008 Jun 2009

https://yhoo.it/2rcqenw

---

[2]Ron Paul, "Ron Paul vs. Alan Greenspan." Testimony before the House Financial Affairs Committee, July 20, 2005.

[3]Thomas E. Woods, *Meltdown: A Free-Market Look at Why the Stock Market Collapsed, the Economy Tanked, and Government Bailouts Will Make Things Worse* (Washington, DC: Regnery Publishing, 2009).

CHAPTER 22

Making Depressions Great Again

In 2010, I argued in "America's Second Great Depression"[1] that the US economy was in an economic depression and that it would likely continue for some time until economic policy was reversed. This was one of six papers organized as a symposium in honor of the late Larry Sechrest at the Southern Economic Association's 2009 convention. While this assessment is a matter of debate, there are plenty of important mainstream economists that agree that current conditions have much more in common with an economic depression than normal economic growth.

An economic depression is a multiyear contraction of economic activity noticeably below the economy's potential. Great depressions are even longer and deeper and can be interspersed with periods of contraction and expansion. There is nothing in economic theory that can determine whether an economy is in a recession, depression, or great depression. These labels are a matter of assessment, opinion, and professional standards and are subject to change.

Instead of addressing how "great" current economic conditions are, this chapter examines theories of the business cycle and how well they

---

[1]Mark Thornton, "America's Second Great Depression: A Symposium in Memory of Larry Sechrest," *Quarterly Journal of Austrian Economics* 13, no. 3 (Fall 2010): 3–6.

appear to perform in light of economic policies that have been enacted since 2007 in the United States and the global economy.

The Great Depression was clearly a great depression in both its length and depth. In addition, it was a worldwide phenomenon. As Professor Higgs[2] has shown, the United States never really recovered from the Great Depression until *after* World War II in terms of inflation-adjusted per capita consumption.

I have also suggested that the stagflation of the 1970s (1970–82) was an economic depression. It was certainly long enough, and it was not confined to the United States. Statistically, it might not have been as bad as the Great Depression. There were economic expansions during the period, but the economy failed to keep up with its potential. However, in contrast with the past, it did inflict both high inflation and high unemployment — that is, stagflation — on the population, simultaneously, really for the first time.

It might surprise you to learn that great depressions are not purely monetary phenomena. Throughout this book great attention has been paid to the phenomenon of central banks' artificially low interest rate monetary policy causing a business cycle. However, business cycle expansions and contractions are typically of a much shorter time span than a great depression.

Depressions begin with a considerable period of monetary expansion followed by an economic crisis. Rothbard[3] shows that there was a considerable period of monetary expansion prior to the stock market crash in 1929. Rothbard's calculation of the money supply in the 1920s has been challenged by Timberlake.[4] However, Salerno[5] has shown that even if you remove the "offending" categories from calculations of the money supply — for example, the cash value of life insurance policies — monetary policy in the 1920s was still highly expansionary.

---

[2]Robert Higgs, "Wartime Prosperity? A Reassessment of the U.S. Economy in the 1940s," *Journal of Economy History* 52, no. 1 (March 1992): 41–60.

[3]Murray Rothbard, *America's Great Depression*, 5th ed. (Auburn, AL: Mises Institute [1963] 2000).

[4]Richard Timberlake, "Money in the 1920s and 1930s," *Freeman* (April 1999): 37–42.

[5]Joseph Salerno, "Money and Gold in the 1920s and 1930s: An Austrian View," *Freeman* (October 1999): 31–40. Reprinted in Joseph T. Salerno, *Money Sound and Unsound* (Auburn, AL: Mises Institute, 2010), pp. 431–49.

Turning the crisis into a depression or great depression requires a significant and sustained effort on the part of the government to use various policies in an attempt to stop and reverse the corrective market process — that is, the economic crisis. In other words, the dominant ideology is some variation of Keynesianism, and the government's response to the crisis involves, among other things, an expansionary monetary and fiscal policy. Rothbard[6] showed that President Hoover's policies were intended to keep wages and prices high. This turned an ordinary economic crisis into the Great Depression. Hoover's "New Deal-like" policies included maintaining high prices and incomes, stimulating the economy with public works projects, loans, bailouts, protectionism, and currency devaluation. Herbener[7] shows that the Fed was interventionist, with a low interest rate monetary policy until 1937. Ohanian and Cole[8] and Ohanian[9] empirically verified the Rothbard hypothesis. Hoover's and later Roosevelt's policies became the basis of what would become Keynesian economics.[10] Keynesian ideology was also the dominant force during the stagflation of the 1970s and in the Japanese economy from 1989 to the present.

The alternative approach to business cycle contractions is espoused by the classical economists, the Austrian-school economists, and the real business cycle theorists. This "do nothing" approach involves shrinking government and balancing the budget, expanding resources in the private sector, and a nonexpansionary monetary policy. This was employed by Presidents Woodrow Wilson and Warren G. Harding during the fifteen-month-long depression of 1920–21. This period was one of the most severely deflationary in US history, and yet it is hardly mentioned in history textbooks.

---

[6]Rothbard, *America's Great Depression*.

[7]Jeffrey Herbener, "Fed Policy Errors of the Great Depression," in *The Fed at One Hundred: A Critical Review on the Federal Reserve System*, edited by David Howden and Joseph T. Salerno (Springer, 2014), pp. 43–45.

[8]Lee E. Ohanian and Harold Cole, "New Deal Policies and the Persistence of the Great Depression: A General Equilibrium Analysis," *Journal of Political Economy* 112, no. 4 (August 2004): 779–816.

[9]Lee E. Ohanian, "What—or Who—Started the Great Depression?" *Journal of Economic Theory* 144 (October 2009): 2310–2335.

[10]Arthur Okun, *The Political Economy of Prosperity* (Washington, DC: Brookings Institution, 1970).

James Grant[11] found that the reason this depression was so short was because it largely cured itself before government meddling could begin. Thomas Woods[12] shows that Harding was really a "do something" liquidationist in the sense that he wanted to reduce the size of government and raise interest rates to actively stamp out the inflation from World War I. There has been some quibbling regarding the timing and effect of various policies and policy changes, but Patrick Newman[13] has decisively shown that a liquidationist policy was dominant before the recovery began.

In the chapter to follow, I will present a simplified version of business cycle theories and discuss what those theories would recommend as policy remedies for economic crises, and how well those remedies worked in the wake of the financial crisis. See Bagus[14] for a more in-depth Austrian critique of modern mainstream business cycle theories.

[11]James Grant, *The Forgotten Depression: 1921: The Crash That Cured Itself* (New York: Simon & Schuster, 2014).

[12]Thomas E. Woods, "Warren Harding and the Forgotten Depression of 1920," *Intercollegiate Review* (Fall 2009): 22–29.

[13]Patrick Newman, "The Depression of 1920–1921: A Credit Induced Boom and a Market Based Recovery?" *Review of Austrian Economics* (January 2016): 1–28.

[14]Philipp Bagus, "Modern Business Cycle Theories in Light of ABCT," in *Theory of Money and Fiduciary Media: Essays in Celebration of the Centennial*, edited by Jörg Guido Hülsmann (Auburn, AL: Mises Institute, 2012), pp. 229–46.

CHAPTER 23

String Theories

In 1993, Milton Friedman proposed his famous "plucking model"[1] of the business cycle. To understand this theory, imagine a string or straight rising line on a graph that represents the potential growth of the economy. Also on the graph is another string that represents actual economic growth and follows the potential growth line except for when the second string is "plucked" downward by policy mistakes or external forces. In Friedman's model, after the economy has been plucked economic growth quickly returns to the potential growth string. For Friedman it is important to explain the pluck and economic bust, but not the boom because in his model the boom is normal.

Friedman would recommend no special polices regarding the business cycle other than avoiding policy errors. If monetary policy is too tight, loosen it. In particular, money mattered for Friedman and the monetarists, and Friedman argued that a mistakenly restrictive monetary policy and high real interest rates were responsible for the Great Depression. Garrison[2] provides an effective critique of the plucking model.

---

[1]Milton Friedman, "The 'Plucking Model' of Business Cycle Fluctuations Revisited," *Economic Inquiry* 31, no. 2 (1993): 171–77.

[2]Roger Garrison, "Friedman's 'Plucking Model': Comment," *Economic Inquiry* 34, no. 4 (1996): 799–802.

In the Friedman context, you could try to make an argument that policy makers made an error that brought on the financial crisis, but this would conflict with Friedman's[3] own vision. He appeared on the *Charlie Rose* show on December 29, 2005, the zenith of the housing bubble, and summarized his view of the US economy: "The stability of the economy is greater than it has ever been in our history. We really are in remarkably good shape. It's amazing."

He went on to praise Alan Greenspan and the work being done at the Federal Reserve. Not only did Friedman fail to see the housing bubble, but his recommended policy response of loosening the supply of money and credit did not solve the problem. In fact, a loose monetary policy of zero interest rate policy (i.e., ZIRP) and quantitative easing (i.e., QE), have all failed to get the economic-growth string back to the potential-economic-growth string thus far.[4]

Another string theorist is Ben Bernanke. The former chairman of the Fed was a student of the Great Depression and Friedman's work on that subject. More generally he is considered to be in the camp of the New Keynesian school, which assumes that people have rational expectations about the future but live in an economy with imperfections and market failures. Extending Friedman's work, Bernanke found in his research that the collapse of the banking sector in 1933 was the main reason that the depression was "great." The stock market crash and ensuing economic crisis weakened banks, and many of them failed. After FDR's bank holiday in March 1933 the normal channels of credit turned into a market failure that held back the economy for many years to come. The bank failures were like a weight hung on the actual-economic-growth string preventing it from reconnecting to the potential-economic-growth string. Therefore Bernanke places a great deal of emphasis on protecting the large, systemically important banks and the credit-industry infrastructure. However, he also believes that loose monetary and fiscal policies are necessary for controlling the business cycle.

On the occasion of Milton Friedman's ninetieth birthday, Bernanke delivered extensive remarks on Friedman and Schwartz's[5] work on the

---

[3]Milton Friedman, *Interview on Charlie Rose*, December 29, 2005.

[4]Ryan Murphy, "The Plucking Model, the Great Recession, and Austrian Business Cycle Theory," *Quarterly Journal of Austrian Economics* 18, no. 1 (Spring 2015): 40–44.

[5]Milton Friedman, and Anna J. Schwartz, *A Monetary History of the United States, 1867–1960* (Princeton, NJ: Princeton University Press, 1963).

Great Depression, holding it in the very highest regard. Although some of his conclusions do differ from Friedman and Schwartz, Bernanke[6] closed his remarks on the Great Depression with the following apology and promise: "Let me end my talk by abusing slightly my status as an official representative of the Federal Reserve. I would like to say to Milton and Anna: Regarding the Great Depression, you're right, we did it. We're very sorry. But thanks to you, we won't do it again."

Bernanke was working at the Fed as vice chairman and then chairman during the housing bubble. He repeatedly denied the existence of the housing bubble and often suggested that if a bubble did exist and did pop, he would just lower interest rates. When it became evident that there was trouble in the housing market Bernanke moved aggressively in terms of monetary policy. He used both policies along traditional lines, such as reducing the federal funds rate and the discount rate, and aggressive, untried nontraditional policies, such as quantitative easing and zero interest rate policy. The overall policy response included radical decreases in interest rates, radical increases of liquidity in banks, a bailout of the systemically important banks and industries, and an enormous fiscal stimulus from the federal government, including multiyear trillion-dollar deficit spending. Bernanke soon began speaking of his ability to see "green shoots" in the economy, but many years later the actual-economic-growth string continues to lag badly behind the potential-economic-growth string.

Paul Krugman will here represent the Keynesian school of economics. The Keynesian view of the business cycle is based on social psychology. In the Keynesian view, periods of investment euphoria give way to periods of panic, retrenchment, and depression. If the actual-economic-growth string veers even slightly down from the potential-economic-growth string, then this sets up a potential scenario of dashed expectations, cutbacks, and diminished investment that can lead to layoffs, high rates of unemployment, and a significant decline in aggregate demand. This scenario is caused by what Keynes himself referred to as "animal spirits," which is the irrational fear associated with investment.

When aggregate demand does not keep up with aggregate supply, this leads to lower prices, or price deflation. This can plunge an economy into what Krugman describes as an economic "black hole" from which the

---

[6]Ben S. Bernanke, "Remarks by Governor Ben S. Bernanke," Speech at the Conference to Honor Milton Friedman, University of Chicago, November 8, 2002.

economy will never recover. As such, Keynesian economists and mainstream economists more generally have a phobia of deflation, or "apoplithorismosphobia," which is the irrational fear of price deflation. However, much has been written about why deflation is *not* to be feared.[7]

Krugman has been very vocal since the financial crisis, calling for aggressive fiscal stimulus — that is, for the government to borrow vast amounts of temporarily unused savings and spend it. What the government spends the money on is less important than how much it spends beyond its means. It is important that consumers get money in their pockets, that businesses are put back to work doing something, and that the spending has the biggest possible impact on increasing aggregate demand. Certain important industries should receive bailouts if necessary, and public works programs should be begun in hard-hit areas. In order to guard against the possibility of deflation Krugman also recommends a stimulative monetary policy. Krugman has even argued that a Martian invasion hoax would fix the economy:

> If we discovered that space aliens were planning to attack and we needed a massive buildup to counter the space alien threat and really inflation and budget deficits (concerns) took secondary place to that, this slump would be over in 18 months. And then if we discovered, oops, we made a mistake, there aren't any aliens, we'd be better off.[8]

Krugman[9] even later congratulated Japan for adopting the "moral equivalent of space aliens" in the form of Abenomics (i.e., aggressive monetary and fiscal stimulus), and for rejecting the "austerian orthodoxy" (i.e., balanced budgets).

The problem for Krugman is that with the exception of the fake Martian invasion, all of these policies have been implemented in the United

---

[7]See Philipp Bagus, *In Defense of Deflation* (New York: Springer, 2015); Jörg Guido Hülsmann, *Deflation and Liberty* (Auburn, AL: Mises Institute, 2008); Greg Kaza, "Deflation and Economic Growth," *Quarterly Journal of Austrian Economics* 9, no. 2 (Summer 2006): 95–97; Mark Thornton, "Apoplithorismosphobia," *Quarterly Journal of Austrian Economics* 6, no. 4 (Winter 2003): 5–18; Joseph T. Salerno, "An Austrian Taxonomy of Deflation—with Applications to the U.S." *Quarterly Journal of Austrian Economics* 6, no. 4 (Winter 2003): 81–109, and "Deflation and Depression: Where's the Link?" Mises.org, August 6, 2004.

[8]Paul Krugman, "Krugman Calls for Space Aliens to Fix U.S. Economy?" *Global Public Square*, August 12. 2011.

[9]Paul Krugman, "The Moral Equivalent of Space Aliens," *New York Times*, May 9, 2013

States at unprecedented levels since 2008. In Japan, they have been implemented at higher levels for a longer period of time, to no good effect. Of course Krugman might object that these policies were still not large enough or quick enough to solve the problem. However, that just means his approach is untenable: Keynesians cannot predict a crisis in advance, because their analysis of the economic crisis starts with an unpredictable shock to social psychology; similarly, in the case of RBCT (real business cycle theory), the analysis starts with an unpredictable technological shock, or some other exogenous change.

These theories of the business cycle start with stylized facts that describe business cycles. From this, economists develop a hypothesis concerning what causes the business cycle. From this hypothesis, they develop a policy recommendation that agrees with their ideological perspective. Conservative economists — for example, those of the Chicago school — typically recommend no or limited remedial policy actions when faced with an economic downturn, while liberal economists from Ivy League universities are much more likely to recommend significant government intervention when faced with the same crisis. The most general problem with these approaches is that all of these recommendations have been tried since the beginning of the financial crisis and they have all failed.

CHAPTER 24

What Is Wrong with ABCT?

To reiterate, the Austrian business cycle theory (ABCT) shows that artificially low interest rates produce systematic distortions in the economy. The most important of these distortions is the inducement to build longer structures of production and more roundabout production processes involving advanced or premature technologies. It is during the resulting boom when all the mistakes or malinvestments occur in a temporal cluster. The bust or economic crisis is when these errors are later revealed. While ABCT has been under critical internal review,[1] more recent works[2] have found that ABCT has a "general validity."

Although it is very difficult to model ABCT empirically, several empirical investigations have taken place with supportive results.[3]

---

[1]See Jeffrey Rogers Hummel, "Problems with Austrian Business Cycle Theory," *Reason Papers* 5 (Winter 1979): 41–53, and Jörg Guido Hülsmann, "Towards a General Theory of Error Cycles," *Quarterly Journal of Austrian Economics* 1, no. 4 (1997): 1–23.

[2]Joseph T. Salerno, "Comment on Gordon Tullock, 'Why Austrians are Wrong About Depressions,'" *Review of Austrian Economics* 3 (1988): 141–45. Reprinted in Joseph T. Salerno, *Money Sound and Unsound* (Auburn, AL: Mises Institute, 2010), pp. 325–31; William Barnett and Walter Block, "On Hummel on Austrian Business Cycle Theory," *Reason Papers* 30 (Fall 2008): 59–90; Mihai Macovei, "The Austrian Business Cycle Theory: A Defense of Its General Validity," *Quarterly Journal of Austrian Economics* 18, no. 4 (2015): 409–35.

[3]C. Wainhouse, "Empirical Evidence for Hayek's Theory of Economic Fluctuations," in

ABCT has also been proven useful in analyzing historical business cycles.[4]

The Austrian answer for the economic crisis is similar to the RBCT's (real business cycle theory) rejection of the effectiveness of stimulative fiscal policy and monetary policy. However, ABCT does have a "positive" side to it. In general, government should follow a philosophy of laissez-faire. First, stop the inflation, raise interest rates, and achieve market-determined interest rates. Second, do not enact any policy that attempts to reduce bankruptcy or unemployment. Third, do not attempt to interfere with prices, wages, consumption, and saving.

This would allow the market's corrective process to proceed at a fast pace to end the economic crisis quickly. On the active positive side, government should cut its budget, its taxes, and all types of regulations and prohibitions in order for more resources to be used productively and efficiently in the private sector. Following these policy recommendations would result in an economic crisis that is painful, but short.

The opposite policy approach to laissez-faire, which employs bailouts and monetary and fiscal stimulus, results in economic crises that are much more painful and prolonged. Examples of this include the Great Depression, the stagflation of the 1970s, Japan's lost decade(s), and the current financial crisis. The Austrian policy approach tends to hurt the wealthy

---

Money in Crisis, edited by B. Siegel, (San Francisco: Pacific Institute for Public Policy Research, 1984), pp. 37–71; P. le Roux, and M. Levin, "The Capital Structure and the Business Cycle: Some Tests of the Validity of the Austrian Business Cycle in South Africa," *Journal for Studies in Economics and Econometrics* 22, no. 3 (1998): 91–109; James P. Keeler, "Empirical Evidence on the Austrian Business Cycle Theory," *Review of Austrian Economics* 14, no. 4 (2001): 331–51; Robert F. Mulligan, "A Hayekian Analysis of the Term Structure of Production," *Quarterly Journal of Austrian Economics* 5, no. 2 (2002): 17–33, and "An Empirical Investigation of the Austrian Business Cycle Theory," *Quarterly Journal of Austrian Economics* 9, no. 2 (2006): 69–93.

[4]A.M. Hughes, "The Recession of 1990: An Austrian Explanation," *Review of Austrian Economics* 10, no. 1 (1997): 107–23; Jeffrey M. Herbener, Herbener, "The Rise and Fall of the Japanese Miracle," *Mises Daily*, September 20, 1999; Benjamin Powell, "Explaining Japan's Recession," *Quarterly Journal of Austrian Economics* 5, no. 2 (2002): 35–50; Gene Callahan, and Roger W. Garrison, "Does Austrian Business Cycle Theory Help Explain the Dot-Com Boom and Bust?" *Quarterly Journal of Austrian Economics* 6, no. 2 (Summer 2003): 67–98; Patrick Newman, "The Depression of 1873–1879: An Austrian Perspective," *Quarterly Journal of Austrian Economics* 17, no. 4 (Winter 2014): 474–509, and "The Depression of 1920–1921: A Credit Induced Boom and a Market Based Recovery?" *Review of Austrian Economics* (January 2016): 1–28.

relatively more than the middle and lower income classes, while mainstream policy approaches tend to hurt the middle- and lower-income classes and to help the rich.

When interest in ABCT by the general public increased significantly after the housing bubble burst, it was largely ignored by mainstream economists. Eventually some economists started to make criticisms that were more like witticisms, such as when Nobel Prize–winning economist Paul Krugman labeled ABCT the "hangover theory." More recently ABCT has experienced multiple attacks by notable mainstream economists. This could be a good sign if you believe in an idea often attributed to Mahatma Gandhi: "First they ignore you, then they ridicule you, then they fight you, and then you win."

CRITICISMS OF THE HYDRAULIC VERSION OF ABCT

The hydraulic version of ABCT is the one described by Gottfried Haberler.[5] It could be described as a mainstream translation of ABCT as developed by Mises, Hayek, and Rothbard, with several critical divergences. Nevertheless, this version was surprisingly seized upon by economists in order to criticize ABCT.[6]

Their basic point is that if investment goes up in the boom, consumption should go down; and during the bust when investment goes down, consumption will *ipso facto* go up. They conclude consumption did not go up in the bust — it went down significantly — and therefore ABCT has been disproven by the facts.

Instead of ABCT, what the critics are arguing against is a simple mainstream two-sector overinvestment theory of the business cycle. However, Austrian economists do not embrace an overinvestment theory, but rather a malinvestment theory. During the boom consumption does not go down but goes up for two reasons. First, the lower interest rate

---

[5]Gottfried Haberler, *Prosperity and Depression: A Theoretical Analysis of Cyclical Movements* (Lake Success, NY: United Nations, 1937).

[6]Tyler Cowen, "Paul Krugman on Austrian Trade Cycle Theory," *Marginal Revolution*, October 14, 2008; Bradford DeLong, "I Accept Larry White's Correction...." *Cato Unbound*, December 11, 2008; John Quiggin, "Austrian Business Cycle Theory," *Commentary on Australian & World Events from a Social Democratic Perspective*, May 3, 2009; Bryan Caplan, "What's Wrong with Austrian Business Cycle Theory?" *EconLog*, January 2, 2008.

discourages savings and encourages consumption, and second, and more importantly, the wealth effect or net-worth effect of higher wages, asset prices, stock prices, and real estate prices encourages people to consume more. Consumers draw down their illusionary wealth because on paper they can afford it.

With people drawing down their true wealth they will actually be consuming their savings and wealth, and this implies that there will likely be less overall investment, not more, during the boom. During the bust phase, consumption will be *relatively* strong compared to capital investment, but because of unemployment, lower wages, a negative wealth effect and a general malaise among entrepreneurs, there will hardly be a boom in consumption. The fact that some mainstream economists would base their criticisms on an obscure and flawed presentation of ABCT could be an indication of malicious intentions. Salerno gave an in-depth analysis of this criticism of ABCT.[7]

THE RATIONAL-EXPECTATIONS CRITIQUE — WHY CAN'T ENTREPRENEURS LEARN?

ABCT has been criticized on the basis of rational-expectations theory. The critics argue that rational entrepreneurs could not be continuously fooled by artificially low interest rates. Based on entrepreneurs' past experience and analysis of current market conditions, the critics ask, why would they be systematically fooled by the central bank?[8]

---

[7]Joseph T. Salerno, "A Reformulation of Austrian Business Cycle Theory in Light of the Financial Crisis," *Quarterly Journal of Austrian Economics* 15, no. 1 (Spring 2012): 3–44.

[8]This criticism has already been addressed by several economists, such as Lucas Engelhardt, "Expansionary Monetary Policy and Decreasing Entrepreneurial Quality," *Quarterly Journal of Austrian Economics* 15 no. 2 (Summer 2012): 172–94; Anthony J. Evans and Toby Baxendale, "Austrian Business Cycle Theory in Light of Rational Expectations: The Role of Heterogeneity, the Monetary Footprint, and Adverse Selection in Monetary Expansion," *Quarterly Journal of Austrian Economics* 11, no. 2: 81–93 (2008); William Barnett II, and Walter Block, "Professor Tullock on Austrian Business Cycle Theory," *Advances in Austrian Economics* 8 (2005): 431–43; and Anthony M. Carilli, and Gregory M. Dempster, "Expectations in Austrian Business Cycle Theory: An Application of the Prisoner's Dilemma," *Review of Austrian Economics* 14, no. 4 (2001): 319–30. For a review of these arguments, see Nicolás Cachanosky, "Expectation in Austrian Business Cycle Theory: Market Share Matters," *Review of Austrian Economics* 28, no. 2 (2015): 151–65.

As I have emphasized throughout this book, the distortions in credit markets from artificially low interest rates are not something that is obvious to the casual observer, and the amount of distortion between the market rate and the natural rate is not known definitively by anyone. What we do know is that when you leave your ivory tower and investigate the economy, you will find that some entrepreneurs, bankers, and market analysts have the experience to detect the possibilities of such market distortions.

These people could act more cautiously, withdraw from certain markets, or require greater risk premia in their dealings. The problem for these people is that their competitors are acting in a boom market where everyone is seemingly making large profits and capital gains. Either you join the party or you get replaced. I have seen this displacement effect in the construction industry, banking, and even on CNBC.

ABCT shows that as the amount of loanable funds expands, less creditworthy borrowers will enter the market. Several economists have explored this adverse-selection argument at length.[9] Austrians see entrepreneurs as rational, but they also realize that the success or failure of a venture is dependent on many factors that cannot be known in advance. Easy-credit policies let more entrepreneurs into the process, the results of which are known not instantaneously, but only as or shortly after these long-term capital projects near or reach completion.

WHAT ABOUT NINETEENTH-CENTURY PANICS?

ABCT has also been criticized for blaming the business cycle on the Federal Reserve when in fact there were business cycles in the nineteenth century before the Fed existed. I have already addressed this criticism in chapter 2 on the history of the skyscraper curse. ABCT actually blames the central bank *and* the fractional-reserve banking system. Even mainstream economists agree that the panics from the time of the Civil War to the time of World War I were caused by the National Banking Acts. The acts' requirements ensured that bank deposits were structured in an unstable manner. Many also agree that business cycles prior to the Civil War were caused by the First and Second Banks of the United States, which were pseudo central banks.

---

[9]Evans and Baxendale, "Austrian Business Cycle Theory in Light of Rational Expectations"; and Engelhardt, "Expansionary Monetary Policy and Decreasing Entrepreneurial Quality."

What about Robert Murphy's Prediction of Double-Digit Inflation?

Critics of the Austrian school of economics have been throwing barbs at Austrians such as Robert Murphy because there is very little inflation in the economy. Of course, these critics are speaking about the mainstream concept of the price level as measured by the Consumer Price Index (CPI).

Let us ignore the problems with the concept of the price level and all the technical problems with the CPI. Let us further ignore the fact that this has little to do with Austrian business cycle theory, despite what the critics would like to suggest. The basic notion that more money (i.e., inflation) causes higher prices (i.e., price inflation) is not a uniquely Austrian view. It is a very old and commonly held view by professional economists and is presented in nearly every textbook that I have examined.

This common view is often labeled the quantity theory of money. Only economists with a mercantilist or Keynesian ideology even challenge this view. However, only Austrians can explain the current puzzle: why hasn't the massive money printing by the central banks of the world resulted in higher prices?

Austrian economists such as Ludwig von Mises, Benjamin Anderson, and F. A. Hayek saw that commodity prices were stable in the 1920s but that other prices in the structure of production indicated problems related to the monetary policy of the Federal Reserve. Mises, in particular, warned that Fisher's "stable dollar" policy, employed at the Fed, was going to have severe ramifications. Absent the Fed's easy-money policies of the Roaring Twenties, prices would have likely fallen throughout that decade.

So let's look at the prices that most economists ignore and see what we find. There are some obvious prices to look at, such as the price of oil. Mainstream economists really do not like looking at oil prices: they want them taken out of the CPI along with food prices, and Ben Bernanke says that oil prices have nothing to do with monetary policy and that oil prices are governed by other factors.

As an Austrian economist, I speculate that in a free market economy, with no central bank, the price of oil would be stable. I further speculate that in the actual economy with a central bank, the price of oil would be unstable and oil prices would reflect monetary policy in a manner informed by ABCT.

That is, artificially low interest rates generated by the Fed would encourage entrepreneurs to start new investment projects. This in turn would stimulate the demand for oil (where supply is relatively inelastic in the short run), leading to higher oil prices. As these entrepreneurs would have to pay higher prices for oil, gasoline, and energy (and many other inputs) and as their customers would cut back on demand for the entrepreneurs' goods (in order to pay higher gasoline prices), some of the entrepreneurs' new investment projects would turn from profitable to unprofitable. Therefore, you should see oil prices rise in a boom and fall during a bust. That is pretty much how things work.

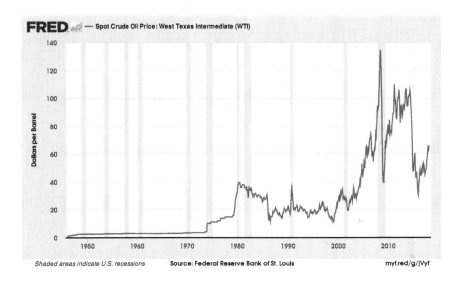

Shaded areas indicate U.S. recessions   Source: Federal Reserve Bank of St. Louis   myf.red/g/JVyf

As you can see, the price of oil was very stable when we were on the pseudo gold standard. The data also show dramatic instability during the fiat paper-dollar standard (post-1971). Furthermore, in general, the price of oil moves roughly as Austrians would suggest, although monetary policy is not the sole determinant of oil prices and obviously there is no stable numerical relationship between the two variables.

Another commodity that is noteworthy for its high price is gold. The price of gold also rises in the boom, and falls during the bust. However, since the last recession officially ended in 2009, the price of gold actually doubled. The Fed's zero interest rate policy has made the opportunity cost of gold extraordinarily low. The Fed's massive monetary pumping created an enormous spike in the price of gold. No surprise here.

Actually, commodity prices increased across the board. The Producer Price Index for commodities shows a similar pattern to oil and gold. The PPI (Producer Price Index) commodity index was more stable during the pseudo gold standard, with more volatility during the post-1971 fiat-paper standard. The index tends to spike before a recession and then recede during and after the recession.

High prices seem to be the norm. The US stock and bond markets are at, or near, all-time highs. Agricultural land in the United States reached an all-time high. The contemporary-art market in New York is booming, with record sales and high prices. The real estate markets in Manhattan and Washington, DC, are both at all-time highs as the Austrians would predict. That is, after all, where the money is being created, and the place where much of it is injected into the economy.

This doesn't even consider what prices would be like if the Fed and world central banks had not acted as they did. Housing prices would be lower, commodity prices would be lower, and the CPI and PPI would be running negative. Low-income families would have seen a surge in their standard of living. Savers would get a decent return on their savings.

Of course, the stock market and the bond market would have seen significantly lower prices. Bank stocks would have collapsed, and the bad banks would have closed. Finance, hedge funds, and investment banks would have collapsed. Manhattan real estate would be in the tank. The market for fund managers, hedge fund operators, and bankers would have evaporated.

In other words, what the Fed chose to do ended up making the rich richer and the poor poorer. If it had not embarked on the most extreme and unorthodox monetary policy in memory, the poor would have experienced a relative rise in their standard of living and the rich would have experienced a collective relative decrease in their standard of living.

There are other major reasons why consumer prices have not risen in tandem with the money supply in the dramatic fashion of oil, gold, stocks, and bonds. It would seem that the inflationary and Keynesian policies followed by the United States, Europe, China, and Japan resulted in an economic and financial environment where bankers were afraid to lend, entrepreneurs were afraid to invest, and everyone is afraid of the currencies they are forced to endure.

In other words, the reason why consumer price-inflation predictions failed to materialize is that Keynesian policy prescriptions such as bailouts, stimulus packages, and massive monetary inflation have failed to work and have indeed helped wreck the economy.

CHAPTER 25

Summary and Conclusion: End the Fed

W hat this book has established is that the central bank causes a variety of economic problems and that Austrian business cycle theory (ABCT) shines a scientific light on what otherwise is a highly complex phenomenon. I have shown that the Skyscraper Index has predicted most of the important economic crises for over a century. I have also shown that Austrian economists have predicted those crises using ABCT.

Now the question arises: what are the problems and what can be done about them? The two most obvious problems with central banking and the monetary inflation that flow from them are the boom/bust business cycle and inevitable price inflation. Embedded in the process of monetary inflation and price inflation is a degenerative process of economic inequality that is so apparent today. This effect on economic inequality and the channels through which it flows are described in further detail by Hülsmann.[1]

Monetary inflation depends on who gets the money and credit first and who gets it last. As fiat money is created by central banks, private banks are in a position to expand the amount of loans they make. The

---

[1]Jörg Guido Hülsmann, "Fiat Money and the Distribution of Incomes and Wealth," in *The Fed at One Hundred: A Critical Review on the Federal Reserve System*, edited by David Howden and Joseph T. Salerno, (New York: Springer, 2014), pp. 127–38.

wealthy have established relationships with the banks, and they have the real estate and assets to provide collateral for the loans. Large, established companies and wealthy individuals are in favorable positions relative to small businesses and people with low or average incomes. The loans allow big companies and wealthy individuals to invest in capital goods during the boom phase of the business cycle. Central banks thereby create artificial inequality and poverty. This is the primary Cantillon effect of redistributing wealth.

We have rarely had a true "free market" in money and banking. The American colonies were controlled by English mercantilist policies. The antebellum era experienced the business cycles created by the First and Second Banks of the United States, which were essentially primitive central banks. Between the end of the Second Bank of the United States and the National Banking System was the era of "free banking." This period best approximates a free market in money and banking because gold and silver coins served as money, entry into the banking business was relatively easy, and bank reserves were kept relatively high compared to demand deposits. Government spending and government intervention were historically very low. This period experienced the highest rates of economic growth in US history, but it was not perfection, as many state free-banking laws contained poisonous provisions that undermined the stability of banking.

The National Bank Acts were passed during the Civil War and "regulated" money and banking until the Federal Reserve Act was passed in 1913. The Fed and WWI effectively ended the classical gold standard and replaced it with the gold exchange standard. In 1933 all privately held monetary gold was confiscated by the federal government, and the nominal book value of gold was changed from $20.67/ounce to $35/ounce. The post-WWII Bretton Woods gold standard allowed other central banks to convert $35 into an ounce of gold, but it also freed the Fed to essentially print gold. This arrangement eventually became untenable when other central banks began converting dollars into gold. President Nixon closed the "gold window" on August 15, 1971.

Since that time the world has been on a fiat monetary system where currencies are not convertible and exchange rates between currencies are "flexible." The power and authority of central banks has continued to expand over time. The money supplies and central bank balance sheets have continued to expand, and the value of currencies has continued to decline. For example, in mid-2008 the total assets of the Federal Reserve were less than $900 billion. By mid-2014 their total assets were over $4,400 billion. The Fed acquired these additional assets of government bonds and mortgage-backed securities by printing electronic dollars. As a reference point, measured in gold, the dollar is currently worth less than two cents of the pre-Fed dollar. The Bank of Japan, the People's Bank of China, the European Central Banks (ECB), and other central banks around the world are pursuing similar policies in an undeclared currency war.

Murphy[2] shows that the Fed's responses to the financial crisis were overwhelming, unprecedented, and of dubious statutory authority. These responses were so egregious that Murphy labels Ben Bernanke the FDR of monetary policy. Despite the Fed's efforts, Murphy concludes the policies have not worked. The ECB has also overstepped its statutory authority from the European Union in response to the European debt crisis, to no avail.

Have these policies worked well? There has been a constant debate since 2008 over whether the economy has recovered and is growing, or whether it is mired in a lingering recession. There are supporters of both views from across the political and economic spectrums. The real dividing line depends on the relationship the person has with the establishment. Supporters of the establishment contend that the economy survived and recovered, while opponents of the establishment generally consider the economy to be broken and regressing.

The battle between these two views is generally undertaken with contending sets of statistics regarding GDP, unemployment, and price inflation. Austrian economics settles the issue by looking at things such as the big increases in government spending, deficit-financed spending, and the questionable value of investments financed with artificially low interest rates since 2008. Austrians argue that the real market value of increased government spending and malinvestments is far less than the dollars expended. Thus the resulting GDP statistics are very dubious. This analysis suggests that the US economy is regressing on a long-term basis and that we are much deeper in debt as a result.

In fact, Engelhardt[3] and others have argued that a central bank facilitates the process of deficit financing and the accumulation of a large national debt. A central bank can always print money to pay for the

---

[2]Robert Murphy, "Ben Bernanke, the FDR of Central Bankers," in *The Fed at One Hundred*, edited by Howden and Salerno, pp. 31–42.

[3]Lucas Engelhardt, "Unholy Matrimony: Monetary Expansion and Deficit Spending," in *The Fed at One Hundred*, edited by Howden and Salerno, pp. 139–48.

national debt, or print money to buy up the national debt, as the Fed is doing today with its various quantitative-easing policies. The US government had a debt of around $370 billion to begin the 1970s. At the end of 2007 the national debt was $9.3 trillion, and it more than doubled before the end of 2015 to a debt of $18.9 trillion and it continues to grow. In 1970 the national debt was the equivalent of 34 percent of GDP. In 2015 the national debt as a percentage of GDP was more than 100 percent. A large national debt is a negative drag on the economy and can even result in hyperinflation. Salerno[4] has shown that central banks also facilitate unnecessary and expensive wars because the central bank can conceal the true costs of war from the citizens.

However, as a best-case scenario, let us make the heroic assumption that all that government spending was really valuable — that is, a dollar of additional government spending produced a dollar of consumer value — and that all those investments made between 2008 and the present will turn out great. If we take the government's measure of the economy (i.e., GDP) and adjust for the government's measure of price increases (i.e., the GDP deflator) and then adjust that figure by the increase in population, we find that the US economy grew at less than 4 percent *over the entire period* from 2008 to mid-2016. Compare that to the years during the free-banking era (1837–62) when inflation-adjusted, per capita GDP growth was 3 percent or even higher *per year*. That is a stark contrast.

It is not a mystery as to what has caused economic malaise in the US economy. In this, we note three important factors. First, the amount of debt that has accumulated in the US economy is enormous. The amount of debt of government, businesses, and consumers has soared over the last forty-five years, and this is no doubt linked to suppressed–interest rate policy and a depreciating currency generated by the Fed. Traditionally, the total amount of debt in the United States was about 1.5 times GDP or less. Today it is about 3.5 times GDP. In other words the debt burden is too high. Second, the personal savings rate in the United States has fallen dramatically. Prior to 1971 the average personal saving rate, as measured by the government, was over 10 percent. Since 1971 the personal saving rate has declined to as low as 2 percent during the housing bubble, although

---

[4]Joseph T. Salerno, "War and the Money Machine: Concealing the Costs of War beneath the Veil of Inflation," *Journal des Economistes et des Etudes Humaines* 6 (March 1995): 153–73. Reprinted in Joseph T. Salerno, *Money Sound and Unsound* (Auburn, AL: Mises Institute, 2010).

it has recovered to an average of over 5 percent since the financial crisis. The Fed's suppressed–interest rate policy and depreciating currency are the major, but not the only causes of the low personal savings rate. Third, the regulatory burden in the US economy has increased enormously over the last half century, and the amount of and burden of regulation has only accelerated since the financial crisis in the form of Dodd-Frank financial regulation and the Affordable Care Act.

The reduction in savings and the increase in regulatory burden have caused the reduction in productivity growth. A lack of productivity growth explains the stagnation in wages and the lack of high-wage job growth. Any remaining income growth has been absorbed by the increased cost of financing debt, higher taxes to finance government debt, and mandated job benefits, such as medical insurance. All of this comes on top of the fact that family incomes have been stagnant or declining for a decade and a half. Meanwhile, billionaires thrive.

With the Fed passing one hundred years of age in 2014, there have been many retrospectives on the general value of this institution. There have been some favorable and encouraging reviews from inside the Fed, but most outsiders have taken an entirely negative stance on the very existence of the Fed and the place of central banking in a healthy and free society.

White,[5] for example, questions the influence and impartiality of the Fed. The Fed spends vast resources on economic policy research, particularly on money, banking, and macroeconomics. This funding, as both carrot and stick, has no doubt produced a status quo bias in academic research on subjects that are the concern of the institution of the Fed. According to White:

> The Fed employed about 495 full-time staff economists in 2002. That year it engaged more than 120 leading academic economists as consultants and visiting scholars, and conducted some 30 conferences that brought 300-plus academics to the podium alongside its own staff economists. It published more than 230 articles in its own research periodicals. Judging by the abstracts compiled by the December 2002 issue of the e-JEL, some 74

---

[5]Lawrence H. White, "The Federal Reserve System's Influence on Research in Monetary Economics, *Econ Journal Watch* 2, no. 2 (August 2005): 325–54.

percent of the articles on monetary policy published by US-based economists in US-edited journals appear in Fed-published journals or are co-authored by Fed staff economists.[6]

White puts the size of the Fed's research staff into perspective by noting that the Fed's staff of economists in 2002 was 27 percent larger than the number of macroeconomists and experts in money and banking employed by the top fifty PhD-granting economics departments in the United States combined. The Fed has numerous research journals that publish an enormous number of articles, but the articles that are published are vetted by the staffs at both the regional Fed banks and the Board of Governors in Washington, DC. This no doubt creates a tremendous bias against criticism of the Fed itself.

White also found that the Fed dominates the editorial boards of the leading academic journals specializing in money, banking, and macroeconomics. At the time of his research, one of the two main editors of the *Journal of Monetary Economics* and eight of the nine associate editors (82 percent) had one or more affiliations with the Fed. At the *Journal of Money, Credit, and Banking*, all three of the main editors and thirty-seven of the forty-three associate editors (87 percent) had Fed affiliations. Therefore not only does the Fed dominate the profession in terms of carrot-and-stick resources, but it also nearly acts as a universal gatekeeper at both the Fed and non-Fed academic journals dealing with money, banking, and macroeconomics. Not only is the Fed political in defense of its institutional power, but DiLorenzo[7] has shown that the "independence" of the Fed from the political process is a complete myth.

Selgin, Lastrapes, and White[8] examined the Fed's track record and found it lacking in comparison to the National Banking system. With the exception of the Fed's role in regulating banks, they examined its roles in controlling inflation and deflation as well as volatility of output and employment; the role of the Fed in the Great Moderation; and the frequency and distribution of recessions, banking panics, and lender-of-last-

---

[6]Ibid., p. 235.

[7]Thomas DiLorenzo, "A Fraudulent Legend," in *The Fed at One Hundred* edited by Howden and Salerno, pp. 65–74.

[8]George Selgin, William D. Lastrapes, and Lawrence H. White, "Has the Fed Been a Failure?" *Journal of Macroeconomics* 34, no. 3 (September 2012): 569–96.

resort lending. They then evaluated the results against prior monetary experience using standard empirical techniques and published research.

They showed that prior to the Fed, the purchasing power of the dollar had long-term stability. In comparison, the Fed has produced powerful bouts of both inflation and deflation and greatly degraded the value of the dollar over the long term. There has also been a trend of increased volatility and decreased predictability of the changes in purchasing power of the dollar, making long-term plans and contracts more difficult. They found that the declining rate of inflation that occurred during the Great Moderation should be attributable to other factors than the Fed's monetary policy. Finally, they showed that the Fed has not reduced panics or improved on its function as lender of last resort. In other words, the Fed has failed to match or exceed the results of the previous monetary regime. Historian Thomas Woods[9] confirms that the problems of the pre-Fed money-and-banking system were the result of various government interventions, but that it was still better than the Fed. Klein[10] and Israel[11] show that the institutional features of a central bank are inherently destabilizing.

Thornton[12] investigated the role of transparency in the conduct of the Fed's monetary policy. Transparency is the notion that central banks reveal information about the concerns, intentions, and policies to the general public and particularly to specialists in markets and other central banks so as to not unintentionally shock markets with negative news. Generally, transparency by central banks has expanded over the last twenty-five years. Research on transparency has shown that increased central bank transparency has produced either positive or negligible effects on things you can measure with numbers, such as stock markets and interest rates. Instead of a statistical examination, Thornton reviewed the public statements prominent Fed officials made to groups of market specialists during 2007, the year between the housing bubble and the beginning of the finan-

---

[9]Thomas E. Woods, "Does U.S. History Vindicate Central Banking?" in *The Fed at One Hundred*, edited by Howden and Salerno, pp. 23–30.

[10]Peter G. Klein, "Information, Incentives, and Organization: The Microfoundations of Central Banking," in *The Fed at One Hundred*, edited by Howden and Salerno, pp. 149–62.

[11]Israel, Karl-Friedrich. "The Costs and Benefits of Central Banking," PhD dissertation, Department of Law, Economics, and Business Administration, University of Angers, France, 2017.

[12]Mark Thornton, "Transparency or Deception: What the Fed Was Saying in 2007," *Quarterly Journal of Austrian Economics* 19, no. 1 (Spring 2016): 65–84.

cial crisis. He found that in these prominent public addresses, Fed officials consistently made misleading statements that often verged on deception. Economist Shawn Ritenour[13] has confirmed that the Fed has consistently used its rhetoric to promote the incorrect view that the Fed solves economic problems, it does not create economic problems.

Given the current scenario and the above analysis, what changes have to be made in order to create an economic environment that produces a stable economy without artificial redistribution of wealth? It would seem that the economic mess might be a web of problems too large and too tangled to solve, but that is not the case.

Let us begin with what are the ultimate goals. It should be clear that given the economic and historical analysis in this book that the goal here is to reestablish genuine markets for money and banking without government regulations and privileges. Market forces alone should regulate money and banking, just like the markets for aspirin, shoes, and cell phones. The following recommendations, couched in this respect, should not be considered a matter of mere opinion.

This seems like a tall task, but the process can begin on day one. The first thing to do is to disband the Federal Open Market Committee (FOMC) and allow the interest rate in the federal-funds market — the federal funds rate, which banks charge other banks for short-term loans — to be determined by market forces. The FOMC consists of the seven members of the Board of Governors in Washington, DC (political appointees), the president of the New York Federal Reserve Bank, and four rotating Federal Reserve District Bank presidents from the remaining twelve Federal Reserve District Banks. Their job is superfluous at best. This central-planning committee is the source of all the problems described in this book. It should be disbanded and its interest-rate–setting authority abolished.

The entire Federal Reserve System should be shutdown. Its legitimate functions, like check clearing, should be privatized. Gold on its balance sheet should be used to redeem Federal Reserve Notes for "gold dollars" equal to some established weight of gold. The Fed's holdings of US government bonds should be cancelled and other assets should be turned over to

[13]Shawn Ritenour, "The Federal Reserve: Reality Trumps Rhetoric," in *The Fed at One Hundred,* edited by Howden and Salerno, pp. 55–64.

the US Treasury. Howden and Salerno[14] offer a similar plan, and Salerno[15] finds that most of the other types of plans to return to a "gold standard" do not work and that a "gold plated standard" does not stabilize the dollar or the economy.

All taxes on capital gains on gold and silver should be eliminated along with taxes on anything else that might emerge as a new type of money — for example, Bitcoin and copper. Legal tender laws should also be repealed so that people are not forced to use any particular type of money. Currently it is possible to deposit dollars into gold banks and make payments using a variety of media, such as checks or debit cards, but you have to pay capital gains taxes if a payment generates a capital gain.

Federal insurance of demand deposits should be eliminated. This would be replaced with banks complying with laws regarding other deposit-taking institutions, such as grain warehouses. They would be forced to use their own capital or money raised by selling bonds to make loans. By charging fees on the use of demand deposits (i.e., checking accounts) and offering interest on bonds, banks would reduce the amount of demand deposits and increase their long-term bonds. This would help solve the perennial problem of banking — borrowing short term, but lending long term. Banks would effectively be 100 percent reserve institutions. Banks would probably receive a great deal of deposits and bond purchases from the now largely irrelevant investment demand for gold, as hoarders of gold would have no reason to hold gold and more reason to invest in gold bonds in order to earn interest, instead of hoarding gold. The personal saving rate would no doubt increase. See Askari (George Washington University) and Krichene (International Monetary Fund)[16] for a full explanation of the nature and history of 100 percent–reserve gold standard reform and the impressive list of noteworthy economists who support it.

None of this would be easy or free of disturbance. The highly leveraged economy would likely face a painful deleveraging process, concentrated in industries that benefitted most from the fiat-money central bank regime.

---

[14]David Howden, and Joseph T. Salerno, "A Stocktaking and Plan for a Fed-less Future," in *The Fed at One Hundred*, edited by Howden and Salerno, pp. 163–69.

[15]Joseph T. Salerno, "Will Gold Plating the Fed Provide a Sound Dollar?" in *The Fed at One Hundred*, edited by Howden and Salerno, pp. 75–90.

[16]Hossein Askari, and Noureddine Krichene, "100 Percent Reserve Banking and the Path to a Single-Country Gold Standard," *Quarterly Journal of Austrian Economics* 19, no. 1 (Spring 2016): 29–64.

There would probably be a massive wave of bankruptcies, foreclosures, defaults, and other legal and entrepreneurial solutions. The national debt would be in precarious shape and would have to be openly repudiated rather than the current process of default by inflation. The national debt could be put under the control of a legal custodian who would make payments from sales of government assets. If Obamacare, Medicaid, Medicare, and Social Security were significantly reformed and replaced with market institutions, the federal government appears to have enough assets to pay off the national debt and to meet its obligations. The federal government would probably not be able to draw additional credit, but forcing future generations to pay for past mistakes is an abhorrent practice. Massive budget cuts would have to be passed in order to balance the budget and to reestablish a market economy free of government intervention. The more government intervention that can be removed, the better the process of economic adjustment and the faster the economy will adjust and grow.

This process would involve deflation or falling prices. Mainstream economists have an unwarranted phobia of deflation. They think that deflation causes economic crises from which an economy cannot ever escape. Austrians have shown that deflation is actually the corrective process by which asset prices and wages fall relative to consumer goods, thus creating profit opportunities for entrepreneurs to reorganize and employ such resources.

With the United States moving to a 100 percent reserve gold standard, the value of the gold dollar would be fixed as a weight of gold. The exchange value would increase relative to other world currencies, and Americans would be made richer by the fact that their incomes and savings would buy more. It would be increasingly difficult to import goods into the United States. This would put pressure on other countries to follow the United States' lead in adopting the gold standard and other monetary reforms. With the United States also cutting back on military and regulatory spending and selling vast amounts of resources to the private sector, the standard of living would quickly recover and the economy would experience high rates of economic growth.

Most people would not want to take the risks imagined by these recommendations. Politicians know this and exploit it. They and mainstream economists have plenty of horror stories to scare everyone else. However,

Salerno[17] has shown that the standard criticisms of the gold standard are baseless.

The truth is the alternative of not reforming the system is much, much worse. As the dollar status as a reserve currency for other central banks worsens, the likelihood that some other government embarks on such a reform process increases. The government is too big, the national debt is too large, savings are too low, the money supply has been expanded too much, and the extent of artificial inequality threatens the fabric of cooperative society. These problems will only get worse over time and will end in hyperinflation, where that fabric is finally set ablaze on a bonfire of worthless paper money and government bonds.

The events in Washington, DC, today in 2018, represent a stalemate between President Trump and the establishment. This stalemate sustains the status quo at a time when there is radical rumbling on both left and right. Despite marginal reforms in taxation and regulation and despite the Fed's announced reversal of policy, nothing remotely has changed to address the calamity that lies ahead, and that I've discussed throughout this book.

---

[17]Joseph T. Salerno, "The 100 Percent Gold Standard: A Proposal for Monetary Reform," in Salerno, *Money Sound and Unsound* (Auburn, AL: Mises Institute, 2014), pp. 333–63.

Bibliography

Abraham, Jesse M., and Patric H. Hendershott. 1994. "Bubbles in Metropolitan Housing Prices." NBER Working Paper 4774. National Bureau of Economic Research. Cambridge, MA.

Ali, M., and Kyoung Sun Moon. 2007. "Structural Developments in Tall Building: Current Trends and Future Prospects." *Architectural Science Review* 50, no. 3.

Alonzo, William. 1964. *Location and Land Use: Toward a General Theory of Land Rent.* Cambridge, MA: Harvard University Press.

Ames, Nick. 2015. "Elevator Installation Prep Begins at Kingdom Tower." ConstructionWeekOnline.com. May 10. http://www.constructionweekonline.com/article-33617-elevator-installation-prep-begins-at-kingdom-tower

Anderson, William. 2000. "New Economy, Old Delusion." *Free Market* 18, no. 8.

Angly, Edward. 1931. *Oh Yeah?* New York: Viking Press.

Arrison, Thomas S., C. Fred Bergsten, Edward M. Graham, and Martha Caldwell Harris, eds. 1992. *Japan's Growing Technological Capability: Implications for the U.S. Economy.* Washington, DC: National Academies Press.

Askari, Hossein, and Noureddine Krichene. 2016. "100 Percent Reserve Banking and the Path to a Single-Country Gold Standard." *Quarterly Journal of Austrian Economics* 19, no. 1.

Atack, Jeremy, and Robert A. Margo. 1996. "'Location, Location, Location!' The Market for Vacant Urban Land: New York 1835–1900." NBER Historical Paper 91. National Bureau of Economic Research. Cambridge, MA.

Bagus, Philipp. 2012. "Modern Business Cycle Theories in Light of ABCT." In *Theory of Money and Fiduciary Media: Essays in Celebration of the Centennial*. Edited by Jörg Guido Hülsmann. Auburn, AL: Mises Institute.

———. 2015. *In Defense of Deflation*. New York: Springer.

Baker, Dean. 2002. *Dangerous Minds? The Track Record of Economic and Financial Analysts*. Washington, DC: Center for Economic and Policy Research.

Baker, Dean, and David Rosnick. 2005. *Will a Bursting Bubble Trouble Bernanke? Evidence for a Housing Bubble*. Washington, DC: Center for Economic and Policy Research. November. http://www.cepr.net/publications/housing_bubble_2005_11.pdf

Barnett, William II, and Walter Block. 2005. "Professor Tullock on Austrian Business Cycle Theory." *Advances in Austrian Economics* 8.

———. 2008. "On Hummel on Austrian Business Cycle Theory." *Reason Papers* 30.

Barr, Jason. 2010. "Skyscrapers and the Skyline: Manhattan, 1865–2004." *Real Estate Economics* 38, no. 3.

———. 2012. "Skyscraper Height." *Journal of Real Estate Finance and Economics* 45, no. 3.

Barr, Jason. 2013. "Skyscrapers and Skylines: New York and Chicago, 1885–2007." *Journal of Regional Science* 53, no. 3.

Barr, Jason, Bruce Mizrach, and Kusam Mundra. 2015. "Skyscraper Height and the Business Cycle: Separating Myth from Reality." *Applied Economics* 47, no. 2. http://www.tandfonline.com/doi/abs/10.1080/00036846.2014.967380?journalCode=raec20

Bernanke, Ben S. 2002. "Remarks by Governor Ben S. Bernanke." Speech at the Conference to Honor Milton Friedman. University of Chicago, Chicago, IL. November 8. http://www.federalreserve.gov/boarddocs/Speeches/2002/20021108/default.htm

———. 2004. *Essays on the Great Depression*. Princeton, NJ: Princeton University Press.

———. 2006a. Speech to the Independent Community Bankers of America National Convention and Techworld. Las Vegas, NV. March 8. https://www.federalreserve.gov/newsevents/speech/bernanke20060308a.htm

———. 2006b. "Reflections on the Yield Curve and Monetary Policy." Remarks before the Economic Club of New York. March 20. https://www.federalreserve.gov/newsevents/speech/bernanke20060320a.htm

Bhatia, Neha. 2015. "Soaring Upwards." ConstructionWeekOnline.com, May 16. Accessed May, 26, 2015. http://www.constructionweekonline.com/article-33675-soaring-upwards

Block, Walter E. 2010. "Who Predicted the Housing Bubble?" LewRockwell.com, December 22. https://www.lewrockwell.com/2010/12/walter-e-block/who-predicted-the-housing-bubble

Bloom, J. L. 1990. *Japan as a Scientific and Technological Superpower.* Springfield, VA: National Technical Information Service.

Bordo, Michael D. 1992. "The Limits of Economic Forecasting." *Cato Journal* 12.

Bordo, Michael D., Peter Rappoport, and Anna J. Schwartz. 1992. "Money versus Credit Rationing: Evidence for the National Banking Era, 1880–1914." In *Strategic Factors in Nineteenth-Century American Economic Growth.* Edited by Claudia Goldin and Hugh Rockoff. Chicago: University of Chicago Press.

Boyle, Elizabeth, Lucas Engelhardt, and Mark Thornton, "Is There Such a Thing As a Skyscraper Curse?" *Quarterly Journal of Austrian Economics* 19, no. 2 (Summer 2016): 149–168.

Brady, Nicholas F. 2002. "Every Market Collapse Is Different." *New York Times,* August 11.

Brooks, John. 1973. *The Go-Go Years: The Drama and Crashing Finale of Wall Street's Bullish 60s.* New York: Allworth Press.

Bruno, Joe B. 2006. "Former Fed Chair Says Housing Boom Over." Associated Press, May 19.

Bureau of the Census. "Price Indexes of New One-Family Houses Sold." http://www.census.gov/const/price_sold.pdf

Caballero, Ricardo J. 2010. "Macroeconomics after the Crisis: Time to Deal with the Pretense-of-Knowledge-Syndrome." *Journal of Economic Perspectives* 24, no. 4.

Cachanosky, Nicolás. 2015. "Expectation in Austrian Business Cycle Theory: Market Share Matters." *Review of Austrian Economics* 28, no. 2.

Cachanosky, Nicolás, and Alexander W. Salter. 2017. "The View from Vienna: An Analysis of the Renewed Interest in the Mises-Hayek Theory of the Business Cycle." *Review of Austrian Economics* 30, no. 2.

Callahan, Gene, and Roger W. Garrison. 2003. "Does Austrian Business Cycle Theory Help Explain the Dot-Com Boom and Bust?" *Quarterly Journal of Austrian Economics* 6, no. 2.

Cantillon, Richard. [1755] 1931. *Essai sur la Nature du Commerce en Général*, translated and edited by Henry Higgs. London: Cass.

Caplan, Bryan. 2008. "What's Wrong with Austrian Business Cycle Theory?" *EconLog*, January 2. http://http://econlog.econlib.org/archives/2008/01/whats_wrong_wit_6.html

Capozza, Dennis, and Yuming Li. 1994. "The Intensity and Timing of Investment: The Case of Land." *American Economic Review* 84, no. 4.

Carilli, Anthony M., and Gregory M. Dempster. 2001. "Expectations in Austrian Business Cycle Theory: An Application of the Prisoner's Dilemma." *Review of Austrian Economics* 14, no. 4.

Chau, K. W., S. K Wong, Y. Yau, and A. K. C. Cheung. 2006. "Determining Optimal Building Height." *Urban Studies* 44, no. 12.

Cheney, David W., and William W. Grimes. 1991. *Japanese Technology Policy: What's the Secret?* Washington, DC: Council on Competitiveness.

Clark, Lindley H., Jr. 1990. "Housing May Be in for a Long Dry Spell." *Wall Street Journal*, January 19.

Clash, The. *Should I Stay or Should I Go.* 1982. Combat Rock. Epic/Sony Records.

Colwell, Peter F., and Roger E. Cannaday. 1988. "Trade-Offs in the Office Market." In *Real Estate Market Analysis: Methods and Applications*. Edited by John M. Clapp and Stephen D. Messner. New York: Praeger.

Corrigan, Sean. 1999. "Will the Bubble Pop?" *Mises Daily*, October 18.

Cowen, Tyler. 2008. "Paul Krugman on Austrian Trade Cycle Theory." *Marginal Revolution*, October 14. http://www.marginalrevolution.com/marginalrevolution/2008/10/paul-krugman-on.html

Cwik, Paul. 2005. "The Inverted Yield Curve and the Economic Downturn." *New Perspectives on Political Economy: A Bilingual Interdisciplinary Journal* 1, no. 1.

———. 2008. "Austrian Business Cycle Theory: Corporate Finance Point of View." *Quarterly Journal of Austrian Economics* 11, no. 1.

DeBenedictis, Luca, and Michele DiMaio. 2016. "Schools of Economic Thought and Economists' Opinions on Economic Policy." *Eastern Economic Journal* 42, no. 3.

Deden, Anthony. 1999. "Reflections on Prosperity." *Sage Chronicle*, December 29.

DeLong, Bradford. 2008. "I Accept Larry White's Correction…." *Cato Unbound*. December 11. http://www.cato-unbound.org/2008/12/11/j-bradford-delong/i-accept-larry-whites-correction

Diamond, Douglas W., and Raghuram G. Rajan. 2009. "The Credit Crisis: Conjectures about Causes and Remedies." *American Economic Review* 99, no. 2.

DiLorenzo, Thomas. 2014. "A Fraudulent Legend: The Myth of the Independent Fed." In *The Fed at One Hundred: A Critical Review on the Federal Reserve System.* Edited by David Howden and Joseph T. Salerno. New York: Springer.

Drabenstott, Mark. 1983. "The 1980s: A Turning Point for U.S. Agricultural Exports?" *Economic Review,* Federal Reserve Bank of Kansas City, April. http://www.kansascityfed.org/publicat/econrev/econrevarchive/1983/2q83drab.pdf

Economist. 2000. "Bubble, Bubble." March 25.

——— . 2015. "Towers of Babel: Is There Such a Thing as the Skyscraper Curse?" March 28. http://www.economist.com/news/finance-and-economics/21647289-there-such-thing-skyscraper-curse-towers-babel

Ekelund, Robert B., George Ford, and Mark Thornton, 2001. "The Measurement of Merger Delay in Regulated and Restructuring Industries." *Applied Economics Letters* 8, no. 8.

Ekelund, Robert B., Jr., and Mark Thornton. 1986. "Schumpeterian Analysis, Supply-Side Economics, and Macroeconomic Policy in the 1920s." *Review of Social Economy* 44, no. 3.

Engelhardt, Lucas. 2012. "Expansionary Monetary Policy and Decreasing Entrepreneurial Quality." *Quarterly Journal of Austrian Economics* 15 no. 2.

——— . 2014. "Unholy Matrimony: Monetary Expansion and Deficit Spending." In *The Fed at One Hundred: A Critical Review on the Federal Reserve System.* Edited by David Howden and Joseph T. Salerno. New York: Springer.

——— . 2015. "Why Skyscrapers? A Spatial Economic Approach." Unpublished manuscript.

Engelhardt, Lucas, and Mark Thornton. 2015. "Skyscraper Height and the Business Cycle: Separating Myth from Reality, a Comment." Working paper at the Mises Institute.

Evans, Anthony J., and Toby Baxendale. 2008. "Austrian Business Cycle Theory in Light of Rational Expectations: The Role of Heterogeneity, the Monetary Footprint, and Adverse Selection in Monetary Expansion." *Quarterly Journal of Austrian Economics* 11, no. 2.

Farrell, Chris. 2005. *Deflation: What Happens When Prices Fall.* New York.

Fisher, Irving. 1932. *Booms and Depressions: Some First Principles.* New York: Adelphi Company.

French, Doug. 2006. "The Dutch Monetary Environment during Tulipmania." *Quarterly Journal of Austrian Economics* 9.

———. 2014. "Arthur Burns: The Ph.D. Standard Begins and the End of Independence." In *The Fed at One Hundred: A Critical Review on the Federal Reserve System.* Edited by David Howden and Joseph T. Salerno. New York: Springer.

Friedman, Milton. 1993. "The 'Plucking Model' of Business Cycle Fluctuations Revisited." *Economic Inquiry* 31, no. 2.

———. 2005. Interview on *Charlie Rose*. December 29.

Friedman, Milton, and Anna J. Schwartz. 1963. *A Monetary History of the United States, 1867–1960.* Princeton, NJ: Princeton University Press.

———. 1965. *The Great Contraction, 1929–1933.* Princeton, NJ: Princeton University Press.

Garrison, Roger W. 1996. "Friedman's 'Plucking Model': Comment." *Economic Inquiry* 34, no. 4.

———. 2001. *Time and Money: The Macroeconomics of Capital Structure.* London: Routledge.

———. 2005. "The Austrian School: Capital-Based Macroeconomics." In *Modern Macroeconomics: Its Origins, Development and Current State.* Edited by Brian Snowden and Howard R. Vane. Aldershot: Edward Elgar.

Glaeser, Edward. 2013. "A Nation of Gamblers: Real Estate Speculation and American History." National Bureau of Economic Research. Cambridge, MA.

Glaeser, Edward L., and Jesse M. Shapiro. 2001. "Cities and Welfare: The Impact of Terrorism on Urban Form." NBER Working Paper 8696. National Bureau of Economic Research. Cambridge, MA.

Glassman, James K., and Kevin A. Hassett. 1999. *Dow 36,000: The New Strategy for Profiting from the Coming Rise in the Stock Market.* New York: Random House.

———. 2002. "Dow 36000 Revisited—Hey, Be Patient." *Wall Street Journal*, August 1.

Goldman, David. 2016. "Amazon Shares Plummet as Profit Disappoints." CNN.com, January 28. http://money.cnn.com/2016/01/28/technology/amazon-earnings

Goodhart, Charles A. E. 1981. "Problems of Monetary Management: The U.K. Experience." In *Inflation, Depression, and Economic Policy in the West.* Edited by Anthony S. Courakis. Lanham, MD: Rowman & Littlefield.

Granitsas, Alkman. 1999. "The Height of Hubris: Skyscrapers Mark Economic Bust." *Far Eastern Economic Review* 162, no. 6.

Grant, James. 1996a. The Trouble with Prosperity: The Loss of Fear, the Rise of Speculation, and the Risk to American Savings. New York: Random House.

———. 1996b. "The Trouble with Prosperity: An Interview with James Grant." *Austrian Economics Newsletter* 16.

———. 2014. *The Forgotten Depression: 1921: The Crash That Cured Itself.* New York: Simon & Schuster.

Greenspan, Alan. 1996. Meeting of the Federal Open Market Committee. September 24.

———. 2002. "Monetary Policy and the Economic Outlook." Testimony before the Joint Economic Committee of the US Congress, April 17. http://www.federalreserve.gov/boarddocs/testimony/2002/20020417/default.htm

———. 2003a. "Testimony of Chairman Alan Greenspan." Federal Reserve Board's semiannual monetary-policy report to the Committee on Banking, Housing, and Urban Affairs. US Senate. February 12. https://www.federalreserve.gov/boarddocs/hh/2003/february/testimony.htm

———. 2003b. "Testimony of Chairman Alan Greenspan: Aging Global Population." Testimony before the Special Committee on Aging. US Senate. February 27.

———. 2005a. "Reflections on Central Banking." Speech given at a symposium sponsored by the Federal Reserve Bank of Kansas City, Jackson Hole, WY. August 26. http://www.federalreserve.gov/Boarddocs/Speeches/2005/20050826/default.htm

———. 2005b. "Mortgage Banking." Speech to the American Bankers Association Annual Convention, Palm Desert, CA. September 26. http://www.federalreserve.gov/boarddocs/speeches/2005/200509262/default.htm

Haberler, Gottfried. 1937. *Prosperity and Depression: A Theoretical Analysis of Cyclical Movements.* Lake Success, NY: United Nations.

Halcomb, Darrin R., and Syed Shah Saeed Hussain. 2002. "Asset Price Bubbles: Implications for Monetary, Regulatory, and International Policies." *Chicago Fed Letter* 1816.

Harford, Jarrad. 2005. "What Drives Merger Waves." *Journal of Financial Economics* 77, no. 3.

Hassett, Kevin. 2002. *Bubbleology: The New Science of Stock Market Winners and Losers.* New York: Crown Business.

Hayek, F. A. 1972. "The Outlook for the 1970s: Open or Repressed Inflation?" In *Tiger by the Tail: The Keynesian Legacy of Inflation*. Edited by Sudha R. Shenoy. Washington, DC: Cato Institute.

———. 1976. *Choice in Currency: A Way to Stop Inflation*. London: Institute for Economic Affairs.

———. 1977. *Denationalization of Money: The Argument Refined*. London: Institute for Economic Affairs.

———. 1979. *Unemployment and Monetary Policy: Government as Generator of the "Business Cycle."* Washington, DC: Cato Institute.

Hays, Kathleen. 2005. "Greenspan Steps Up Criticism of Fannie: Fed Chief Says Company and Freddie Mac Have Exploited Their Relationship with the Treasury." CNN.com. May 19. http://money.cnn.com/2005/05/19/news/economy/greenspan_fannie

Helsley, Robert, and William Strange. 2008. "A Game-Theoretic Analysis of Skyscrapers." *Journal of Urban Economics* 64, no. 1.

Hendershott, Patric H., and Edward J. Kane. 1992. "Causes and Consequences of the 1980s Commercial Construction Boom." *Journal of Applied Corporate Finance* 5, no. 1.

Henderson, Jason, Brent Gloy, and Michael Boehlje. 2011. "Agriculture's Boom-Bust Cycles: Is This Time Different?" *Economic Review* (4th quart.).

Herbener, Jeffrey M. 1999. "The Rise and Fall of the Japanese Miracle." *Mises Daily*. September 20. https://mises.org/library/rise-and-fall-japanese-miracle

———. 2014. "Fed Policy Errors of the Great Depression." In *The Fed at One Hundred: A Critical Review on the Federal Reserve System*. Edited by David Howden and Joseph T. Salerno. New York: Springer.

Hershey, Robert D., Jr. 1995. "U.S. Farms Out Compiling of Leading Indicators." *New York Times*, September 8.

Higgs, Robert. 1987. *Crisis and Leviathan: Critical Episodes in the Growth of American Government*. New York: Oxford University Press.

———. 1992. "Wartime Prosperity? A Reassessment of the U.S. Economy in the 1940s." *Journal of Economy History* 52, no. 1.

———. 2005. *Resurgence of the Warfare State: The Crisis Since 9/11*. Oakland, CA: Independent Institute.

Holcombe, Randall G. 1995. *Public Policy and the Quality of Life: Market Incentives versus Government Planning*. Westport, CT: Greenwood Press.

Holcombe, Randall G., and Benjamin Powell, eds. 2009. *Housing America: Building Out of a Crisis*. New Brunswick, NJ: Transactions Publishers.

Howden, David. 2014. "A Pre-History of the Federal Reserve." In *The Fed at One Hundred: A Critical Review on the Federal Reserve System*. Edited by David Howden and Joseph T. Salerno. New York: Springer.

Howden, David, and Joseph T. Salerno. 2014a. *The Fed at One Hundred: A Critical Review on the Federal Reserve System*. Edited by David Howden and Joseph T. Salerno. New York: Springer.

———. 2014b. "A Stocktaking and Plan for a Fed-less Future." In *The Fed at One Hundred: A Critical Review on the Federal Reserve System*. Edited by David Howden and Joseph T. Salerno. New York: Springer.

Hoyt, Homer. 1933. *One Hundred Years of Land Values in Chicago: The Relationship of the Growth of Chicago to the Rise in Its Land Values, 1830–1933*. Chicago: University of Chicago Press.

Hughes, A. M. 1997. "The Recession of 1990: An Austrian Explanation." *Review of Austrian Economics* 10, no. 1.

Hülsmann, Jörg, Guido. 1999. *Scöne neue Zeichengeldwelt* (Brave New World of Fiat Monies). Postface to Murray Rothbard, *Das Schein-Geld-System* (Gräfelfing) Resch.

———. 1997. "Towards a General Theory of Error Cycles." *Quarterly Journal of Austrian Economics* 1, no. 4.

———. 2000. "Scöne neue Zeichengeldwelt [Brave new world of fiat monies]." 2000. In Murray Rothbard, *Das Schein-Geld-System (Gräfelfing) Resch*.

———. 2008. *Deflation and Liberty*. Auburn, AL: Mises Institute.

———. 2012. *Theory of Money and Fiduciary Media: Essays in Celebration of the Centennial*. Auburn, AL: Mises Institute.

———. 2014. "Fiat Money and the Distribution of Incomes and Wealth." In *The Fed at One Hundred: A Critical Review on the Federal Reserve System*. Edited by David Howden and Joseph T. Salerno. New York: Springer.

Hummel, Jeffrey R. 1979. "Problems with Austrian Business Cycle Theory." *Reason Papers* 5.

Hunter, William C., George G. Kaufman, and Michael Pomerleano, eds. 2003. *Asset Price Bubbles: The Implications for Monetary, Regulatory, and International Policies*. Cambridge, MA: MIT Press.

Huxtable, Ada Louise. 1992. *The Tall Building Artistically Reconsidered: The Search for a Skyscraper Style*. Berkeley: University of California Press.

Investors' Business Daily. 1999. "Edifice Complex." May 6.

Israel, Karl-Friedrich. 2017. "The Costs and Benefits of Central Banking." PhD Dissertation, Department of Law, Economics, and Business Administration, University of Angers, France.

Jenkins, Holman W., Jr. 1999–2000. "Of Bulls and Bubbles." *Policy Review* 98.

Johnson, Chalmers, Laura D'Andrea Tyson, and John Zysman, eds. 1989. *Politics and Productivity: The Real Story of Why Japan Works*. Cambridge, MA: Ballinger.

Jordan, Jerry L. 1997. Minutes to the Federal Open Market Committee Meeting. November 12.

Kaza, Greg. 1999. "Downsizing Detroit: Motown's Lament." *Chronicles: A Magazine of American Culture*, November 20.

———. 2006. "Deflation and Economic Growth." *Quarterly Journal of Austrian Economics* 9, no. 2.

———. 2010. "Note: Wolverines, Razorbacks, and Skyscrapers." *Quarterly Journal of Austrian Economics* 13, no. 4.

Keeler, James P. 2001. "Empirical Evidence on the Austrian Business Cycle Theory." *Review of Austrian Economics* 14, no. 4.

Kennedy, Robert C. 1869. "Gold at 160, Gold at 130." *Harper's Weekly*. October 16. https://www.nytimes.com/learning/general/onthisday/harp/1016.html

Kim, Sukkoo. 2002. "The Reconstruction of the American Urban Landscape in the Twentieth Century." NBER Working Paper 8857. National Bureau of Economic Research. Cambridge, MA.

Klein, Peter G. 2008. "The Mundane Economics of the Austrian School." *Quarterly Journal of Austrian Economics* 11, nos. 3–4.

———. 2014. "Information, Incentives, and Organization: The Microfoundations of Central Banking." In *The Fed at One Hundred: A Critical Review on the Federal Reserve System*. Edited by David Howden and Joseph T. Salerno. New York: Springer.

Kodama, Fumio. 1991. *Analyzing Japanese High Technologies: The Techno-Paradigm Shift*. London: Pinter Publisher.

Koretz, Gene. 1999. "Do Towers Rise before a Crash?" *Business Week*, May 17.

Kostigen, Thomas. 2006. "Skewed Views: If the Rich Are Doing So Well, How Much Worse Off Are the Rest of Us?" *MarketWatch*. May 23.

Krugman, Paul, 2005a. "Running Out of Bubbles." *New York Times*. May 27. http://www.nytimes.com/2005/05/27/opinion/27krugman.html

———. 2005b. "That Hissing Sound." *New York Times*. August 8. http://www. nytimes.com/2005/08/08/opinion/08krugman.html?

———. 2011. "Krugman Calls for Space Aliens to Fix U.S. Economy?" *Global Public Square*. August 12. http://globalpublicsquare.blogs.cnn. com/2011/08/12/gps-this-sunday-krugman-calls-for-space-aliens-to-fix-u-s-economy

———. 2013. "The Moral Equivalent of Space Aliens." *New York Times*. May 9. http://krugman.blogs.nytimes.com/2013/05/09/the-moral-equivalent-of-space-aliens

Landau, Sarah Bradford, and Carl W. Condit. 1996. *Rise of the New York Skyscraper: 1865–1913*. New Haven, CT: Yale University Press.

Lawrence, Andrew. 1999a. "The Skyscraper Index: Faulty Towers!" *Property Report*, January 15.

———. 1999b. "The Curse Bites: Skyscraper Index Strikes." *Property Report*, March 3.

le Roux, P., and Levin, M. 1998 "The Capital Structure and the Business Cycle: Some Tests of the Validity of the Austrian Business Cycle in South Africa." *Journal for Studies in Economics and Econometrics* 22, no. 3.

Lereah, David, Inman News. 2004. "Real Estate Prices Post Double Digit Gains." *Ocala Star-Banner*. May 22.

Liebowitz, Stan J. 2002. *Rethinking the Network Economy: The Real Forces That Drive the Digital Marketplace*. New York: Amacom.

Liebowitz, Stan J., and Stephen Margolis. 1999. *Winners, Losers, & Microsoft: Competition and Antitrust in High Technology*. Oakland, CA: Independent Institute.

Lloyd, Carol. 2006. "Home Sweet Cash Cow: How Our Houses Are Financing Our Lives." SFGate.com. March 10. http://www.sfgate.com/cgi-bin/article. cgi?file=/gate/archive/2006/03/10/carollloyd.DTL

Loeffler, Gunter. 2013. "Tower Building and Stock Market Returns." *Journal of Financial Research* 36.

Lucas, Robert E., Jr. 1987. *Models of Business Cycles*. New York: Basil Blackwell.

McCarthy, Jonathan, and Richard W. Peach. 2004. "Are Home Prices the Next 'Bubble'?" *FRBNY Economic Policy Review* (December).

McCloskey, Donald. 1992. "The Art of Forecasting: From Ancient to Modern Times." *Cato Journal* 12.

McCulloch, J. H. 1981. "Misintermediation and Macroeconomic Fluctuations." *Journal of Monetary Economics* 8.

Macovei, Mihai. 2015. "The Austrian Business Cycle Theory: A Defense of Its General Validity." *Quarterly Journal of Austrian Economics* 18, no. 4.

Mayer, Christopher. 2000. "The Meaning of Over-valued." *Mises Daily*. March 30.

———. 2003. "The Housing Bubble." *Free Market* 23, no. 8.

Mises, Ludwig von. [1908] 1981. *The Theory of Money and Credit*. Indianapolis, IN: Liberty Classics.

———. 2016. "The Economist Eugen v. Böhm-Bawerk, on the Occasion of the Tenth Anniversary of His Death." (In *Neue Freie Presse*, Vienna, August 27, 1924). Karl Friedrich Israel, trans. *Quarterly Journal of Austrian Economics* 19, no. 2.

———. [1928] 2006. "Monetary Stabilization and Cyclical Policy [Geldwertstabilisierung und Konjunkturpolitik]." In *The Causes of the Economic Crisis: And Other Essays before and after the Great Depression*. Edited by Percy L. Greaves. Auburn, AL: Mises Institute.

———. 1962. *The Ultimate Foundations of Economic Science: An Essay on Method*. Princeton, NJ: D. Van Nostrand.

———. 1968–1970. Lecture. The Problems of Inflation. Mises Institute. Auburn, AL. https://mises.org/library/problems-inflation

Mishkin, Frederic S., and Eugene N. White. 2003. "Stock Market Bubbles: When Does Intervention Work?" *Milken Institute Review: A Journal of Economic Policy* 5 (2nd quart.).

Mulligan, Robert F. 2002. "A Hayekian Analysis of the Term Structure of Production." *Quarterly Journal of Austrian Economics* 5, no. 2.

———. 2006. "An Empirical Investigation of the Austrian Business Cycle Theory." *Quarterly Journal of Austrian Economics* 9, no. 2.

Murphy, Robert P. 2014. "Ben Bernanke, the FDR of Central Bankers." In *The Fed at One Hundred: A Critical Review on the Federal Reserve System*. Edited by David Howden and Joseph T. Salerno. New York: Springer.

Murphy, Ryan H. 2015. "The Plucking Model, the Great Recession, and Austrian Business Cycle Theory." *Quarterly Journal of Austrian Economics* 18, no. 1.

Murray, Charles. 2000. "Bubble Trouble." *Research Reports* 67, no. 11.

Newman, Patrick. 2014. "The Depression of 1873–1879: An Austrian Perspective." *Quarterly Journal of Austrian Economics* 17, no. 4.

———. 2016. "The Depression of 1920–1921: A Credit Induced Boom and a Market Based Recovery?" *Review of Austrian Economics* (January). http:// link.springer.com/article/10.1007/s11138-015-0337-5

Norman, Mike. 2003. "Dismal Science May Get a Little Sunnier." *Special to the Street.* April 21.

Ohanian, Lee E. 2009. "What—or Who—Started the Great Depression?" *Journal of Economic Theory* 144 (October).

Ohanian, Lee E., and Harold Cole. 2004. "New Deal Policies and the Persistence of the Great Depression: A General Equilibrium Analysis." *Journal of Political Economy* 112, no. 4.

Okun, Arthur. 1970. *The Political Economy of Prosperity.* Washington, DC: Brookings Institution.

Papadakis, Maria. 1988. *The Science and Technology Resources of Japan: A Comparison with the United States.* Washington, DC: National Science Foundation.

Patrick, Hugh. 1986. *Japan's High Technology Industries: Lessons and Limitations of Industrial Policy.* Seattle: University of Washington Press.

Paul, Ron. 2005. "Ron Paul vs. Alan Greenspan." Testimony before the House Financial Affairs Committee, July 20.

Paul, Ron, Lewis Lehrman, and Murray N. Rothbard. 1982. *The Case for Gold: A Minority Report of the U.S. Gold Commission.* Washington, DC: Cato Institute.

Pesek, William, Jr. 1999a. "Want to Know Where the Next Disaster Will Hit? Look Where the World's Biggest Skyscraper's Going Up." *Barron's,* May 17.

———. 1999b. "To the Sky: Does Chicago Skyscraper Augur a U.S. Market Crash?" *Barron's* 79, no. 39.

Pierre, Andrew J., ed. 1987. *A High Technology Gap?: Europe, America, and Japan.* New York: New York University Press.

Piketty, Thomas. 2014. *Capital in the Twenty-First Century.* Cambridge, MA: Harvard University Press.

Powell, Benjamin. 2002. "Explaining Japan's Recession." *Quarterly Journal of Austrian Economics* 5, no. 2.

Quiggin, John. 2009. "Austrian Business Cycle Theory." *Commentary on Australian & World Events from a Social Democratic Perspective.* May 3. http:// johnquiggin.com/index.php/ archives/2009/05/03/austrian-business-cycle-theory

Reisman, George. 1999. "When Will the Bubble Burst?" *Mises Daily*. August 18.

———. 2000. "It May Be Bursting Now, and Faulty Economic Analysis May Cost Investors Dearly." Capitalism.net, February 26.

Ritenour, Shawn. 2014. "The Federal Reserve: Reality Trumps Rhetoric." In *The Fed at One Hundred: A Critical Review on the Federal Reserve System*. Edited by David Howden and Joseph T. Salerno. New York: Springer.

Robbins, Lionel. 1934. *The Great Depression*. London: Macmillan.

Rockwell, Llewellyn H., Jr. 1999. "Stock Market Bailout." *Free Market* (November).

Roll, Richard. 1992. "Volatility in U.S. and Japanese Stock Markets: A Symposium." *Journal of Applied Corporate Finance* 5, no. 1.

Rothbard, Murray N. 1962. *Man, Economy, and State*. Auburn, AL: Mises Institute.

———. [1963] 2000. *America's Great Depression*. 5th ed. Auburn, AL: Mises Institute.

———. 1969a. *Economic Depressions: Their Cause and Cure*. Lansing: Constitutional Alliance of Lansing Michigan.

———. 1969b. "Nixon's Decisions." *Libertarian Forum* 1, no. 8.

———. 1970. "The Nixon Mess." *Libertarian Forum* 2, no. 12.

———. 1971. "Nixonite Socialism." *Libertarian Forum* 3, no. 1.

———. 1984. "The Federal Reserve as a Cartelization Device." In *Money in Crisis: the Federal Reserve, the Economy, and Monetary Reform*. Edited by Barry N. Siegel. San Francisco, CA: Pacific Institute for Public Policy Research.

———. 1995. *Economic Thought before Adam Smith: An Austrian Perspective on the History of Economic Thought*. Vol. 1. Brookfield, VT: Edward Elgar.

Rouanet, Louis. 2017. "Monetary Policy, Asset Price Inflation and Inequality." Master's Thesis. School of Public Affairs. Institut d'Etudes Politiques de Paris.

Rubinstein, Dana. 2015. "Where the Transit-Build Costs Are Unbelievable." *Politico*. March 31.

Salerno, Joseph T. 1987. "The 100 Percent Gold Standard: A Proposal for Monetary Reform." In *Supply-Side Economics: A Critical Appraisal*. Edited by Richard H. Fink. Frederick, Maryland: University Publications of America.

———. 1988. "Comment on Gordon Tullock, 'Why Austrians are Wrong About Depressions.'" *Review of Austrian Economics* 3. Reprinted in Joseph T. Salerno, *Money Sound and Unsound*. Auburn, AL: Mises Institute. 2010.

———. 1995. "War and the Money Machine: Concealing the Costs of War beneath the Veil of Inflation." *Journal des Economistes et des Etudes Humaines* 6 (March). Reprinted in Joseph T. Salerno, *Money Sound and Unsound*. Auburn, AL: Mises Institute. 2010.

———. 1999. "Money and Gold in the 1920s and 1930s: An Austrian View." *Freeman* (October): 31–40. Reprinted in Joseph T. Salerno, *Money Sound and Unsound*, 431–49. Auburn, AL: Ludwig von Mises Institute, 2010.

———. 2003. "An Austrian Taxonomy of Deflation—with Applications to the U.S." *Quarterly Journal of Austrian Economics* 6, no. 4.

———. 2004. "Deflation and Depression: Where's the Link?" Mises.org. August 6. https://mises.org/library/deflation-and-depression-wheres-link

———. 2010. *Money Sound and Unsound*. Auburn, AL: Mises Institute.

———. 2012. "A Reformulation of Austrian Business Cycle Theory in Light of the Financial Crisis." *Quarterly Journal of Austrian Economics* 15, no. 1 (Spring): 3–44.

Salo, Jackie. 2015. "World's Tallest Skyscraper Is Saudi Arabia's Kingdom Tower? Jeddah Building Projected to Break Height Records." *International Business Times*, December 1. http://www.ibtimes.com/worlds-tallest-skyscraper-saudi-arabias-kingdom-tower-jeddah-building-projected-break-2207083

Samuelson, Paul A. 1966. "Science and Stocks." *Newsweek*, September 19.

Saravia, Jimmy A. 2014. "Merger Waves and the Austrian Business Cycle Theory." *Quarterly Journal of Austrian Economics* 17, no. 2.

Saucier, Chantel, and Mark Thornton, eds. 2010. Richard Cantillon, *An Essay on Economic Theory*. Auburn, AL: Mises Institute.

Selgin, George. 1992. "Bank Lending 'Manias' in Theory and History." *Journal of Financial Services Research* 6, no. 2.

Selgin, George, William D. Lastrapes, and Lawrence H. White. 2012. "Has the Fed Been a Failure?" *Journal of Macroeconomics* 34, no. 3.

Sennholz, Hans. 2000. "Can the Boom Last?" *Mises Daily*. July 31. https://mises.org/library/can-boom-last

Shapiro, Robert. 2004. "Spin Cycle: Why Has the Business Cycle Gone Topsy-Turvy?" Slate.com. April 15.

Shenoy, Sudha R., ed. 1972. *Tiger by the Tail: The Keynesian Legacy of Inflation*. Washington, DC: Cato Institute.

Shiller, Robert. 1992. "Volatility in U.S. and Japanese Stock Markets: A Symposium." *Journal of Applied Corporate Finance* 5, no. 1.

——— . 2000. *Irrational Exuberance*. Princeton, N.J.: Princeton University Press.

——— . 2004. "Are Housing Prices a House of Cards?" Project-Syndicate.org. September. http://www.project-syndicate.org/commentary/shiller17

——— . 2005. *Irrational Exuberance*. 2nd ed. Princeton, NJ: Princeton University Press.

Shostak, Frank. 1999. "Inflation, Deflation, and the Future." *Mises Daily*. October 5. https://mises.org/library/inflation-deflation-and-future

——— . 2003. "Housing Bubble: Myth or Reality?" *Mises Daily*. March 4. http://www.mises.org/story/1177

——— . 2004. "Who Made the Fannie and Freddie Threat?" *Mises Daily*. March 5. http://www.mises.org/story/1463

Skousen, Mark. 1991. *Economics on Trial: Lies, Myths, and Realities*. Homewood, IL: Business One Irvin.

Siegel, Barry N., ed. *Money in Crisis*. San Francisco: Pacific Institute for Public Policy Research.

Spiegel, Matthew. 2002. "2000 A Bubble? 2002 A Panic? Maybe Nothing?" Yale School of Management. New Haven, CT. http://faculty.som.yale.edu/MatthewSpiegel/editorial/CrashorPanic.pdf

Sumner, Scott. 2012. "If I buy T-bond, their price rises. If the Fed buys T-bonds, their price (usually) falls." TheMoneyIllusion blog. December 7. http://www.themoneyillusion.com/?p=18037

Tatsuno, Sheridan. 1986. *The Technopolis Strategy: Japan, High Technology, and the Control of the Twenty-First Century*. New York: Prentice Hall Press.

——— . 1990. *Created in Japan: From Imitators to World-Class Innovators*. New York: Harper & Row Publishers.

Television Post. 2015. "Prince Alwaleed Sells 5.6% Stake in News Corp for $188 Million." March 2.

Thornton, Mark. 1998. "Richard Cantillon and the Origins of Economic Theory." *Journal of Economics and Humane Studies* 8, no. 1.

——— . 1999. "Review of *The Synergy Trap: How Companies Lose the Acquisition Game*, by Mark L. Sirower." *Quarterly Journal of Austrian Economics* 2, no.

1.

———. 2003. "Apoplithorismosphobia." *Quarterly Journal of Austrian Economics* 6, no. 4.

———. 2004? "The Japanese Bubble Economy." LewRockwell.com. May 23, 2004. http://archive.lewrockwell.com/thornton/thornton24.html

———. 2004a. "Bull Market?" LewRockwell.com. February 9. http://archive. lewrockwell.com/thornton/thornton11.html

———. 2004b. "Surviving GreenSpam." LewRockwell.com. February 16. https:// www.lewrockwell.com/2004/02/mark-thornton/surviving-greenspam/

———. 2004c. "Housing: Too Good to Be True." *Mises Daily*. June 4. http:// www.mises.org/story/1533

———. 2004d. "Who Predicted the Bubble? Who Predicted the Crash?" *Independent Review* 9, no. 1.

———. 2005a. "Is the Housing Bubble Popping?" LewRockwell.com. August 8. http://archive.lewrockwell.com/thornton/thornton27.html

———. 2005b. "Skyscrapers and Business Cycles." *Quarterly Journal of Austrian Economics* 8, no. 1. https://mises.org/library/skyscrapers-and-business-cycles-4

———. 2005c. "What Is the 'Dark Side' and Why Do Some People Choose It?" *Mises Daily*. May 13. https://mises.org/library/what-dark-side-and-why-do-some-people-choose-it

———. 2006. "Cantillon on the Cause of the Business Cycle." *Quarterly Journal of Austrian Economics* 9, no. 3.

———. 2007. "New Record Skyscraper (and Depression?) in the Making." *Mises. org Blog*. August 7. https://mises.org/blog/new-record-skyscraper-and-depression-making

———. 2009. "The Economics of Housing Bubbles." In *Housing America: Building out of a Crisis*. Edited by Randall G. Holcombe and Benjamin Powell. New Brunswick, NJ: Transactions Publishers.

———. 2010a. "America's Second Great Depression: A Symposium in Memory of Larry Sechrest." *Quarterly Journal of Austrian Economics* 13, no. 3.

———. 2010b. "The Austrian School on Business Cycles: 100 Years of Being Right." Lecture. Mises Institute. Auburn, AL. March 12. https://mises.org/library/austrian-school-business-cycles-100-years-being-right

———. 2014. "The Federal Reserve's Housing Bubble and the Skyscraper Curse." In *The Fed at One Hundred: A Critical Review on the Federal Reserve System*.

Edited by David Howden and Joseph T. Salerno. New York: Springer.

———. 2015. "Where Is the Skyscraper Today?" *Mises Daily*. February 24. https://mises.org/library/where-skyscraper-curse-today

———. 2016. "Transparency or Deception: What the Fed Was Saying in 2007." *Quarterly Journal of Austrian Economics* 19, no. 1.

Timberlake, Richard. 1999. "Money in the 1920s and 1930s." *Freeman* (April).

Tucker, Jeffrey A. 1994. *Henry Hazlitt: A Giant of Liberty*. Auburn, AL: Mises Institute.

Tyson, Laura D'Andrea, and John Zysman. 1989. "Preface: The Argument Refined." In *Politics and Productivity: The Real Story of Why Japan Works*. Edited by Chalmers Johnson, Laura D'Andrea Tyson, and John Zysman. Cambridge, MA: Ballinger Publishing Company.

Tyson, Laura D'Andrea, John Zysman, and Giovanni Dosi. 1989. "Trade, Technologies, and Development: A Framework for Discussing Japan." In *Politics and Productivity: The Real Story of Why Japan Works*. Edited by Chalmers Johnson, Laura D'Andrea Tyson, and John Zysman. Cambridge, MA: Ballinger Publishing Company.

US Congressional Budget Office. 2003. "CBO's Economic Forecasting Record: An Evaluation of the Economic Forecasts CBO Made from January 1976 through January 2001." Washington, DC: US Congressional Budget Office (October).

Vedder, Richard, and Lowell Gallaway. 2000. "The Austrian Market Share in the Marketplace for Ideas, 1871–2025." *Quarterly Journal of Austrian Economics* 3, no. 1.

Vinzant, Carol. 2002. "Two Schools of Thought on Economics." *Chicago Tribune*. September 3.

Voigt, Kevin. 2010. "As Skyscrapers Rise, Markets Fall." CNN.com. January 8. http://www.cnn.com/2010/WORLD/asiapcf/01/08/skyscrapers.rise.markets.fall

Wanniski, Jude. 2000. "Letters to Clients." March 30 to April 19.

Wainhouse, C. 1984 "Empirical Evidence for Hayek's Theory of Economic Fluctuations." In *Money in Crisis*. Edited by B. Siegel. San Francisco: Pacific Institute for Public Policy Research.

White, Lawrence H. 2005. "The Federal Reserve System's Influence on Research in Monetary Economics." *Econ Journal Watch* 2, no. 2.

Willis, Carol. 1995. *Form Follows Finance: Skyscrapers and Skylines in New York and Chicago*. New York: Princeton Architectural Press.

Wilson, David. 2016. "Cisco, Apple Fail to Reach $1 Trillion. Is Amazon Next?" Bloomberg.com. May 9. http://www.bloomberg.com/news/articles/2016-05-09/cisco-apple-fail-to-reach-1-trillion-is-amazon-next-chart

Wood, Christopher. 1992. *The Bubble Economy: Japan's Extraordinary Speculative Boom of the '80s and the Dramatic Bust of the '90s.* New York: Atlantic Monthly Press.

Woods, Thomas E. 2009a. *Meltdown: A Free-Market Look at Why the Stock Market Collapsed, the Economy Tanked, and Government Bailouts Will Make Things Worse.* Washington, DC: Regnery Publishing.

——— . 2009b. "Warren Harding and the Forgotten Depression of 1920." *Intercollegiate Review* (Fall).

——— . 2014. "Does U.S. History Vindicate Central Banking?" In *The Fed at One Hundred: A Critical Review on the Federal Reserve System.* Edited by David Howden and Joseph T. Salerno. New York: Springer.

Zarnowitz, Victor. 1992. *Business Cycles: Theory, History, Indicators, and Forecasting.* Chicago: University of Chicago Press.

——— . 1999. "Theory and History Behind Business Cycles: Are the 1990s the Onset of a Golden Age?" NBER Working Paper 7010. National Bureau of Economic Research. Cambridge, MA.

Zijp, Rudy van. 1993. *Austrian and New Classical Business Cycle Theories: A Comparative Study through the Method of Rational Construction.* Brookfield, VT: Edward Elgar.

Zweig, Jason. 2011. "Super Bowl Indicator: The Secret History." *Wall Street Journal.* January 28. http://blogs.wsj.com/marketbeat/2011/01/28/super-bowl-indicator-the-secret-history

Index

THE MISES INSTITUTE

Civil War II is a work of fiction. Any resemblance to current events or people is entirely coincidental.